FROM AXONS TO IDENTITY

FROM AXONS
TO IDENTITY

Neurological Explorations
of the Nature of the Self

TODD E. FEINBERG, M.D.

W. W. NORTON & COMPANY

New York • London

For information about permission to reproduce selections from this book, write to
Permissions, W. W. Norton & Company, Inc., 500 Fifth Avenue, New York, NY 10110

For information about special discounts for bulk purchases, please contact W. W. Norton
Special Sales at specialsales@wwnorton.com or 800-233-4830

Manufacturing by Quebecor World Fairfield Graphics
Book design by Charlotte Staub
Production manager: Leeann Graham

Library of Congress Cataloging-in-Publication Data

Feinberg, Todd E.
    From axons to identity : neurological explorations of the nature of
the self / Todd E. Feinberg. — 1st ed.
        p.   cm. — (The Norton series on interpersonal neurobiology)
    Includes bibliographical references and index.
    ISBN 978-0-393-70557-7 (hardcover)
    1. Identity (Psychology)   2. Self.   3. Personality disorders.   4.
Neuropsychology.   I. Title.
    BF697.F443 2009
    155 2—dc22   2008052428

W. W. Norton & Company, Inc., 500 Fifth Avenue, New York, N.Y. 10110
www.wwnorton.com

W.W. Norton & Company Ltd., Castle House, 75/76 Wells Street, London W1T 3QT

1   2   3   4   5   6   7   8   9   0

CONTENTS

ACKNOWLEDGMENTS

THIS BOOK is the product of many years of thought and writing. In my career in clinical work and research it has been my privilege to work with and learn from so many brilliant people, too many to name. Some in particular are Kenneth Heilman, who was my first teacher in behavioral neurology, and the late Dr. Edwin Weinstein, who first introduced me to the possibilities of integrating neurological concepts with dynamic-defensive operations. For this particular book, I had wonderfully instructive e-mail correspondence with several researchers and theoreticians who generously shared with me their insights in their respective fields, including Tim Allen, Bud Craig, Derek Denton, Phoebe Cramer, Michael Lewis, Tom Mandel, Bjorn Merker, Rudolf Nieuwenhuys, Georg Northoff, Stanley Salthe, Allan Schore, Mark Solms, and Marjorie Taylor. Marsel Mesulam was an invaluable resource, particularly on the neuroanatomical issues, and Dr. David Roane has been a frequent collaborator in my clinical research over the years. I owe all these wonderful explorers a great debt, but of course the opinions expressed here and whatever mistakes I have made are my own. A special thanks is owed to Jill K. Gregory, MFA, CMI who provided the beautiful illustrations, and Marilyn Rivera and Michael Rothman for manuscript assistance.

Grants from the Gerald J. and Dorothy R. Friedman New York Foundation for Medical Research have been instrumental in supporting our clinical and research programs. A special thanks is owed to Betty Yarmon and her late husband, Mort, and Jane Friedman, all of whom have been, and continue to be, immensely supportive of our Center. I also wish the thank my wonderful agent and steadfast supporter Deirdre Mullane, whose sharp literary eye and insights were so helpful in shaping this work, and my exceptional editor at W. W. Norton, Deborah Malmud, who guided this project from its inception and made working on it more pleasure than work. And finally, once again, my mom Gloria and dad Mort, my wife Marlene, and kids Rachel and Josh, for helping me grow my self.

INTRODUCTION

From Axons to Identity

IF I ASK YOU, "Who are you?" chances are you will tell me your name. But if I ask you to tell me more about yourself, to explain who you think yourself *to be*, how you view your personal identity in a broader sense, then I can expect a range of answers. Some people identify themselves by their careers, others by their place in a family, some by their ethnicity or country, others by their religion. And if I ask you, "What are you doing right now?" there is no single "correct" answer. You might say you are sitting in a chair, waiting for dinner, preparing for a lecture, or reading this book. And if I ask you, "Where are you at this very moment?" your answer might range from your kitchen to your home to your city. My point is that there is enormous leeway in how we view ourselves, a viewpoint that can change from moment to moment, and is to a large extent dependent upon who is asking the questions and for what reasons. It is also very much related to what a person wants to express about him- or herself.

Although it may seem clear what we mean when we refer to "ourselves," in fact the status of the self as an object of study is a matter of considerable controversy. There are nearly as many conceptions of the self, or what is sometimes referred to as "a sense of self," as there are writers on the subject. One reason for this continuing debate is that how one views the nature of the self will depend upon one's particular intellectual background and approach. Whether the adopted perspective is grounded in philosophy, religion, literature, psychology, sociology, or neuroscience—to name a few of the common approaches—will influence one's speculations on the nature of the self. Indeed, the ideas generated from these diverse viewpoints are often unrelated or mutually incompatible.

The philosopher Galen Strawson, who has written extensively on the subject, describes these multiple perspectives on the nature of the self:

> It is difficult to know where to begin, because there are many different notions of the self. Among those I have recently come across are the cognitive self, the conceptual self, the contextualized self, the core self, the dialogic self, the ecological self, the embodied self, the emergent self, the empirical self, the existential self, the extended self, the fictional self, the full-grown self, the interpersonal self, the material self, the narrative self, the philosophical self, the physical self, the private self, the representational self, the rock bottom essential self, the semiotic self, the social self, the transparent self, and the verbal self.[1]

In one recent bit of extraordinary academic sleuthing, the psychologists Mark Leary and June Tangney identified sixty-six different terms to refer to some aspect of identity or the self.[2]

In the face of these many ways of thinking about the self, one further question that immediately comes to mind is whether and how one might distinguish the idea of "consciousness" from the concept of the self. This problem is made all the more complex because there are as many meanings of the word "consciousness" as there are definitions of the self. I believe the succinct definition provided by the philosopher John Searle to be sufficient: "Consciousness consists of inner, qualitative, subjective states and processes of sentience or awareness."[3] By almost any criteria, a definition of "the self" will require that for there to be a self, there must also be consciousness, in order for that self to come into being and continue to exist. But certainly the idea of the self goes beyond simple awareness, as the many forms of the self described above make clear.

When the self is considered from the standpoint of neuroscience, one primary concern is how awareness is integrated and organized into a coherent whole, since that whole is what is emphasized when we refer to "the self" or "the mind." Here the emphasis is not upon any single momentary act of perception or motor response, but rather upon the totality of the brain's functions into unified experience and action. Indeed, one major reason why the self seems so difficult to explain on a purely neurobiological basis is that, while we experience a unified consciousness, there appears to be an essential difference between the unified mind and the divisible brain. We know the nervous system is composed of millions of neurons grouped into numerous larger structures. The question is, how do all of these physically connected but materially separable structures function as the seamless whole that we experience as our unified selves? In this volume the problems of the unity of the self and the unity of mental phenomena in general will be considered as essentially the same problem with the same solutions, and these aspects of the problem of the self will be one of our primary interests.

Thus, for the purposes of our neurological explorations, I will define the self essentially by its coherence: *The self is a unity of consciousness in perception and action that persists in time.* While we may possess awareness at any single point in time, the self is something that at least subjectively feels like it endures beyond the passing moment. Whether and in what sense this is true or not is subject to debate, but for our purposes we'll argue that the self, at least as subjectively experienced, has a temporal aspect and that there is "something that it is like to be me" that I experienced yesterday and today, and will experience tomorrow. This temporal feature suggests also that for all the temporal "me's" to be integrated into a unified self, there must be some aspect of higher order self-awareness—the awareness of the "me" as an enduring entity—that serves as the basis of one's continuing identity. This aspect of the self is sometimes referred to as the "narrative self" and its existence requires some degree of self-awareness as well as the ability to episodically recall personal experiences and integrate them into a coherent self-related story.[4]

I believe we now have sufficient knowledge of the workings of the brain to discern in broad outline how the neurological self is constructed from the "wetware" of the nervous system. However, understanding the neural substrate of a self is not the same thing as understanding how a person experiences an identity as it persists through time. It is here, I believe, that the clinical cases are most instructive. As Sigmund Freud pointed out many years ago, at a time when neurology was still a young science, neuropsychiatric disturbances offer a unique opportunity to study a range of disturbances of the "ego":

> Pathology has made us acquainted with a great number of states in which the boundary lines between the ego and the external world become uncertain or in which they are actually drawn incorrectly. There are cases in which parts of a person's own body, even portions of his mental life—his perceptions, thoughts and feelings—, appear alien to him and as not belonging to his ego; there are other cases in which he ascribes to the external world things that clearly originate in his own ego and that ought to be acknowledged by it. Thus even the feeling of our own ego is subject to disturbances and the boundaries of the ego are not constant.[5]

Disruptions in the nature of the self among some neurological patients can provide a gateway to the understanding of what parts of the brain contribute to the formulation of the self.[6] I have studied these cases for over two decades, and still find these endlessly fascinating disorders a great source of insight into how the brain creates individual identity. In the neurological patient, seemingly straight-forward questions such as "Who are you?" "Where are you?" or "Who are these people around you?" may bring forth such surprising and peculiar responses that they seemingly defy explanation.

During the course of my clinical practice and research as a neurologist and psychiatrist, as I found myself increasingly analyzing my patients' responses in the way that a psychoanalyst interprets a patient's description of a dream, it became apparent to me that when I posed questions such as these to my patients, although ostensibly relating objective truth, they were actually revealing personal feelings that went well beyond the bare facts about themselves. More specifically, I have been especially intrigued by the role brain pathology plays in these transformations of the self, and what we can learn from these cases about how the brain creates the self. I realized that by linking the region of the brain that was affected by brain disease with the particular disorder of the self that ensued, I could recreate—in reverse, as it were—how nature builds a self from neural tissue.

I have learned that, in order to pursue these intriguing questions, one must pay very close attention to what the patient actually says. I have found that in many cases, especially when my explorations in the neurology of the self were in their infancy, I needed to view an hour long videotape of a clinical interview over a hundred times before the meaning of the patient's narrative became clear. For this reason, whenever possible, I report the verbatim interviews here so that the reader can hear what I heard, these extraordinary stories told in the patients' own words. It is the best way of conveying why I think about these cases the way I do, and what led to the theories I propose to explain them.

Consider my patient CM, a woman in her forties with a right hemisphere stroke and paralysis on the left side of her body, who displayed a rather common condition among right hemisphere stroke patients called *asomatognosia*, a disorder we will consider at greater length later on. In asomatognosia, the patient expresses the belief that an arm that has been paralyzed—usually the left—as the result of damage to crucial regions of the brain is no longer her own, no longer thought of as part of her body. In some cases the patient may simply ignore the arm as if it does not exist, but other patients will strike the arm or attempt to throw it out of the bed. Other patients adopt a kindly or parental attitude toward the limb and coddle it as one might an infant. When I asked CM to tell me what was wrong with her left arm, she replied:

CM: *I told my brother let's cut it off* [her left arm] *and sell it to somebody else to pay the medical bills. . . . It should move but I cannot move it . . . it's like a bum, a lazy bum . . .*

TEF: *You refer to it as a bum?*

CM: *Lazy bum . . . lazy bum . . .* [looking at her arm] *I say to you lazy bum you're not moving! You should be moving . . . you're not moving . . . come on lazy bum move, move up my leg, don't make me help you . . .*

The attitude of disdain and a feeling of alienation toward the arm displayed by CM was evident in another patient of mine, PG, a gentleman in his eighties, who after a right temporoparietal stroke that resulted in a dense paralysis of the left side, complained about his weakness and expressed his annoyance at not being able to return home. I held his right hand up on his right side and asked him to identify it:

TEF: *What do you call this? Do you have any special name for this?*

PG: *A dummy hand.*

TEF: *I'm sorry?*

PG: *A dummy hand.*

TEF: *Why do you call it that?*

PG: *Because it's just a dummy. . . .*

It is a somewhat surprising fact that in spite of the profound disturbance of a personal sense of an integrated self that such rejection of a part of one's own body represents, asomatognosia is actually quite common in the early aftermath of right hemisphere damage.

In this sense we can appreciate how sensitive our personal sense of who the self is, and that it changes in response to a condition of the brain.

There is in fact a wide array of self-related disturbances in neurology, and I will be discussing many of them later in this book. For instance, one striking group of patients harbor consistent delusional beliefs about imaginary friends, persecutors, or relatives. Some of these fictitious entities may be seen in the mirror, as in the case of a patient who screamed at her mirror image and referred to her reflection as the "whore" and the "tramp." Other patients describe people who are completely fictitious, such as a man who spoke of an imaginary child that he and his wife were planning to adopt. In this group we consider how the phantom beings function as "alter egos" of the patient, so that the man who was about to adopt a "phantom child" said the poor child had been "in and out of hospitals" for years and that the doctors claimed the child had all sorts of medical issues, but these statements were actually true of the patient himself.

I begin, in chapter 1, by describing many of these *neuropathologies of the self,* such as *anosognosia, asomatognosia, delusional misidentification,* and *Capgras* and *Fregoli syndromes.* These conditions affect not only the patients' sense of their own personal identities but also how they feel related to others around them and to the world in general. The study of these cases raises some perplexing questions, and this work has led me to explore some of the central themes I consider in this book: What makes these previously normal individuals develop, subsequent to brain damage, such extreme forms of behavior? Why are these strikingly odd and seemingly improbable syndromes so consistent from one individual to the next? And what can these disorders teach us about the way the brain creates personal identity and a sense of self?

Although for over a hundred years these disorders have been characterized as examples of discrete syndromes, a problem that has always intrigued me is whether there is an underlying mechanism, or

integrated viewpoint, or unifying theme common to these conditions. For me personally, there was an extraordinary "aha moment"
when I came to the stunning realization that while I and other investigators had largely approached the solution to the mystery of
neurological disturbances of the self from the perspective of the
adult brain, what was missing was a greater appreciation of how
these conditions related to *the hierarchical development of the self in the
child*. Not only are the childhood patterns of behavior related to the
adult neurological disorders of the self, but this relationship can be
used as a kind of Rosetta Stone for deciphering the origins and
meaning of the adult disturbances in self-related functions.

Using this principle, in chapter 2 I outline the hierarchical development of self awareness and psychological defenses in the child,
and relate these to psychological defenses in the adult. It turns out
that many of the defenses and forms of thought that are utilized in
the normal course of development by the child may also reappear in
the adult under conditions of stress or mental illness. Indeed, when
these defenses are present in the adult, authorities often consider
them instances of *immature* defenses and thought processes. With
this unified schema as a roadmap, in chapter 3 I demonstrate that
there are also striking similarities between the patterns of behavior
that are displayed by children in early stages of normal psychological development and the seemingly bizarre neurological disorders
that we witness in adults with brain damage. In particular, the developmentally immature psychological defenses of the child may
make a repeat appearance in the psyche of the brain-damaged adult.
For example, if a patient who is quite ill says that in actuality it is
the person in the next bed who is really sick, we say that the patient
is using the defenses of *denial* and *projection*. If the patient insists that
his paralyzed arm is actually his brother's that was sewn on by the
hospital surgeons last night, that is an example of *distortion*. And if
the patient says he has two left arms, one strong and healthy and the
other a "withered chicken wing," that is called *splitting*. As we shall

see, denial, projection, distortion, and splitting are also immature defenses that may be seen in the course of development. Thus, the
brain damage in the adult cases does not create "new people," but actually reveals aspects of the self that were in reality lying dormant in
the brain throughout adult life—what I call "the brainchild within"—
and therefore these clinical conditions can be understood as representing a return of the adult mind to hierarchically lower, earlier
developing, and less mature patterns of thought and behavior,

In chapter 4, I examine what these findings tell us about one of
the earliest and fundamental concerns of Sigmund Freud, the relationship between brain functions and psychological defense. According to my hypothesis, in the course of normal brain maturation,
approximately between the ages of 3 to 8 years, there is a shift from
immature defensive operations and the relatively unconstrained use
of fantasy to mature defenses and reality-oriented modes of thought.
This shift depends in large measure upon maturational processes
that are occurring within the right hemisphere. Once these hierarchically mature brain regions develop, the emergence of more mature defenses characteristic of the adult are made possible, and the
unbridled fantasy of the child is no longer overtly expressed. However, analysis of clinical cases leads me to conclude that in the
presence of right frontal damage, we witness a disturbance in *ego
boundaries* and the *self-observing ego*—the ability to take an outside perspective on one's experience. The loss of these important functions
creates a state of *ego disequilibrium* that disturbs the normal balance
between the hemispheres and allows the expression of these previously dormant mental potentialities. Furthermore, the preservation
and activation of the verbal defenses, including such immature operations as verbal denial, projection, splitting, and fantasy, must
therefore depend upon the functioning of the relatively intact left
verbal hemisphere. Therefore, it may be that these immature defenses as well as the operation of fantasy, under normal circumstances, may be lateralized to the intact left hemisphere.

The relationship between the brain and the self, however, goes beyond the clinical conditions I describe here. In an effort to provide a comprehensive "neurology of the self," in chapters 5 through 8 I also address a series of central and interrelated questions about the underlying brain functions that make a self possible. Once again, an essential theme I will emphasize in our search is my belief that the reason for our current lack of understanding of the relationship between consciousnesss, the self, and the brain is that we have not paid sufficient attention to the *hierarchical arrangement of the nervous system*. Nervous systems have evolved toward the creation of a hierarchy of brain structures of ever increasing complexity and abstractness, and by understanding the nature of these hierarchies many mysteries about the self and consciousness may be resolved.

In chapter 5 I first present a neurological model of the self that integrates some of the functional features of the self within the anatomy of the brain. The emphasis here again is on the hierarchical aspects of the nervous system, and we will explore how lower and more primitive brain regions are related to and integrated with higher brain structures in order to make more advanced aspects of the self possible. I develop the argument that the functioning of the nervous system can be understood as the result of the two great developmental trends, a *medial-lateral trend* in which the nervous system expands from its center outward, like the growth rings of a tree, and a *caudal-rostral trend* that results in the hierarchical growth of later developing and more complex neurological sructures upon those with more simple and basic organization and function. Progressive growth under the influence of the medial-lateral trend in both evolution and in the course of development of the individual gives rise to an *interoself system* that is primarily involved with the internal milieu and homeostatic needs of the organism, and an *exterosensorimotor system* that is primarily concerned with the organism's interactions with the environment. A third system—the *integrative self system*—serves to assimilate the interoself systems with the extero systems, and integrate the organism's internal needs with the external environment. It is within the integrative self systems that the most advanced aspects of the self and those we consider the most characteristic of the human individual take center stage.

Having established the basic hierarchical neural architecture of the self, in chapters 6 through 8 I examine some of the fundamental scientific enigmas of our era, such as how the brain maintains mental unity and the unique design features displayed by the brain that make the self and consciousness possible. I suggest that it is through a deeper understanding of the nature of neural hierarchies that the biological basis of the wholeness of self and consciousness can be explained. Further, I will show how this hypothesis leads to a solution for what is commonly known as the mind-body problem—why consciousness and the self seem so different in form and function from the material brain. Since the time of Descartes, there has been an enormous amount written on this topic, and yet there is no consensus on how to frame this question, much less on how to answer it. In this part of the book I offer some solutions.

In chapter 6 I argue that we can begin to solve the mind-body problem and the mystery of consciousness by understanding how neurobiological hierarchies operate when compared to other hierarchies found in nature. In this analysis we consider two basic types of hierarchies, *non-nested* or *control hierarchies* and *nested* or *compositional hierarchies*. A non-nested hierarchy has a structure that is roughly designed in the shape of a pyramid in which lower more basic levels of the hierarchy converge upon higher levels. In this type of organization, lower levels of the hierarchy are not physically composed of higher levels, but higher order properties are created by the integrated effects of lower upon higher levels. This arrangement also allows centralized control of the entire system to emanate from the top of the pyramid. In contrast to a non-nested hierarchy, in a *nested* or *compositional hierarchy* any given level of the organization is entirely composed of the constituent parts of the lower levels of which it is comprised. All living organisms functionally operate in the manner of a nested hierarchy in which the elements comprising the lower levels of the hierarchy are physically combined or *nested* within higher levels. In this way increasingly complex wholes are created from smaller and less complex units.

When we analyze the functions of the nervous system that involve consciousness, we observe some extraordinary features. On the one hand, there is centralization of neural activity in which the highest levels of the hierarchy display more abstract and integrated responses patterns when compared to lower levels—a feature of non-nested hierarchies. However, at the same time lower order elements contributing to conscious experience are nested within and emerge in awareness as part of a nested totally of perception and action. Therefore, where consciousness and higher order aspects of the self are concerned, the neural hierarchy displays features of *both* non-nested and nested hierarchies. As far as I have been able to determine, only the nervous system *simultaneously* operates in both a nested and non-nested fashion and in this regard appears to be unique among biological and non-biological systems.

In chapter 7, I attempt to show how this feature of the operation of the brain holds the key to understanding three fundamental enigmas of consciousness—the problems of *mental unity*, the *qualia problem*, and the problem of the *intentionality* of consciousness. Using the principles of the neural hierarchy I have outlined, I present what I call the *Neural Hierarchy Theory of Consciousness (NHTC)* as a way to explain these unique and perplexing problems regarding the relationship between the brain and consciousness. The principles presented within this model lead me to the conclusion that it is exclusively within the parameters of the nested neural hierarchy that consciousness and the higher order aspects of the self are made possible. I will also explain why these three critical features of higher awareness are only possible as aspects of higher selves.

Finally, in chapter 8, I explain why my analysis leads naturally to the conclusion that we must conceive of our personal consciousness as a *process.* We generally conceive of ourselves as discrete entities, things, and that is certainly true to an extent. We have material bodies that include material brains, things that can be weighed and measured, touched and divided. But here I will present my belief that many of our commonsense notions of what we are as selves are misguided and the true nature of the self, as others have suggested before me, is not what the brain *is,* but what it *does.* The self, what you may think of as "you," is an ever-changing process that cannot be located in any specific physical component of the brain itself. It is only by appreciating this dynamic that we can understand how we progress from axons to identities.

CHAPTER ONE

Damaged Brains, Damaged Selves

IN THE COURSE of my daily practice as a neurologist, I see many clinical patterns that pose no particular intellectual problem in their familiarity. But every so often, usually quite unexpectedly, I will come across a patient whose symptoms are so unusual or an excited colleague will call me about what we sometimes refer to as a "fascinoma"—a case wonderously unusual and unexplained—that I feel compelled to drop everything and dig into the analysis of that case in an effort to explore what it can teach us about the brain-self enigma. It is to these patients and their clinical conditions that I now turn.

Among the many cases of self-related disorders that neurologists have observed, the numerous types fall into a number of broad categories. First are disorders of the *bodily self*. These are conditions that transform the manner in which a person views or acts upon the nature or limits of his or her physical being. These disorders reflect confusion about the properties of the patient's own body and affect the question, "What physically am I?" Second, there are disturbances of the *relational self*, or how the individual thinks about or interacts with other objects and persons in the world, and their personal and autobiographical significance with reference to the patient. The relational self addresses questions such as, "Who are you to me?" and "How am I related to the objects in the world?" Third, there are perturbations of the *narrative self*; that is, how one describes one's past and present circumstances and relates one's personal history. Here one seeks answers to questions such as "How did I get here?" or "What has happened to me?"[1] Finally, there are disorders of *personal identity and the global sense of self*. This is a large group of conditions that concerns the feeling of one's sense of self with reference to basic personal identity in the world. These are questions, literally, of "Who am I?"

The first three self-related disorders are relatively common among patients with neurological disease as well as among psychiatric patients, while the last type of disturbance is more common in purely psychiatric conditions. In neurological patients, not knowing who one is only occurs with advanced and severe neurological disease. However, confusion about one's personal identity may occur among certain psychiatric patients, such as those with dissociative disorders like fugue states or serious psychotic conditions including schizophrenia.[2] In the following pages, I'll describe in some detail a number of cases that I have studied, as well a number of reports from other researchers, that illuminate the remarkable nature of this loss of self in any of its dimensions.

Disorders of the Bodily Self

One of the first disorders of the self and self-awareness to be described in the neurological literature, *anosognosia* was reported by celebrated neurologists Gabriel Anton and Joseph Babinski as early as the turn of the twentieth century, when neurological science was in its infancy.[3]

Anosognosia

The term "anosognosia" literally means "lack of knowledge of the existence of disease." Patients with this condition may be unaware of many aspects of their medical situation for a variety of reasons; however, the most common and classic variety of anosognosia is unawareness of left hemiplegia, or paralysis of the entire left side of the body. In this syndrome, the patient typically has an acute lesion, most commonly due to a stroke, in the non-dominant hemisphere of the brain. In most right-handed persons, this would be a stroke in the right hemisphere that leads to a paralysis of the opposite (contralateral) left limb of the body. The majority of patients with anosognosia for left hemiplegia also display *hemispatial neglect*, in which they ignore the left side of the body as well as the extrapersonal space on the left. These patients will also experience significant sensory loss on the left side of the body, and problems determining where the affected limb is in space if they are not directly looking at it.

My patient AP, a man in his seventies who sustained a stroke of his right hemisphere in the temporoparietal region and experienced paralysis of the entire left side, presents a straightforward case of anosognosia. Although he admitted that he had had a stroke and was in the hospital, he denied that there was anything wrong with his left arm or leg:

TEF: *What happened to you?*

AP: *They brought me here.*

TEF: *What kind of problems were you having? Do you remember? What kind of problems are you having now? Do you feel fine . . . ?*

AP: *Yes.*

TEF: *Nothing is bothering you?*

AP: *There's a pain in my back.*

TEF: *Is there anything wrong with your arms or your legs?*

AP: *I don't remember . . .*

TEF: *As far as you're concerned you're not aware of any problems with your arms or your legs?*

AP: [shakes his "no"]

TEF: *Is there anything wrong with your arms?*
AP: *Nothing.*
TEF: *If you wanted to could you walk right out of this place?*
AP: *It's possible.*

Though AP seemed to be unaware of his paralysis, he did not express other delusions about his arm, his current location, or his present medical situation. In the simplest varieties of anosognosia for hemiplegia, patients may admit to having had a stroke, and when the paralysis is specifically pointed out to them they may actually acknowledge the defect. In contrast, a sub-group of anosognosic patients seems not only unaware that the limb is paralyzed, but persists in this belief even if the paralysis is demonstrated to them right before their eyes. Indeed, some of these patients deny they are ill in any way in spite of being told repeatedly of their condition and finding themselves in the hospital surrounded by doctors, nurses, flowers, and concerned family members.

To explain away the disparities between the situation as they understand it and what they are being told, such patients may demonstrate confabulation, which has been broadly defined as a statement that is made without a conscious effort to deceive but is clearly erroneous; or alternatively, as statements or actions that involve unintentional but obvious distortions.[4] Early clinical observations of confabulation were made as far back as 1892 in patients with what is now known as Wernicke-Korsakoff syndrome, an observation that was subsequently confirmed by later investigators.[5] Subsequently, many varieties of confabulation have been noted in a wide range of types and clinical settings.[6] Anosognosic patients are often confabulatory about the paralyzed arms, their illness, their current location, or the people around them.

My patient PM, a woman in her sixties who developed an acute left hemiplegia due to a large right hemisphere stroke that extended from the frontal to the parietal regions, demonstrated this sort of profound denial coupled with a confabulatory tendency.[7] Through-out weeks of hospitalization, and in spite of having been told re-peatedly that she had suffered a stroke and her left side was paralyzed, PM denied her illness and her disability:

TEF: *OK. What are you doing here?*

PM: *Checking out why I fell over a coffee table.*

TEF: *Is there anything wrong with you now?*

PM: *No.*

TEF: *Nothing at all? You're fine? You're in the picture of health?*

PM: *I would say that I'm well enough to go home!*

TEF: *Could you just get up and walk out of here?*

PM: *Yes I could.*

TEF: *Are you having any difficulty walking?*

PM: *No.*

TEF: *OK. So what are you doing here?*

PM: *You all tell me I have a weak left side.*

TEF: *I'm sorry?*

PM: *You all say I have a weak left side.*

TEF: *We all say you have a weak left side?*

PM: *And I don't agree!*

TEF: *And you don't agree?*

PM: *No.*

TEF: *Why?*

PM: *Because I know I don't!*

TEF: *It feels fine?*

PM: *Yes.*

TEF: *There's no weakness over there?*

PM: *No* [She is asked to raise her right arm, which she does.]

TEF: *Now raise the other arm for me. Raise your left arm for me. Can't you do that for me?* [Pause] *Did you do it? Did you raise it?*

PM: *I did now.*

TEF: *You did now? Do you have any difficulty raising it?*

PM: *No.*

TEF: *OK then. Why don't you touch your nose?* [touches nose with right hand]

TEF: *Why don't you touch it with the other hand? Can you touch it with the other hand?*

PM: *Yes.*

TEF: *Could you do it for me?* [no movement] *Are you doing it?* [Again, no response]. . . . *You know, it would seem to me that if you couldn't touch your nose with your left hand, that there might be some weakness over there. How does that sound to you?*

PM: *No.*

TEF: *You adamantly disagree? You are absolutely certain there's no weakness over there? Could you tell me why you won't touch your nose with your left hand? Is there a reason for that?*

PM: *Because I think I'm a comedian . . . and I'd probably make an obscene gesture.*

TEF: *You know I can't help but notice it looks to me like you have some degree of paralysis of your left arm. Would you believe me if I told you that you did?*

PM: *No . . . because I know I could drive to work tomorrow and work with both hands! . . . I answer the telephone and take messages constantly. . . .*

TEF: *And you'd have no difficulty doing that?*

PM: *No.*

[The next day]

TEF: *Is there anything wrong with you? What are you doing here?*

PM: *Playing games.*

TEF: *Are you fine? Is there anything bothering you? Are you perfectly well?*

PM: *I'm well enough to go home.*

TEF: *Do you want to go home?*

PM: *Very much so.*

TEF: *Are you having any difficulty moving your arms or legs?*

PM: *Not at all.*

TEF: *Could you raise them for me?* [She raises the right arm.]

TEF: *Can you raise the other one?*

PM: *Yes.*

TEF: *Then why don't you pick it up for me?*

PM: *Because I don't like to be told!* [I hold up her left arm and show it to her

on her right side. She denies any weakness, and I ask her to hold it up
for me]
TEF: *Let's try it.* [When I let go, the arm drops to the bed.]
PM: *Are you holding it up for me?*
PM: *Yes.*
TEF: *But it's falling.*
PM: *Because I'm not trying very hard.*

PM's responses here go well beyond simple unawareness of her
condition. She is in total denial of her paralysis, her inability to
walk, her inability to perform her usual work activities, and confabulates about or otherwise rationalizes her inability to move the arm.
She is indeed delusional about her paralysis and current situation.

There is another interesting aspect to PM's personality. According
to reports from her family, PM was a very "private person" who
rarely discussed her problems with others. Even before her stroke, a
tendency toward denial was a characteristic behavior as well. She
was reluctant to go to doctors, would attempt to minimize problems
in general, and according to her daughter "would never want anyone
else to know what's going on with her." The daughter observed that
years ago when her mother had a brief surgical procedure that required hospitalization, although PM had many friends and family,
she didn't want anyone to know about her hospitalization and kept
it a secret from nearly everyone except her children and husband. I
asked PM about this experience:

TEF: *Why didn't you want people to know you were in the hospital?*
PM: *It's a sign of weakness and I didn't want to be weak! . . . Hospitals are only good
for emergencies and having babies. . . . I don't want people fawning all over me
. . . I don't like that . . . it's not part of my personality.*

In subsequent chapters I will argue that there is an important relationship between the patient's personality before a brain injury and

their current sense of their self that deserves our attention. At this point, however, I want to emphasize the following points. First, there are a range of neurological factors that potentially contribute to the production of the anosognosic response, including generalized confusion, the loss of position sense in the paralyzed limb, and most significantly hemispatial neglect.[8] However, there remain some important and perplexing questions. For example, why do some patients deny their impairments while other patients with similar lesions and degrees of hemispatial neglect do not?[9] Additionally, it has been demonstrated that one can temporally reverse the neglect in some anosognosic patients yet the anosognosia itself improves only in some.[10] This suggests that neglect alone cannot entirely account for anosognosia. Furthermore, why do some patients persist in denying their impairments even when the paralysis is clearly demonstrated to them, with the arm held out before them on the non-neglected side?[11] And why do some patients actually admit the lack of movement in the limb but offer rationalizations to explain away their failures?[12] Finally, how do we explain other varieties of anosognosia, such as unawareness of blindness (known as Anton's syndrome), unawareness of aphasia (language disturbances) and memory disorders, and even unawareness of other neurological conditions such as chorea (uncontrollable quick movements of the limbs and body)?[13] For these and other reasons, many researchers have speculated that the most extreme cases of anosognosia cannot be explained solely by the *loss* of certain faculties and abilities that are often present in ansognosic patients, and other factors must be involved.

Asomatognosia and Somatoparaphrenia

If anosognosia involves the denial of bodily illness, one of the most perplexing neurological perturbations of the self is a condition called *asomatognosia,* in which the patient denies ownership of a part of the body itself.[14] Although some patients have been reported to disown the entire body, or one half of the body (and even in one case the penis), by far the most common variety of the syndrome occurs in patients with damage to the non-dominant, usually right hemisphere of the brain, who consequently deny ownership of a paralyzed left limb. In these cases patients also typically demonstrate hemispatial neglect, and they are commonly, but not necessarily, anosognosic of their condition.

When I work with this group of patients, I always elicit the asomatognosic response in the same way. In order to minimize the effect of the left hemispatial neglect, I approach the patient from the right side, grasp the patient's paralyzed left arm and hand, and bring it as much as possible onto the patient's right, non-neglected side. I then ask the patient a series a question regarding the identity of the limb, such as: "What is this?" "Who does this belong to?" and "Do you have a name for this?"

In the simplest cases a patient only appears confused about the identity of the arm. He or she may profess ignorance, tell me that they are not sure, or state that it could be my arm. When corrected, and told explicitly that indeed this is their own arm, many patients will readily change their minds and admit ownership of the limb. This simple degree of confusion is understandable, and not terribly interesting from a neuropsychological point of view, given that the patient has profound hemispatial neglect and nearly complete loss of sensation in the arm due to damage to the sensory regions of the right hemisphere. Additionally, the acute patient often displays varying degrees of generalized confusion that could contribute to misidentification of the arm.

As with anosognosia, however, there is a wide range of asomatognosic responses that vary in their degree of intensity. Some patients have a much more profound disturbance in their sense of ownership or personal relatedness to the limb. In these cases, patients adamantly deny that the limb belongs to them. Even when they are told explicitly that the limb is theirs, or when the connec-

Table 1-1. Examples of personification and misidentification of left paralyzed limbs

Responses from women	**Responses from men**
PEOPLE	

"My (now deceased) husband's hand"[16]	"My brother's arm"[27]
"My mother's arm"[17]	"Paralyzed brother's arm"[19]
"My son's arm"[17]	"Belonged to his daughter"[20]
"My (now deceased) husband's hand"[18]	
"My (now deceased) husband's arm"[18]	
"That's an old man"[19]	
"Her daughter"[22]	
"Belongs to the nurse"[22]	
"Belongs to Mrs. D" (a friend and nurse)[22]	

NICKNAMES

"Little Susie"[16]	"Little Monkey . . . Lucky"[24]
"Toby"[19]	

METAPHORS

"Pet Rock"[16]	"A piece of dead meat"[24]
"Dummy"[24]	"A cow's foot . . . like Long John
"Nothing but a bag of bones"[16]	Silver"[21]
"Stock option"[16]	"A canary claw, yellow and shriv-
"Reptile"[19]	eled"[25]
"It's the strange hand"[16]	"A sack of coal"[23]
"Lazy bum"[26]	"Dead hand"[28]
	"Dummy hand"[29]

tion of the paralyzed arm is traced to the shoulder, they still will deny it belongs them, or provide some delusional or confabulatory explanation for how the arm came to be attached to them. When the patient displays these more extreme forms of asomatognosia, the term *somatoparaphrenia* is sometimes applied.[15]

For patients who develop asomatognosia or somatoparaphrenia, the forms of misidentification and personification roughly fall into three categories[16-29] (Table 1-1). The limb may be identified as belonging to another person, usually a relative of the patient. Several women identified the arm as belonging to their deceased husbands, but the range of responses included claims that the arm belonged to a son, a daughter, a nurse, or a friend. Men tended to misidentify the arm as belonging to a son or brother, but one man attributed it to his mother-in-law.

Another group of patients employed the use of metaphor in their misidentifications in a way that tended to express the patient's feelings about the limb. While the term "metaphor" has numerous meanings, one useful definition for our purposes states that "The essence of metaphor is understanding and experiencing one kind of thing in terms of another."[30] In neurological cases, patients with self-related disturbances may relate confabulations about elements of their lives, which they deny directly, in a metaphorical form. These may be derogatory ("dummy," "a canary claw, yellow and shriveled") or expressive of the patient's feelings that the limb was useless ("nothing but a bag of bones," "lump of lead," "sack of coal"). Patient CM, whom we discussed earlier, used this form of metaphorical language about her paralyzed left arm to both personify it and express disgust when she urged her arm, "*come on lazy bum move, move up my leg, don't make me help you. . . .*"

Perhaps as a result of the dire circumstances in which these individuals find themselves, the metaphors they use often relate to death. These patients may describe their left arm as appearing "dead" or say that the arm is "dead tired." There are some patients, however, who seem to believe the arm is literally dead. A patient I examined, GS, had this response when I showed him his left hand:

GS: *Part of a dead hand . . . It belonged to me once . . .*
TEF: *Who does it belong to?*
GS: *The hospital.*
TEF: *Who does it belong to? Is it yours?*
GS: *It was once.*

TEF: *So let's just say for one more time then, what is this now? Tell me what it is.*
GS: *A dead hand . . . A dead hand . . .*

GS went on to describe the hand as "the Devil's hand" and requested that it be cut off.

My patient SK who had a left hemisphere paralysis after a right hemisphere stroke also spoke about her arm in metaphorical fashion. While on the one hand she gives the arm the comical, somewhat sarcastic, designation of a "pet rock," she also alludes to death in her account:

SK: *It took a vacation without telling me it was going. It didn't ask, it just went.*
TEF: *What did?*
SK: *My pet rock.*
TEF: *You call that your pet rock?*
SK: *Yeah.*
TEF: *Why do you call it your pet rock?*
SK: *Because it doesn't do anything. It just sits there.*
TEF: *When did you come up with that name?*
SK: *Right after it went plop. I thought I'd give it a nice name even though it was something terrible.*
TEF: *Do you have any other names for it?*
SK: *Her. She belongs to me so she's a her. She's mine but I don't like her very well. She let me down.*
TEF: *In what way?*
SK: *Plop plop rock rock nothing. I was on my way home out the door and then she went and did this* [pointing to her left arm]. *She didn't ask if she could* [shaking her head back and forth]. *I have to be the boss not her* [pointing to her left arm].
TEF: *Is that its actual name? Would you say that is its real name?*
SK: *For now. It doesn't deserve any better. I could paint it if I wanted to.*
TEF: *Is it a real pet rock though?*
SK: *No, it's my hand.*
TEF: *So why do you refer to it as a pet rock? What do you mean by that?*
SK: *It lays there like a lump. It doesn't do anything. It just lays there. Its like when you're Jewish and you go to Jewish cemetery and put a rock on the tomb and it*

just lays there. It is supposed to say "I was here." [pointing to her arm] *It's saying I'm here. But I'm not. I'm only sort of here. I'm not really here.*

Another patient included numerous metaphorical allusions to death in his descriptions of his paralyzed left arm. A man in his thirties who was artistically inclined, JK had been living and working in America for several years, though his family, with whom he was very close, remained overseas. After JK underwent surgery to drain a brain abscess of his right hemisphere, he developed a left-side paralysis, left hemispatial neglect, and dense loss of sensation on the left side. When I examined JK, I held his left arm up to him and asked him to identify it:

TEF: *What is this?*

JK: *It's supposed to be my arm, but I think it's my brother's arm. I tell that to everyone but they don't believe me. My brother was on the wrong track for a while, and he got involved with some gangsters. They chopped off his arms and threw them in the river. I found this in my coffin.* [touching the left arm] *Some people thought I was dead and it was there.*

After some further questioning, I returned to this theme:

TEF: *Now what about, you mentioned something about being in . . . you found it in your coffin. Tell me about that.*

JK: *I don't know why I was in a coffin . . . after I was carried to the hospital. . . . I was in a coffin . . . that's what I remember . . . I was laying next to this arm* [pointing to left arm]. *. . . I was in a coffin.*

TEF: *And that's how you found it?*

JK: *Yeah that's how I found it . . .*

TEF: *Were you alive?*

JK: *I was alive . . . I didn't die . . . I found the arm in the coffin.*

As JK misidentifies his arm, gives it a separate identity, and confabulates about how it was attached to him, his statements are particularly rich in metaphor and meaning. Furthermore, the boundaries between his physical being and that of an emotionally significant other have been partially dissolved—both figuratively and literally. Another case I examined, ML, a woman in her seventies who was admitted to the hospital with an acute stroke and left-side paralysis, also viewed her arm as literally dead, and related it to a husband who had died years ago:[31]

TEF: *What is this about your husband's hands? Did you have your husband's hands?*
ML: *I did.*
TEF: *Tell me about that. What happened?*
ML: *He left them.*
TEF: *He left them to you?*
ML: *He didn't want them.*
TEF: *OK. Well, did he leave them to you in his will?*
ML: *He just left them like he left his clothes [tearfully].*
TEF: *So they were in the house? Tell me about them.*
ML: *Up until the other day. They used to fall on my chest. I said "I got to get rid of them!"*
TEF: *Yes.*
ML: *So I did.*
TEF: *So what did you do?*
ML: *Put them in the garbage.*
TEF: *You put them in the garbage?*
ML: *Yes . . . two days ago.*
TEF: *Where are they now?*
ML: *Still in the garbage . . . a black hand, with a plastic cover . . . you'll find them there. Be careful, though . . . the nails are very long . . . and very sharp. How come nails grew on dead hands?*
TEF: *I don't know . . . How do you figure that?*
ML: *I don't understand; if it's dead, it's dead. I don't know.*
TEF: *How do you account for that?*
ML: *I can't . . . maybe they're not completely dead.*
TEF: *What would that mean?*
ML: *Nothing at all.*

TEF: *Why did you get rid of them?*

ML: *They were bothering me. They used to fall on my chest when I slept . . . and they're very heavy. And the nails used to scratch me.*

TEF: *Sounds like they were alive!*

ML: *No . . . they were dead, dead, dead! I tell you, you can take my word for it.*

TEF: *How many years did you have them?*

ML: *Maybe two. Since I was sick.*

TEF: *Since you were sick you had them? Why did you throw them out?*

ML: *Because I thought they were hard luck.*

TEF: *Why did you get rid of them after all those years?*

ML: *Because I got the stroke . . . and I thought maybe I'd die here like he did!*

As in the case of JK, the boundaries between ML's feelings about herself and her paralyzed arm and those about a loved one are merged. Both patients deny the true nature of the arm and identify this part of the self with something else personally significant in the world. Another type of asomatognosic response, with an even more fanciful attitude toward the paralyzed limb, was first described by the great British neurologist Macdonald Critchley. In this case, the patient with a left hemiplegia and left hemisensory deficit refers to his left arm as if it possessed an identify separate from himself: Critchley's patient, who called his arm "Little Monkey" and "Lucky," also tried to feed it.

My own patient SK who called her arm a "pet rock" also referred to it as "Little Susie," similarly misidentifying her limb as another individual.[32] At one point during an interview she grasped her left hand with her right, shook it and began to sing "Wake Up Little Susie":

SK: *Wake up! Time to go home. What are we gonna tell your mama? What are we gonna tell your papa? What are we gonna tell your friends when they say ooh la la wake up little Susie, it's time to go home.* [Then she held her left hand to her cheek and hugged it and kissed it and fondled it and petted it. She said she's a good girl.]

TEF: *What was that?*

SK: *Wake up little Susie, remember the Everly Brothers?* [pointing to her left arm] *that's her, that's little Susie. She been out all night long she has to go home. That's it she's done she's gotta go home or they're gonna think she's the town whore* [laughing].

TEF: *Why would you say that?*

SK: *Because she's not behaving* [She wiggled her arm again, pulling on her fingers as if to rouse it]. *Wake up little Susie!*

[She later went on to tell me why she had developed this idea about her left arm being little Susie].

SK: *It's a coping mechanism. It's like laughter is the best medicine. If you can't laugh what have you got? I thought I could bring her back with some loving kindness. So I sang it "Wake Up Little Susie," which is one of my favorite songs from the Everly Brothers.*

TEF: *What's the theme of that song?*

SK: *A girl and her boyfriend were out too late at night. And the entire town is gonna be talking about them, that she's being a slut. So it's a way of avoiding getting in trouble. And then he says what are you gonna tell your mama, what are you gonna tell your papa, what are you gonna tell your friends when then they say ooh la la wake up little Susie it's time to go home.* [Then she lifts her left arm] *I wanna go home.*

These cases of asomatognosia and confabulation share a number of important features. In the case of JK and ML their feelings about the self are merged with their feelings about a relative. Critchley's patient treats the arm like a comical plaything or a doll, while SK half-jokingly identifies the arm with a character from a song. All cases therefore represent a merging of feelings about the self—their arm—with those about someone or something else. But in these neurological cases, the metaphorical usage and the merging of the self with the outside world take on a particular intensity as the boundaries between the self and the world appear to partially dissolve. We shall see that this disturbance in ego boundaries is common in patients with right hemisphere pathology, and is an important key to understanding how these confabulations are created.

Disorders of the Relational Self

Beyond the disorders relating to the self in the body, there exists a broad group of conditions known as *delusional misidentification syndromes* (DMS), in which a patient consistently misidentifies persons, places, objects, or events in the world around him.

Delusional Misidentification Syndromes

The most commonly reported form of misidentification for persons is known as Capgras syndrome, first reported in 1923 by the French psychiatrists Joseph Capgras and Reboul-Lachaux.[33] The essence of the disorder lies in the delusional belief that a person or persons have been replaced by "doubles" or imposters. A related type of misidentification is Fregoli syndrome, first described in 1927 and named after the Italian actor Leopoldo Fregoli, who was known for his quick changes on stage, which involves the belief that a person who is well known to the patient is really impersonating, and hence taking on the appearance of, a stranger in the patient's environment.[34]

There have been various attempts to broadly classify the various types of DMS. One early theory held that Capgras syndrome represents a negative illusion (a negation of actual identity) while Fregoli represents a positive illusion (an assertion of false identity). Another theory suggested that Capgras syndrome is a result of "hypoidentification," that is, patients "under-identify" or fail to identify what is familiar, while Fregoli syndrome is the manifestation of "hyperidentification," where the novel is misidentified or "over-identified" as familiar.[35] In my own research, I've suggested that the DMS cleave along a dimension of *personal relatedness*, in which alienation and affiliation is based upon the pattern of identification between the self and other persons, objects, events, or experiences. In this view, Capgras syndrome represents an *under-personalized* response and Fregoli syndrome an *over-personalized* misidentification.[36] I prefer this approach because it emphasizes the emotional and motivational aspects of the condition. DMS patients *know* who the misidentified person should be, but they experience a disturbance or transformation in their emotional relatedness and connectedness to the misidentified entity.

A typical patient I've examined with the Capgras syndrome was FP, a woman in her eighties in the early stages of Alzheimer's disease, who began to misidentify her sister, who was her closest relation and friend, and who was gradually becoming her caretaker as well. Her sister's proper name was Mary, but she was known as Paula. FP typically called her sister Paula, but she began to claim that someone named Mary, who was not her sister, was posing as Paula and trying to take her place in the house. I interviewed FP about these "doubles" with her sister Paula present in the office:

PAULA: *I would say nine times out of ten she.... I'm the " other" person. I am not her sister Paula. I am "Paula someone else."*

TEF: *But they both have the same name though?*

FP: *No ... she stole it* [pointing to Paula] *She snatched it! It's not her real name ... You remember you said—when we were on our way out—"Here's the girl now and she was coming down the steps, and you said "which one is she?" And I said "Well, I don't know which one" but she is always there you know ... she is a lot of help to me but sometimes she aggravates me and then I can't see ...*

PAULA: *There is always a third person in the room and it could be Mary, it's not her sister, but it's Mary this girl ... it's not Mary her sister, it's Mary a stranger, it's somebody else that wants to horn in and take Paula's place.*

FP: *You do that don't you?*

PAULA: *No honey ... I tried to tell you it's just a hallucination that you have ...*

FP: *There are five Paulas now and they have all gone off the hook. Believe me. Five of them, yes. And I think they are almost all in this room now! And I'm so aggravated with the whole bunch of them. . . . I call you Mary, I call you any other name, but you will hang on to Paula. I said why would anyone want a rotten wily name that you can't even bother about?*

FP also had significant memory and visuospatial impairment, which is a frequent ingredient in similar cases of the disorder. However, her misidentification was selective and exclusive to her sister, and she never misidentified me or anyone else in her environment. This selectivity is critical. One feature I have repeatedly observed among Capgras patients is that the person who is misidentified is the person whom the patient is most dependent upon. The misidentification is therefore particularly disappointing and frustrating to the family member who is managing the patient's care, since that is the person the patient most commonly claims is an imposter. In many instances, the son or daughter who spends the most time with the parent, the one who absorbs the brunt of the responsibility for the patient's care, and often the one who must absorb the occasionally difficult and sometimes abusive behavior of the patient, is the one whose identity is denied. The issue of the ambivalent feelings of the patient toward the primary caretaker appears to play an essential role in the development of the condition in these cases.

In another variant of the Capgras syndrome in neurological patients, *Capgras syndrome for inanimate objects,* the patient does not misidentify people but rather displays selective misidentification and doubling of familiar objects.[37] I examined LR, a woman in her eighties also in the early stages of Alzheimer's disease, who displayed this condition.

TEF: *Which things in the apartment have been switched?*
LR: *Everything, the doors have been taken out . . . they are old, dirty, and beat up . . . not my chairs. But I'm glad they are there . . .*
TEF: *They look older you're saying.*
LR: *I don't think I know they are older.*

TEF: *Now what about your clothes?*

LR: *They're changed . . .*

TEF: *And your children's clothes have been changed as well?*

LR: *Oh yes.*

TEF: *Now why would somebody do this?*

LR: *I don't know . . . I have no idea, why would somebody do this. There were these "drug people" that got mixed up in our lives for a while there but we got rid of them. But I can't see drug people doing that. They would more take something. They would steal it! It doesn't make sense at all. I know my clothes. I know my things. . . . My daughter thinks I'm crazy. All of them think I'm senile. That I'm saying things and doing things that are not so. But I know I'm not senile! I'm far from being senile. And I'll never get senile! Can someone drive you senile? There's nothing they can do to your health in that area to make you senile?*

TEF: *No . . . Tell me about that bag* [LR had a pocketbook on her lap].

LR: *It's not my bag . . . not the right size for one thing. And the color is completely wrong too. I don't buy navy blue bags. It's a different color, and a different manufacturer. Two people don't cut alike. Two people never make the same thing. The person must have who made the switch.*

TEF: *Is that your shirt?*

LR: *No. I never bought a shirt like this in my life. . . . OK you think I'm crazy? No! You think somebody is trying to drive me crazy? Maybe there is something there in that area . . . I don't know . . . I don't think so.*

I have observed that Capgras patients also display memory and visuospatial impairment, as well as unawareness—*even denial*—of these impairments. When such patients are corrected regarding their errors, they often respond with anger, despairing that no one believes them, that everyone else is crazy or trying to trick them. Thus, suspiciousness and the feeling that there is some sort of ruse or deception at play is common.

Patients with memory and visuospatial impairments may also exhibit the opposite of the Capgras syndrome, or the Fregoli syndrome. Unlike the Capgras case where personal relatedness to the familiar is lost, in the Fregoli syndrome, rather than denying the identity of a familiar person or environment, these patients mis-identify unfamiliar persons or objects as personally familiar or related to them. For example, many people who were employed prior to a brain injury produce confabulations that are temporally displaced memories about their employment. Thus, hospitalized patients will often claim they are at a work site, at the office, on a construction job, etc. Many of these neutral confabulations are banal, changing from moment to moment and day to day, and contain no particularly unbelievable or bizarre elements. They are most often a condensation of the patient's memories before the injury with some aspect of their ongoing experience.

Such was the case of OE, a man in his fifties who sustained bilateral frontal damage as a result of a traumatic brain injury with resulting profound amnesia for past and present events. He was previously employed as a manager in a large company involved in employee training and planning, although when asked he could not actually recall what kind of work he did or his home address, and he gave the ages of his children as approximately ten years younger than their actual ages. When examined, the patient produced confabulations that were a combination of his past work experience and his current experience in the rehabilitation facility where he was now housed:

EX: *And so where are you living now?*

OE: *I'm staying right here in the hotel I came from.*

EX: *And why are you in a hotel at this point?*

OE: *I'm staying there for my company there to try to help with my situation.*

EX: *And what do you do at the hotel?*

OE: *I'm responsible for the training situation right now.*

EX: *Who else is there?*

OE: *My wife is there and there is a whole set of people. Their operations, procedures, do the stuff for them that they can't do.*

EX: *What do you do there specifically?*

OE: *Involved with serving and eating . . . I set procedures to handle the daily one per day. So anyone we send through the training in the morning we have to have breakfast for, then we have to have lunch for, then we have to have dinner for . . . so we write that what everyone has to go through what the procedures are.*

EX: *And these people who you direct procedures for, why are they there?*

OE: *They are there because that's what we want them to do. We want them to handle these operations in order to handle our products.*

It is often the case in this type of confabulation that *both* persons and the environment are over-identified, that is, seen as familiar when they are not, as was the case with patient LA, a man in his early forties with a right frontal brain hemorrhage who claimed he was at work, and misidentified multiple staff workers as people from his workplace. My colleague, neuropsychologist Dr. Joseph Giacino, conducted this interview in a rehabilitation facility:

JG: *What are you doing here?*

LA: *I'm working.*

JG: *OK. And what are you working at?*

LA: *I'm trying to learn from them.*

JG: *OK. Is this part of your job?*

LA: *Yes.*

JG: *And what's your job?*

LA: *I'm a computer person.*

JG: *So that's what you're doing here? Computers? . . . And you're at work here?*

LA: *Yes.*

JG: *Do you get paid your regular salary?*

LA: *Yes.*

JG: *Where are we right now?*

LA: *We're at* [name of his company] *in New York . . . My office is right around the corner* [pointing]. *If they have problems with their computers I solve them.*

JG: [Pointing to a therapist of the facility that the patient had previously claimed he knew] *And you know her from . . . ?*

LA: *Yes* [names his company] . . .

JG: *Co-worker? What's her job?*

LA: *Her job is to do research on certain items and them bring them to* [his company]
*... She works with somebody else ... She comes to me for the type of information
I need to connect for her ... that's the time we have connection. Otherwise there isn't
any connection ... when she has problems with her computer she comes to me.*

Delusions and Fantasies about Imaginary
Persons: Foes, Friends, and Family

Among the many other variants on the basic theme of misidentification that are included within the broad classification of DMS,
there is one particular group of conditions that is particularly relevant to the study of the self.[38] In these patients, the affected individual may or may not misidentify specific persons in the environment,
but whether or not there is misidentification of specific persons, the
patient holds a delusional or confabulatory belief that a fictitious
person exists in the world that is in some fashion significantly related to the individual. One of these syndromes occurs when the patient believes that his or her mirror reflection represents such a
fictitious person. In another variety, the patient creates an imaginary
relative who may be a duplication of someone the patient is actually
related to, such as a child, brother, or cousin. Finally, there are other
cases when the patient imbues an inanimate object with a human
identity. For the purpose of analysis, I will divide these syndromes
into three groups: *delusional persecutors, imaginary companions,* and *phantom relatives.* As with patients who experience anosognosia and asomatognosia, each of these variants displays specific patterns that
supply clues to the underlying mechanisms behind their creation.

Delusional Persecutors

Among those who display such unusual delusions and fantasies,
there is an intriguing and surprisingly homogenous group of patients who harbor intensely held, delusional, and often persecutory
beliefs about their reflected image. Although the syndrome affects

both sexes, the most severely delusional and persecutory cases have been described in women.[39]

The first well-described example of this syndrome was the case reported in 1968 of a 61-year-old New Zealand woman of European descent who may have been in the early stages of dementia. Her major complaint was that there was a woman in her home who was her double and who followed her about the house and imitated her in every way. This woman, however, could only be seen in the mirror:

> She could only see her if she looked in the mirror. She did not know what this woman was called, calling her an old hag, an ugly hag or usually this thing. This woman did not speak to her verbally but only in gesture or by mimicry. . . . The woman was there because she wanted love and affection from the patient, but the patient could not give her affection and she was very much afraid of this double . . . she would say emphatically that it was not her but that terrible ugly old woman who followed her everywhere and frightened her. She could not escape, try as she would, from the presence of this hag. . . . She had on occasion thrown a bucket of water and other solid objects at her mirror image to try and persuade it to leave the house.[40]

As in this case, the majority of patients identified with this syndrome are diagnosed with dementia and harbor paranoid beliefs about the "other person" in the mirror. In one such case the patient believed the woman in the mirror was following her and stealing her possessions.[41] In another instance, a woman who suffered from Alzheimer's disease displayed a similar constellation of behaviors:

> The patient had a history of self-consciousness about her physical attractiveness and was disturbed by her reflection in the mirror. She interpreted her reflection as another woman who was constantly present in her apartment, occupying her bed, interfering in her activities, stealing her things and claiming her possessions. The patient described the intruder as a crude and unpleasant woman who spoke Hungarian, the patient's native language.[42]

In the case of another 61-year-old woman with probable Alzheimer's disease, the woman in the mirror appeared to be hostile toward her. She would become upset and tearful upon seeing "the woman" and sometimes would hide from her. The patient even claimed that one day the intruder chased the patient from her home. She wondered why "the woman" was not at her own home "cleaning the toilets," which the patient claimed was "the woman's" only responsibility.[43] In another case of an 82-year-old woman with dementia and evidence of bilateral brain disease (that was greater on the right side), the patient had a similar reaction to her mirror image, although she referred to the mirror image as "the girl." While she was being examined at the hospital, she was given a small hand held mirror and exclaimed:

> That girl! What is she doing here? I thought she was only back home! She launched into a tirade implicating "the girl" in a scheme to move into her home and drain her resources. "I just can't afford to feed two people!"[44]

A number of other varieties of persecutory presences may occur in patients with selective brain damage or dementia. One particularly common variety is called the *phantom boarder syndrome,* a condition that is seen most often in association with Alzheimer's disease, in which the patient believes a person or persons have invaded the home.[45] The phantom is not typically seen in the mirror, and in some cases may not be seen at all, but is believed to be living upstairs or in the attic. J-P Hwang and his colleagues studied fifty-six patients with dementia and phantom boarder syndrome admitted to the geropsychiatric ward of the Veterans General Hospital in Taipei, Taiwan, where they found that the phantom boarder may often be identified as a friend or relative, an intruder or stranger, or a deceased person or ghost. Some patients were afraid that the phantom would do them harm or even kill them. Others had more indifferent reactions, and there were also some who interacted with the phantom in a pleasant fashion and even had it to dinner.[46]

In one of my own patients, this delusion took the form that he believed his body was actually physically inhabited by a diabolical being. This patient, GT, was a man in his sixties, a highly functioning individual with an excellent job who had never seen a psychiatrist until he had a stroke within his right hemisphere that caused minimal weakness on the left side. At the time I interviewed him, he was cognitively entirely normal. But he described to me how, about a year after his stroke, he began to experience the belief and physical sensation that there was a malevolent entity that inhabited his body and tortured him:

GT: *Well right now there is something right around my neck, strangling me and he's screaming he's ranting like I'm warning you you're going to be dead by midnight tonight. He's screaming at me now, I can hear him. . . . he puts dust in my ears, and my nose and mouth . . . he's in the shape of an amoeba. He gets pretty big . . . it's not alive but it talks to me . . . right now he's pounding on my chest from the inside. . . . he's twisting my head around and what he does too I don't know how he does this—it's an illusion—but he takes my head and he twists it right off and he throws it like a basketball . . . he takes my medication and throws it in the air . . . he shoots tacks at me at night. . . . he's in my mouth right now . . . he stays in there all day . . . no one else can see him but me . . . he says it's me, he is me . . .*
TEF: *He is you? What do you mean by that?*
GT: *I'm asking him now. . . . I'm asking him now . . . he's telling me he's going to follow me to my grave and be with me forever! . . . he's become part of me already. He's with me every day, all through the day and the night . . . he hates the news and he hates music, so whenever I try to watch the news or listen to music he gets crazy. . . . He hates my left side that was affected by the stroke . . . like right now he's pulling it back . . . he's making it move right now* [he moves his left arm back and forth] *. . . he says he's number one and I'm number two. . . . he flies into my rectum and I try to flush him down the toilet. . . . it's a man, my age . . . he's like me, my age. looks like me.*
TEF: *So he's your age, he's a man, and he looks like you . . .*

GT: *He does sometimes like I tell him sometimes he's in the shape of an amoeba . . .*
and he'll take it and slap it on my face and later he'll peel it off. . . . he makes a
cast of my face. . . . he says he is me.

The patients I have described with delusional persecutors develop
these beliefs in the setting of brain pathology. However, there is no
evidence that the persecutory aspects of the symptom have any specific neuroanatomical features that distinguish this group from patients that have more friendly fantasy companions that I describe
next. In other words, while the brain pathology is essential in creating the delusion, there may be other factors, such as the patient's personality, that determine whether the imaginary person is perceived
as friend or foe.

IMAGINARY COMPANIONS

As we have seen earlier in the case of SP, who developed a close and
personal relationship with the "other" self in the mirror, not all
imaginary figures are hostile. In a similar case, an 80-year-old
woman with dementia also saw a friendly presence in the reflection:

> She was unable to recognize herself in the mirror, calling her reflec-
> tion "my friend." Although she used the mirror when washing and
> grooming, she continued to maintain that it was her "friend" whom
> she was viewing in the mirror and who was also engaging in wash-
> ing and grooming routines . . . she did not think that her "friend"
> looked identical to her but did agree that there was some resem-
> blance.[47]

British researchers Michael Shanks and Annalena Venneri described another group of patients who, like those with the mirror
companion syndrome, claim the existence of *delusional companions.*[48]
In these three cases, all of them women who had Alzheimer's disease
with predominantly right parietal, temporal, or frontal hemisphere
dysfunction, the patients treated teddy bears or other soft toys or

dolls as if they were real. In one case, an 81-year-old unmarried woman, AS, developed a relationship with a large teddy bear. She spoke to it, took it on drives with her, and tried to get it to eat, drink, and read the newspaper. She described the teddy bear as "a super person very interested in what is going on" and as "a very attractive little youngster." For her, the teddy seemed to serve the role as a companion and friend. In the case of AL, 85 years old and also unmarried, the patient called her teddy bear "Doreen" and said of her, "She is a dear little girl and she's got a dearly loving heart." AL gave "Doreen" an allowance of one pound per week, and she noted that at age 9 "dolls grow up quickly, you know!" When asked if "Doreen" was really alive she explained, "No, she does not breathe or anything like that, I sometime wonder myself whether she is alive, I wish she were, she would make a lovely companion!" Finally, in the case of ST, a 74-year-old widow claimed her deceased husband was actually alive. More remarkably, she kept thirty soft toys and dolls that she would place on her coffee table "so that they could watch television." ST claimed that they were able to speak to her and move about the apartment.

In addition to the common denominator that all of the women in these cases suffered right hemisphere dysfunction, all three patients were socially isolated and the delusional companions were an important source of emotional comfort and companionship. Thus, in these delusional companion cases, as in the mirror cases, there appears to be an interaction between neurological, neuropsychological, and socioemotional variables in the creation of the full-blown syndrome.

While these delusions may be most common among women, one of my patients, KP, a gentleman in his eighties, developed an unusual relationship with his own inner voice. Though he had had no prior psychiatric episodes, he had longstanding bilateral hearing loss and used hearing aids and was referred to our center because he was experiencing hallucinations of a voice or voices singing:

KP: *I don't think it keeps me awake . . . I fall asleep . . . this guy's singing or whatever*
   he does. . . . he sounds like he does a lot of regular normal music and he hums a

lot "la lala lala lala lalalala." . . . He even sang once "Fiddler on the Roof" because I sang it once, because I mentioned it. He copies, if I should sing something—I like to sing—I sing to myself . . . sometimes I hum, but as soon as I do
that he will come and do the same thing. Copies the ones I do. . . . I know all the
songs he knows . . . sometimes he ad libs some of the words. . . . A week later I went
to New Jersey and there it was again. He followed me there!

TEF: *Is this a person who is singing this or is it coming from your head?*

KP: *It sounds like a person that is singing it.*

TEF: *Is it your imagination or is it real?*

KP: *No it's real.*

TEF: *It's real . . . how can someone be singing in your head?*

KP: *I don't know . . . [laughs] . . . and every once in a while a woman comes . . . very
seldom . . . when I sit by the television and he's in another room, I don't hear him
because the television blocks him out . . . but as soon as I shut down the television
and I go to bed he starts . . .*

TEF: *Is it always the same person?*

KP: *99 percent.*

TEF: *Do you know his name?*

KP: *[laughs] He never told me . . . I wish I knew his name!*

TEF: *It's not your name? He doesn't have the same name as you?*

KP: *No, he has his own name. . . . One song was "If I Was a Rich Man."*

TEF: *From Fiddler?*

KP: *Fiddler on the Roof. Yeah, there are many songs he sang. Very popular songs.
All songs that were famous.*

TEF: *He did "Rich Man"? That was one of them?*

KP: *Because I was humming it. I was singing it. So he copied it . . . when I stopped
he starting singing it . . . with every song, with everything I do, if he hears it, he
probably will sing it.*

I interpret KP's experience as a form of personification of his own
experiences of himself. Although the inner voice does not have the
fullness of personality of some of the other fantasy people I have described, it is clear in listening to KP that the voices in his head have
become separate individuals who are distinct from his own ego. He

does not tell me that he hears his own voice inside his head singing, but rather there are other people who sing to him.

PHANTOM RELATIVES

Finally, among those harboring beliefs about fictitious persons that we might describe as delusions, confabulations, or even fantasies, are those who claim the existence of a fictitious relative. In some cases, the phantom is the duplication of an actual, and usually close, relative; in other cases, it appears in the form of a belief in a phantom child.

In 1956, Edwin Weinstein and his colleagues first described patients with brain damage who expressed delusional beliefs about children, the most common of which was the mistaken belief that the patient was a parent of a fictitious child.[49] These astute clinicians observed that a unique feature of this particular variety of delusion was that these patients often attributed to the "phantom child" the same illness or disability that they themselves had. One woman with a brain tumor and resulting blindness claimed during her illness that she had a child who was "sick and blind," and a 21-year-old soldier with a traumatic brain injury and weakness of both legs claimed that he had a 3-year-old "daughter" who had leg paralysis as a result of polio. In other cases, the "phantom child" embodied significant personal issues besides or in addition to personal illness. For example, one woman who felt that she was being mistreated by the nursing staff claimed that she had a "baby" that the nurses had "harmed and even killed." As in asomatognosia, in which the patient may claim the affected limb is dead or belongs to a dead person, the phantom child is often said to be dead or ill. This belief often parallels the patient's sense of his or her own threatening personal medical condition. These self-referential delusions and confabulations occur in a variety of clinical settings yet demonstrate particular repeating patterns.

For instance, in another case, a 42-year-old Englishman, RJ, was involved in a serious car accident that resulted in intracranial hemorrhages involving both frontal lobes.[50] Despite the seriousness of his condition and the fact that he was in the hospital and rehabilitation for many months, he repeatedly denied the seriousness of his own injuries. RJ had a real brother, Martin, an adult who was still in communication with the patient. However, after his injury, RJ confabulated that he had had two brothers, both named Martin, but that one Martin had been killed in a car accident.

One of my patients who exhibited phantom child delusions was a 65-year-old female, LK, who had suffered a brain aneurysm that resulted in damage to her frontal lobes bilaterally and also displayed significant memory and cognitive impairments.[51] She was divorced and had no children. When I inquired why she was in the hospital, she described that she was there to visit her "niece" whom she described as a "child" and "a little girl." She claimed that the niece had an aneurysm, and also insisted that she had an aunt and six cousins all with "aneurysms on top of their heads."

LK tended to deny or minimize her own neuropsychological deficits and displayed poor insight into her surgery and illnesses. Initially, she denied any surgery or illness entirely, but rather attributed similar problems to her relatives:

TEF: *So you came to visit somebody. Who did you come to visit?*

LK: *I came to visit my aunt.*

TEF: *Your aunt . . . and what was wrong with her?*

LK: *She couldn't think straight.*

TEF: *She couldn't think straight? Why?*

LK: [Patient now reaches up and feels the top of her head, which was shaved and had a long line of surgical staples] *Something was wrong on top of her head . . . causing her . . . an aneurysm . . . not to think straight.*

TEF: *Your aunt had an aneurysm?*

LK: *Yeah. And an aneurysm is blood on top of your head.*

TEF: *What hospital was she in?*

LK: *This one.*

TEF: *You're kidding? She was in the same hospital as this one? Is she here now?*
LK: *I think so.*
TEF: *Where is she?*
LK: *You got me! I don't know exactly where, but I know she is in this hospital.*

At various times, LK expressed the belief that she had an aneurysm, that her cousins had aneurysms, or that her aunt had an aneurysm. Much of the time, however, it seemed that she herself felt well, and that it did not seem to her that what she had been told about her operations and illness was actually true:

TEF: *You're saying that the doctors told you had an aneurysm, and that everything was going to be fine.*
LK: *Right.*
TEF: *But something happened? What happened?*
LK: *I assume something happened.*
TEF: *And now there's a disparity between the two things?*
LK: *Yes.*
TEF: *You don't feel ...*
LK: *Like I had an operation to save my life. I feel I had an operation to save someone else's life!*
TEF: *What would that mean?*
LK: *I don't know. I have no idea what that little statement meant.*
TEF: *Does that make any sense?*
LK: *No ... It absolutely doesn't make any sense. .... It doesn't make any sense!*
TEF: *But that's the way you feel?*
LK: *Yes.*
TEF: *Say it again.*
LK: *I feel like I had an operation for an aneurysm that I do not believe I had, do not believe they took out, and I'm walking around with an aneurysm that's half gone and half not gone. I feel half safe and half not safe. Does that make sense?*

In one of the most interesting and complex cases of this nature, examined by Dr. Joseph Giacino, SC suffered bilateral damage to his frontal lobes as the result of a ruptured anterior cerebral artery aneurysm.[52] After the injury, he experienced an array of neuropsychological impairments including problems with attention, memory, and executive functioning (i.e., the ability to plan ahead, regulate his actions, and exercise judgment and reason). In spite of the seriousness and incapacitating nature of his cognitive difficulties, SC denied that he had any cognitive impairment. Indeed, when he was asked why he was in the rehabilitation facility, he claimed he was "a guest" with the "optimists club" to "help out."

SC was the biological father of three children, and the severe nature of his intellectual difficulties led to the break-up of his marriage. In spite of the fact that he was separated from his wife, he claimed the existence of a child they were planning to adopt. During the course of an interview with Dr. Giacino, he asserted that the adopted child "has problems" and complained about the way the doctors were treating "the child":

SC: *I feel like I've got a little more ability than they give me credit for.*

JG: *So one last question: Has this aneurysm or the consequences of this aneurysm changed your life in any way at all?*

SC: *No.*

JG: *So basically your life is the way it was before?*

SC: *Yeah, like the way it was before. We have another baby . . . we've just adopted, and I have three children of my own. I've got my own house.*

JG: *When did you adopt a baby?*

SC: *We haven't gotten the final result, but about a month ago.*

JG: *They said you could have the baby?*

SC: *But the baby has problems now. They're trying to sort out the problems before, you know, somebody really adopts it . . . the baby. They want to make sure it's the right direction.*

JG: *Who's actually adopting the baby?*

SC: *Me and my wife.*

JG: *Have you seen the baby at all?*

SC: *Well, we've seen pictures. And I've seen the baby in person, too.*

JG: *And where does the baby live now?*

SC: *The baby lives with the mother, and I think it's the mother of the boy that was dumped . . . and the mother would like to have the baby. I guess [since] she lost her sons he might as well have the baby. That's a little problem there.*

JG: *You said before the baby has some problems.*

SC: *That's what the psychologists are telling the guy who is in charge of the hospital. You know it's like they say certain things I go along with and certain things I don't go along with. I think there's too much pressure on the kid to really give an honest answer. I don't think a kid who is 6 or 7 years old is capable of giving you the right answer.*

JG: *What kind of problems does this child have?*

SC: *I don't know . . . to tell you the honest truth, I don't know. I know this kid has been in the hospital off and on for a couple of years, and they kind of rate them as far as progress goes or things like that.* [The patient was being rated during the interview.]

JG: *How do they rate them?*

SC: *I guess they must rate them when they don't hear the things they want to hear . . . like the kid is not accomplishing anything, which I think is very unfair to basically analyze a kid that way.*

JG: *Let me ask you . . . tell me what this child looks like?*

SC: *Looks like me. But my kids all look the same. Put it this way. . . . They favor my complexion and everything like that. Beautiful looking kid. My wife's a beautiful looking woman. . . . Right now the child isn't a child's age . . . the child is 34 . . . 35 years old. You know what I mean?*

During the same interview the patient spoke about his intentions to adopt his niece as well.

SC: *We were going to adopt my niece. If we could adopt the niece instead of making her be on her own . . . this is my wife's brother's child. . . .*

JG: *So why would you adopt your wife's brother's child?*

SC: *We were going to adopt my niece. If we could adopt the niece instead of making her be on her own . . . this is my wife's brother's kid. . . .*

JG: *Your wife's brother's child? And why would you consider adopting?*

SC: *Because they are getting divorced . . . this has been going on for the last four or five years* [this was basically true of the patient] *and I think the kid is a brilliant kid. I don't believe . . . they are making the kid out to be some kind of nut but she isn't. She is a very intelligent girl. She has proven herself in school . . . she is leading the whole school as far as achievement is concerned. I believe . . . this all came to a head when the father decided in very short time . . . he got a divorce from his wife, the kid was separated from the family, and the father remarried. . . . the family got split up and she was denied some of her, what she thought were her rights when the divorce did come. In other words, the kid was out! The kid feels bitter. You know I could feel for the kid . . . all of a sudden she ain't got a brother, she ain't got a father, she got no brothers or sisters, and the family's split up. So its very easy to understand how they feel . . .* [at this point he becomes tear-full].

Clearly, although SC denies his own neurological impairments and personal problems, he attributes these problems to a phantom child. His complaints about the way the doctors treat him in the beginning of the interview resemble his complaints about the treatment of the child at the end. In this entirely unconscious process, SC's own deficits are denied, and then projected onto the fictitious phantom. In a similar fashion, his confabulations that some people are trying to make his niece out to be a "nut" but she's really "a brilliant kid" and "very intelligent" reflect his own feelings that his intelligence is underestimed by those around him. Likewise, his comments about the niece's bitterness at being abandoned reflect his own abandonment by his wife.

Another patient studied by Dr. Giacino displayed a similar form of confabulation. CB was a woman in her early forties who had a ruptured anterior cerebral artery aneurysm that resulted in a significant bifrontal subarachnoid hemorrhage. The bleed produced a profound memory defect within both her short- and long-term autobiographical memory. Although her problems were actually the result of the brain injury from the ruptured aneurysm, she confabulated that she thought she had shot herself through the mouth in a failed suicide attempt, an act she claimed that her niece, whom she was particularly fond of, had also committed. We do not know the niece's exact medical history, but there was no indication anyone had shot herself.

JG: *You were talking about [the rehab hospital] and you said "That's where I first met you" pointing to me.*

CB: *... I know I met you. And it was at a hospital. And you were with Mary Lou, my niece. She's the one that had I know she has surgery here* [pointing to her nose] *... she shot herself in the mouth.* [making gesture of a gun with her hand and pointing it into her mouth] *... And she's got fingers missing. ... she's had some amputated and others cut off.* [She discussed further her niece's hospitalizations and medical problems, and that Dr. Giacino is supposed to "work on her fingers." The patient claimed she was currently "visiting her niece" in the rehab hospital for her medical problems.]

JG: *How many* [rehab hospitals] *have you been in?*

CB: *Me? One down where I shot myself ...*

JG: *Can I ask you something you just said? You said "That's where I shot myself."*

CB: *Well supposedly I did. You see I'm getting, I'm hearing contradictions on this* [pointing to her upper lip with a gun gesture] *... I'm hearing I took a gun ... a shotgun. ... But then I'm thinking, that if I took a shotgun and put it in my mouth, I wouldn't have a roof and there should be stitches, and I really really don't think that I'd be here talking to you!*

JG: *Well who is it who thinks you shot yourself?*

CB: *Well first it was me, because believe it or not, it did cross my mind ... and that's what, God, everybody's been telling me.*

JG: *Everybody's been telling you what?*

CB: *That I shot myself!*

JG: [After some further questioning] *You know I'm going to interrupt you and go back a second, and tell you that because you've been saying that I met you at the hospital that your niece was at, who shot herself right?*

CB: *No ... she didn't ... that's what people are also telling her too. I think the family really needs ... thinks we want to shoot somebody and they get it into their heads that we go around shooting ourselves. Or they want to kill us. I don't know!* [laughing]

JG: [After more discussion of a possible self-inflicted gun shot wound] *It sounds like your feeling is that people have told you that you shot yourself but you don't see any evidence for that. So do you think you shot yourself?*

CB: *No. I don't think I have the nerve. Not to take a gun . . . No, I'm too afraid of bullets and too afraid of guns . . . I might have stabbed myself, or taken pills, the easy way . . . out.*

JG: *Were you depressed?*

CB: *I've been depressed. . . . yes* [nodding her head].

JG: *You have? To the point where . . . have you ever had suicidal thoughts before?*

CB: *Oh yes* [nodding her head] *but I don't think I have the nerve* [laughing exuberantly].

Like CB, who attributed her wounds to her niece, another patient, who had extensive frontal lobe injury that especially involved his right hemisphere, consistently spoke of his son as having gone through experiences that closely paralleled his own actions and feelings.[53] The patient, BB, was the father of two sons and spoke frequently about masculine themes, about the importance of being strong. BB's speech was peppered with his virtual obsession with the words "girls" and "boys" and "daughters" and "sons." (I have frequently observed the repetitive use of a particular words, or phrases, or concepts, in patients with frontal brain damage.) During his stay in a rehabilitation facility which had patients of both sexes, he produced the following narrative:

BB: *My son was a patient here . . . I thought he busted something in his back. He hurt his back real bad and thought he was going to have to do something but they only had a few harnesses on him he didn't really do too bad and he was in here about a week . . . he hurt himself at work. . . . I got a little upset because there are two boys I had, I had no girls, they said to me "your daughter is hurt" and I said to them "I don't have a daughter, I have boys" and apparently what happened was for some reason, whatever the reason was, they had an opening in a group that had some girls in it and he wanted to get in that so I thought I don't know what*

whatever was going through my brain and they had him in the group and it was
a girls' group and [son's name] was in the girls' group and I was bustin' his chops
about being in the girls' group. That's a girls' group, that's for girls. There are girls
who really want to get in there. What the hell are ya doing that for?" He says
"Dad I gotta do this, that's what happened, that's the case, they had to make a de-
cision, they asked me if I would take it and I did," and he was in it . . . but then he
got out of it! . . . It was a group to be like I'm in now. Let's say there is like the four
of us in a group and it was Mary's [who is Mary?] group and it was all girls.
. . . He said "Dad I'm not a girl!"

BB showed other misidentifications regarding women, claiming one aide on the floor and another female patient on the floor were his daughters-in-law.

In addition to their fantasies about phantom children, nieces, aunts, and other relatives, patients may also confabulate about best friends to whom they are particularly close. SA was a 36-year-old man suffering from alcohol abuse, a seizure, and a traumatic brain injury that created bilateral frontal hematomas much greater on the right (a brain pathology quite similar to that of patient SC). Like patient SC, SA also suffered from memory problems but denied his cognitive impairments. SA had a stormy hospitalization, and during a period of acute agitation wrist restraints were applied to secure his wrists to the bed to keep him from pulling out his intravenous lines and catheters.

SA later spoke frequently of his best friend from college named Gary. At the time of interview, although SA denied current physical issues regarding his bound wrists, and denied any current financial or insurance issues, he ascribed to Gary problems regarding Gary's wrists and insurance coverage:

SA: *Well, there is a thing called hell week and in any event as some sort of initiation*
or hazing, one of my friends had something wrong with his hands, and well, I
guess I'm sort of here in his place. . . . Gary is a friend of mine. . . . We were best
friends. . . . Gary had this problem with both his wrists and is having this problem
with the insurance company, and I more or less admitted to him that my wrists

> *are not as good as they were in college, and when it comes to this situation I am*
> *more or less playing or depicting Gary.*
> TEF: *What does this have to do with fraternities?*
> SA: *It's not so much that as much as having mutual responsibilities.*
> TEF: *Like what?*
> SA: *Sergeant at Arms . . . you know . . . more or less someone who stands guard, picks*
> *up things here and there.*
> TEF: *What happened to Gary's wrists?*
> SA: *He had something done medicinally to them and his insurance company isn't*
> *covering it. . . .*

SA recalled that his own wrists had been restrained earlier in his hospitalization, but it was Gary who now had a problem with his wrists, and his reference to a "Sergeant at Arms" as someone who "picks things up" is a telling metaphorical representation of SA's preoccupation with his wrist restraints. In this narrative, the patient's identity is partially merged with Gary's, and their problems are mutual.

Phantom relatives may also appear as reified memories or ghosts of lost loved ones. In what Venneri and co-workers have described as the *nurturing syndrome*, patients—in their report both women—developed the delusion that a deceased spouse is still alive.[54] They first describe the case of CS, a 78-year-old woman with early dementia who after her husband's death claimed he would visit her at her home. During these visits they would sit and sew together. She also hallucinated seeing him sitting on the sofa. Later, she became paranoid about the husband's behavior and absences and became suspicious that he was having an affair with a younger woman. She became morbidly attached to a photograph of him which she tried to feed to the point that the mouth on the photo was worn away. The patient was so certain that her husband was alive that she asked for a refund on his funeral expenses.

The second case was KC, a 71-year-old woman, who also suffered from a progressive dementia. She too denied her husband's death and interestingly also took to talking to and feeding his photograph. Of note is that both patients showed frontal brain area dysfunction on metabolic brain images (SPECT Scans), especially within the right hemisphere.

In summary, the imaginary others serve many functions for these patients. In some cases, as with SC, the imaginary person acts as a surrogate, enabling the patient to displace his own problems and unpleasant circumstances upon an alter ego. This mechanism also enables these individuals to express to others how they feel about themselves, and how they feel about how others are treating them. The imaginary person may also be a friend, a companion that the mind makes available to the patient through tough or lonely times. And finally the companion may be a malevolent force, an expression of fear and paranoia that emerges in the context of frightening and inescapable circumstances. Thus, although the precipitating factors that begin the process of the delusion are neurological, psychological factors surely shape and fashion the nature and content of the belief.

Disorders of the Narrative Self

Symbolic Representations of Personal Experiences

There are, in addition to disorders of the self focused on the body or in relationship with others, beliefs that patients express about themselves that occur as a manifestation of a *delusional confabulation* about the individual's personal experiences. One of my early mentors, psychoanalyst and neurologist Edwin Weinstein, was among the first to analyze this self-related symptom in patients with neurological damage. In his work, Weinstein pointed out that the fantastic narratives some patients produce that seem to be the simple result of memory failure may actually be "metaphorical or symbolic repre-sentations" of the patient's current life circumstances.

Among these patients, the most enduring delusional confabula-tions are produced with reference to some emotionally and person-ally significant aspect of their lives. Thus, questions directed at the patient regarding the nature of the patient's illness or family are most likely to result in these metaphorical narratives. In his reports, Weinstein emphasized that the language the patient used to de-scribe their recent *past* histories were clues to their *current* feelings about themselves and their present situations.

Weinstein described this type of confabulation in the case of a 42-year-old Air Force officer, a veteran of the Korean War, who was in-volved in a jeep accident while stationed in Korea. His neurological impairments included weakness in the right arm and difficulty with speech and the ability to read and write. While he admitted his im-pairments, he seemed indifferent to them, and when asked how he came to sustain his injuries, this is how he described his accident:

> *I had a big job overseas. I was an intelligence officer in the Air Force. The man I relieved was a captain and his assistant a first lieutenant. I was sent to check on their security. They were just as Commie as if painted with a red brush. I had to write out everything I found so that it could be read at court in a court-martial for these men some day. I wrote it out and turned it into headquarters. I had enough written so that any jury in its right senses would give those guys 20 years in jail apiece, they were just that Commie. Those two were riding with me on the day the shell exploded in my jeep. I can remember now that I stopped to look at my road map over there in Korea.*[55]

As Weinstein points out, the mention of *intelligence, reading, writing,* and *right senses,* and I would add *remembering, head, checking,* and *looking,* were all allusions or metaphorical references to the patient's current problems and circumstances.[56] Weinstein also described a soldier who, having suffered a stroke that resulted in left side weakness and visual defects, claimed that he been injured in World War I and "bro-

ken his leg" and had been "blinded by headlights." Another patient
with a bleeding aneurysm, who had become sexually impotent, "in-
variably mentioned that someone had tried to revive him by pouring
cold water on his genitals."[57]

More recently, patient LA with Fregoli syndrome for misidentification of persons and places, described earlier, denied his
obvious physical impairments in spite of the fact that he was interviewed while he was in a wheelchair and was receiving daily
physical therapy for a severely impaired gait. The actual circumstances of his illness (a ruptured arteriovenous malformation)
were repeatedly explained to him, but when he was asked what
had happened to him he consistently responded with a dramatic
confabulation:

LA: *A couple of days ago people been telling me the things that happened to me and*
it's possible that something happened to me. . . . People been telling me that they
think there was a big explosion in one place I was at and that destroyed my mind.
And that is one of the reasons I'm having now. . . . What do you call a person that
is sleeping and starts to walk?

TEF: *Sleep walking.*

LA: *Yeah I started to do that . . . and that is causing all the disturbances in my mind.*
. . . People are saying, somebody said I was in a room like next door, a big explo-
sion in there and I was in there, and that was going to destroy my mind, my per-
sonality. That might be what it is. . . . They said also that I was going to be
sleeping and I was going to awake. But I didn't wake up and I started to walk
[starts to cry]. I never had it before. . . . The doctor said I was going to be sleep-
ing and start walking in my sleep, and I don't understand because I never had it.

TEF: *Are you sleep walking now?*

LA: *Not according to my parents and not according to me.*

TEF: *How is your actual walking?*

LA: *My actual walking is good.*

TEF: *Fine? So you can run and dance and jump?*

LA: *No problem. . . .*

So here we have a man who cannot walk, and feels like he is in a
dream, who is preoccupied with the idea that he is "sleepwalking."

This is the essence of the metaphorical confabulation, wherein personal concerns are expressed in terms of a metaphor for the actual experiences of the self. In another case, patient TP, who had a severe deficit in episodic memory and frontal lobe damage, denied that he had experienced or undergone an operation to repair a ruptured aneurysm. Instead, he claimed he had been involved with experiments in which "materials" that were supposed to be "contained" had "escaped" from their "containers."

TP: *I woke up this morning and tried to get my things together and there was a knock on the door and there was a local person wanting to ask me questions about this, so I was intrigued that it had gotten the interest of the local people so quickly . . . we had been involved last night in releasing—well I shouldn't say releasing because that wasn't the intent—but we had transferred some of the materials last night from one kind of container to another kind of container and it's inevitable in a thing like that that some of these things are going to be released. One of the most expensive parts of our project is paying for the laboratory facilities to be able to do that without releasing or if elements are going to released they are released under the most rigid circumstances so they can be collected again and not released into the at. . . . Well anyway we tried an experiment last night in which some of these materials—I stress materials that are not of danger to human, animal, or plant life—did escape . . . and we did our best to destroy them but weren't able to destroy all of them and some of them apparently did get to the point where they were encountered by people who lived in the fairly remote area where we are. . . .*

Whatever the psychological importance for TP of "releasing"—perhaps he wishes to be released from the rehabilitation center—it is clear that it forms a central concern in his narrative.

Disorders of Personal Identity and the Global Sense of Self

Finally, the process of dissociation may also be the source of a number of self-related clinical syndromes.

Dissociation

In the context of clinical pathology, the *DSM-IV-TR* defines dissociation as "A disruption in the usually integrated functions of consciousness, memory, identity, or perception of the environment. The disturbance may be sudden or gradual, transient or chronic."[58] In addition to the neuropathologies of the self that we have already considered in which a specific, well-defined injury or progressive disease of the brain could be identified, the dissociative disorders may also occur as a result of purely psychiatric conditions. One difference between the two is that the conditions I have described earlier generally leave the overall sense of the patient's personal identity intact. Even the patient who sees a mirror companion or neglects half of the body still does not deny his or her own essential personal identity. Also, dissociative disorders are, at least in theory, reversible.[59] When the patient recovers from a dissociative episode, the "forgotten" memories or aspects of the true identity return to awareness. Thus the past memories are not destroyed, though they are—most often temporarily—irretrievable during the period of dissociation.

The conditions that may be included under "dissociative phenomena" range from such everyday states as daydreaming or performing an action without being explicitly aware of it, to pathological states such as Dissociative Identity Disorder (DID; multiple personality disorder), psychogenic amnesia, and fugue states. Given the wide range of these disorders, psychologist Etzel Cardeña has provided a useful schema for organizing and distinguishing the various reported states and conditions of dissociation into various subtypes.[60]

One group he calls *dissociation as the absence of conscious awareness of impinging stimuli or ongoing behaviors.* Included here are any behaviors or perceptions that occur outside an individual's awareness, such as listening to the radio while driving, or being explicitly unaware of shifting gears or road or weather conditions. Cardeña argues that including all the states of subliminal, preconscious or implicit awareness is an overextension of the term "dissociation." Certainly for the purposes of relating dissociation to the neuropathological or neuropsychiatric cases of self-related disruptions, these instances of simple perception without awareness are least relevant.

Another of Cardeña's sub-types is *dissociation as the coexistence of separate mental systems that should be integrated in the person's consciousness, memory, or identity.* In these cases, the term "dissociation" "applies to mental processes, such as sensations, thoughts, emotions, volition, memories, and identities, that we would ordinarily expect to be integrated within the individual's stream of consciousness and the historically extended self, but which are not."[61] As Cardeña points out, this form of dissociation is the one that comes closest to the pathologies described in the clinical literature since French psychologist Pierre Janet, who is credited with the earliest scientific descriptions of the condition in the late nineteenth century.[62] This definition is also most in line with the current characterizations of dissociation such as DID (previously Multiple Personality Disorder), in which the patient behaves as if he or she has more than one identity, dissociative amnesia in which the patient cannot recall significant personal information or life periods, and dissociative fugue states in which the patient appears to be unable to recall his or her identity and travels far from home. Within this group Cardeña would also include trances, possession states, and hypnosis.

Among the neurological patients I have examined, the case of RD, who saw a persecutor reflected in the mirror, comes closest to representing a dissociative disorder.[63] While perhaps in the early stages of dementia, RD was brought to my office by her husband because whenever she viewed her reflection, she became agitated and claimed that a strange and malevolent woman was following her. There were times when she became so violent toward the mirror image that she attacked her own reflection. Although she was a prim and proper churchgoing wife and mother, when she beheld her reflection she would suddenly become animated and violent:

RD: *Did you hear the story? Eh? Did you hear it? Now you get out . . . get home where you belong. You don't belong here . . . you don't live here. Out! . . . That's her, that's her. Yeah, that's her . . . sure that's her. She has no name . . . I never heard her name . . . never, never! I never! She never told me her name. No, no . . . you can't go in the house! No, you can't go in the house! She never let me know, had a lot of problems with her . . . Yeah, not this here one. Then she starts calling me these kind of names, street walker . . . cannot stand her . . . I don't know, she's just an old bag . . . she's a bag. Yeah, and you, and you. Heh, I'm not afraid of you. Go ahead . . . I don't know she's just an old bag. Yeah, she's a bag . . . yeah, afraid to say it. . . . You want to know who she is? You want to know who she is? Because you're a . . . that's what you are. We know where you live. Where do you live? You know what? You're a good for nothin'. You know what? You're a good for nothin' . . . Yeah, where you walk . . . yeah, you little bitch . . . yeah. Now you know where you're gonna go? You're gonna go home . . . and when we get home, you know what? We're gonna find her right around the . . . we'll find her walkin' right around the windows. In the windows where she watches . . . listens to what we do. I can't stand her . . . she's been walking around the house, around the area for a long time . . . you know that? All the time she bothers everybody. I always wanted to hit her! I'm gonna kill her.*

Although RD did not experience a loss of her own personal identity, or a loss of personal memory, she treated her mirror image as if it had an entirely separate identity, although clearly the person in the mirror was implicitly recognized, since only her own reflection was misidentified. The "old bag" and the "little bitch" viewed in the mirror was in this regard similar to the multiple identities that patients with Dissociative Identity Disorder possess.

RD's behavior is also similar to what Cardeña defines as a third type of dissociation in which there is *an alteration in consciousness wherein disconnection/disengagement from the self or the environment is experienced.* In these disorders there is a global alteration in the individual's *phenomenal experience* of his or her circumstances, which might take the form of global detachment of the self from the world, *derealization,* and global detachment of the self from itself, *depersonaliza-*

tion. Interestingly, Cardeña includes the experience of a personal "double" within this sub-type:

> Perhaps the most intriguing and unusual forms of depersonalization is the "double" syndrome, in which a person may actually "perceive" and even interact with an external double of him- or herself, a phenomenon that has fascinated writers and psychologists alike including Otto Rank, Edgar Allan Poe, and Fyodor Dostoevsky.[64]

Some of the cases I have examined resemble other forms of dissociative phenomena that are commonly known as déjà vu, deja vecu, jamais vu, and other related experiences. In these cases something that is actually unseen or unfamiliar to the patient is felt to be overly familiar—as in déjà vu experiences[65]—or something that should be familiar to the patient is felt to be alien, as in jamais vu experiences.

One example of this symptom I have also seen in patients who experience a doubling of their experiences in time, as if everything that is happening to them has already happened in that past. In one such case, AR had a history of multiple small strokes, and one larger one on the right three years prior to my examining him. During our interview, he reported persistent feelings that resembled déjà vu experiences:

AR: *In other words when I leave here I'm going to get behind cars and I've seen the same cars, the same people . . . like today, coming here . . . the same trucks, everything I've seen before even though I'm just doing it today . . . they say I'm crazy! . . . Like it's just taking place now—the World Series. I knew everything that was going to happen as it happened. Not before. . . . I seen it, just like I'm seeing you right know. . . . I saw you exactly what you're wearing, the sweater, and this is the first time I'm here. I never saw you before today but I've seen you before as I see.*

TEF: *How is that possible?*

AR: *I don't know you tell me!*

TEF: *It's not [that] you're clairvoyant?*

AR: *No . . . otherwise I'd win the lottery!*

TEF: *On the other hand when you see it, it looks familiar.*

AR: *It doesn't look familiar, it is! I've seen it! . . . I think the world is crazy and I'm sane.*

TEF: *Does it seem at all possible to you let's say it's you and not actually the world?*

AR: *No, I think the world is crazy and I think I'm sane.*

TEF: *Now you know you haven't seen me before, but I look familiar to you now. You've seen me before and the same stuff and I'm wearing . . . totally no difference?*

AR: *And him too. . .* [indicating a medical resident in the room].

TEF: *Dressed the same way exactly? How can this be?*

AR: *You tell me!*

TEF: *I don't know!*

AR: *You don't know! If I knew I wouldn't be here! I told you the world's crazy except for me. I never saw you before as far as I know, but the way you're dressed your shoes, tie, sweater, pants, the bag over there, the coffee cup, the thing that looks like a brain of a head . . . everything I've seen before now. As I see it I've seen it before. In other words if you asked me in the other room before I came in here what's in here I couldn't tell. But now that I'm looking I've seen it, even though it's my first time here . . . you tell me what's wrong! . . . I've never seen you before except just now. I've seen you before now.*

When AR went to the movies, he was convinced he had seen the films previously. He said he was only willing to go again because his wife hadn't seen them before. He got into arguments with toll takers on the highway because he was convinced he had paid twice, and had frequent arguments with his family regarding the truth of these odd recurrences. In fact, he began to think that his wife "was losing it" because her memory was failing! He thought *she* might be getting demented or developing Alzheimer's disease.

Another patient I examined, MG,[66] showed an enduring alteration in her phenomenal experience of her environment similar to jamais vu. Like patient LR, with Capgras syndrome for inanimate objects, who believed all the objects in her apartment had been switched with fakes, MG also spoke of a global dissociation from her environment:

*Basically it was substituted as I had once read in a mystery story and everything
was done precisely as that mystery story had it . . . so the mystery story became
alive for me . . . even the posters I had on my wall in the closet. . . . And in the
kitchen closet I noticed a difference . . . the types of dishes that were there, were
arranged as I would never arrange it. . . . Well, I basically size them, and then
there were cups and glasses that were not quite the same . . . pattern I don't use
dishwash cloths, wash cloths that way.*

During the time that MG was being treated, her psychosis abated
and she began to realize that there really was only a single apartment. She described to me the eerie quality of her experience:

*Because as the film disappears . . . and dissipates . . . and the dreamlike experience
dissolves. I know that there is one, but there must have been the illusion of two.
. . . To dispel an illusion that I'm in a horrible place and until I concretely resolve
. . . until I completely resolve what I feel is an illusion and I am beginning to
think it was an illusion. . . .*

In summary, some of the delusional misidentification syndromes
that we have discussed, in the cases of RD, AR, and MG, for example,
seem to represent global alterations between the self and the world
that are generally considered varieties of dissociative disorders. In
spite of the clear similarities between the dissociations that occur in
psychiatric and neurological cases, however, while the psychiatric
dissociation cases are felt to be reversible—for instance by some sudden psychological insight or relief from stress—this does not seem to
be the case in the neurological cases. Unless the underlying neurological pathology that triggered the inset of the disorder is corrected,
the symptom or syndrome in the neurological cases are often irre-
versible.

Although in this chapter I have described a wide range of conditions
that in the medical and scientific literature go by many names, my
interest has always been to find the common factors that bind these
disorders. These conditions all affect the way the individual relates

to his or her self and others, but the question is, what do they have in common? Do they share any neuropathological features? What can they teach us about the neurological basis of the self? While various theories have been offered to explain one or another of these conditions, at this point we lack a coherent model that identifies a single underlying mechanism or draws them together with an overarching theme. In the following chapters I will attempt to enumerate the common causal factors among these conditions in order to arrive at a "unified theory" to explain their occurrence.

CHAPTER TWO

The Growth of the Ego
and Its Defenses

MOST OF MY WORK has focused on adult disorders of the self that occur as a result of either some injury to the brain or some degenerative brain disease such as dementia, as in a number of the cases we have just seen. In this work, I have noted numerous similarities between these conditions and some common childhood patterns of behavior and thought; however, I did not dwell on the full extent of these parallels. More recently, I have come to the opinion that, not only are these parallels between my patients' misbeliefs and narratives and childhood defenses and patterns of thought significant, these two domains of behavior *are nearly identical* and that somehow understanding this relationship is the key to understanding how some of these perplexing neuropsychiatric conditions come into being.

Let's take, for example, the case of my patient SP, a woman in her sixties, who treated her mirror image as a companion.[1] Partially deaf since childhood, SP was able to hear with a hearing aid but had also learned sign language as a child. Thus, she communicated both by signing and spoken language. After she sustained a right hemisphere stroke, SP recovered neurologically but her son brought her to me with the complaint that she had begun to sign to and communicate with "the other S" whom she saw in the mirror. According to SP this "other S" was her same age, had a similar background in terms of education and upbringing, and even had a son with the same name as her son! This is how SP described this unusual situation:

SP: *Well, she's all right . . . sounds funny for me talking from one to another, because you know she was a new person to me, and I'm surprised. She was all right, but she's very nervous, she likes to do her own ways . . . she never knew that she couldn't hear so good, and she's not a very good lip reader. I had to do mostly in sign language for her, to make her understand . . . she copies every word I say like this, like this motion . . . she doesn't even know the sign language very well, and I was confused a little bit, you know, because I wanted her. I thought she knew the sign language very well, so I won't have to repeat it twice, but then I found out that she's not that bright. I hate to say that . . . I don't want to brag, but she's a nice person; but one thing about her . . . I see her everyday through a mirror, and that's the only place I can see her. When she sees me through the mirror, she looks a little then she comes over and talks to me, and that's how we began becoming friends through our sign language. She was very nice. . . .*

Taken on one level, one might argue that SP had developed a vascular dementia on the basis of one or more strokes, and was simply confused about the nature of her mirror image. Indeed it is not uncommon for patients who develop dementia to mistake the nature of mirror reflections in general. However, with SP this was not the case. Her misrecognition of mirror images was selective, and if I stood behind her in the mirror, she never spoke of the "other doctor Feinberg," or if she saw her son in the mirror, she never misidentified him. Rather, she developed an entire delusional system that only involved her own mirror image. Indeed she would admit that she was looking in the mirror, and yet her delusions about her reflection were impervious to this realization.

Another significant feature of SP's case was the type of emotional attachment that formed with her reflection. Due in part to her deafness and her partial reliance on sign language, SP had lived a somewhat isolated life, spending many hours alone in her apartment. It was during these periods that she developed her beliefs about the "other SP." The mirror image was not merely a case of mistaken identify, the "other SP" grew to seem like a companion. They would converse, exchange points of view, even argue at times. As in some of the cases we discussed in the last chapter "the other SP" had become SP's friend.

When I focused upon this aspect of SPs behavior, I began to realize that the puzzling and seemingly incredibly bizarre conditions I had studied for years became understandable as manifestations of childhood patterns of behavior. Further, I have come to believe that an appropriate interpretation of these mechanisms could have important implications for our understanding of how ego mechanisms are neurologically constructed in the first place. It follows therefore that to fully understand the adult neuropathologies of the self, we must first look at the ontological development and hierarchical structure of the self and self-awareness.[2]

The Growth of Self Awareness

Developmental psychologist Michael Lewis at the Institute for the Study of Child Development, Robert Wood Johnson Medical School in New Jersey has proposed a particularly useful account of the development of self-recognition, social emotions, and a theory of mind (ToM) that is well suited to the hierarchical organization of the nervous system and the self, and that fits nicely into the other aspects of the hierarchical organization of self-systems and the nervous system that I will examine in depth later on.[3]

According to Lewis's model, we can discern at least three stages in the social-emotional development of the infant and child (Figure 2-1). In the first stage, the infant possesses and displays what are commonly known as the *fundamental* or *primary emotions*. Although the exact number of primary emotions is still debated, these emotional

Figure 2-1. A hierarchical model of the emergence of self-awareness, self-metarepresentation, self-conscious emotions, and related behaviors. Basic schema adapted from Lewis et al., 1989; Lewis, 1992, 1997.

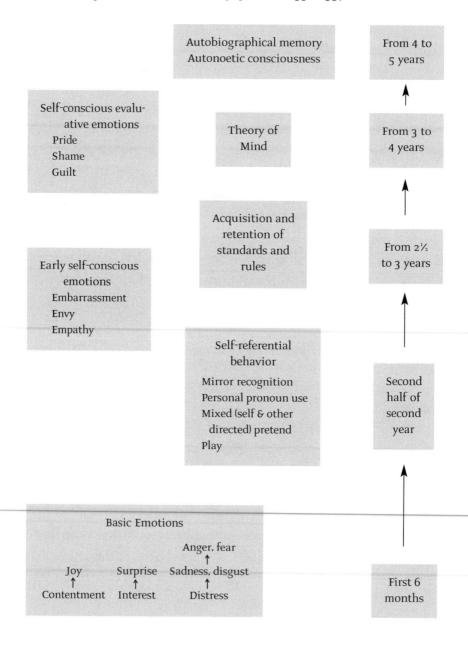

behaviors emerge during the first six months of life.[4] Expressions of interest, joy, physical distress, and disgust may be present at birth or appear shortly afterward, anger may appear by 4 weeks, surprise by 6 weeks, and by 10 weeks, given the appropriate stimuli, the infant may also display fear and sadness.[5] By one year, in normal children the primary emotions, which are expressed in a cross-culturally stereotyped fashion and therefore assumed to be "hard wired" into the developing nervous system, have all made their appearance.

In the next stages of development, the *secondary* or *self-conscious emotions* emerge. The appearance of the secondary emotions requires a new cognitive leap on the part of the infant's developing brain and intellectual functions: the emergence of nascent self-awareness. During the latter half of the second year, a cluster of behaviors emerges that indicates that the infant is becoming self-aware, or as Lewis puts it, "Self metarepresentation, sometimes referred to as the mental state or the idea of 'me' involves the knowledge of the recursive relation 'I know that I know' as opposed to the nonrecursive relation 'I know' that defines the sense of agency present at younger ages."[6]

One behavioral marker particularly important as an indicator of this stage of mental development is the emergence of visual self-recognition, as demonstrated in a number of similar experiments performed in primates to determine the presence or absence of self-recognition.[7] In the "rouge test," the researcher surreptitiously applies a spot of rouge on the child's forehead or nose. When the child is then exposed to a mirror, the experimenter notes whether the child visually inspects and touches the marked spot on his or her face, which is taken as an indicator that the child has developed some degree of self-recognition.[8] In neurologically normal children, mark-directed behavior emerges between 15 months and 2 years, with most children showing the behavior by 18 months of age. Lewis and co-worker Douglas Ramsay also found that around the same age, children who showed positive evidence of mirror self-recognition also demonstrated other signs of self-metarepresentation.

In one investigation, Lewis and Ramsay studied a group of children at ages 15, 18, and 21 months to determine the developmental relationship between mirror self-recognition and two other markers of
self-metarepresentation: the use of the personal pronoun (e.g. *me,
mine, I, I'm, myself*) and the presence of self-directed or other-directed
play. Among developmental psychologists, there is a general agreement that there exists a shift in play behaviors during the middle of
the second year. Before this period, the child's play is comprised of
actions that are wholly self-directed, such as pretending to drink
from a cup, to actions that are both symbolic as well as other-directed, for instance the child now puts the cup to a doll's lips. In the
normally developing child, play from that point on will involve both
self and other-directed pretense. Indeed, as children developed mirror self-recognition they also increased their use of personal pro-
nouns in speech and displayed more other-directed symbolic play.

Lewis and Ramsay concluded that these behaviors can be related
to a fundamental emergence of a cluster of self-metarepresenta-
tional abilities that occurs during the second year of life. Children at
this stage possess the mental capacity to understand that "I know
that my play is not real."[9] Put another way, they expressed the concept that "I know that I know," or demonstrated a theory of their
own mind. Ramsay and Lewis point out as well that at the same age
range, children begin to demonstrate an increase in imitation, and
other research has indicated a developmental relationship between
self-recognition and imitation.[10] This raises the question of whether
the development of the mirror neuron system, which likely plays a
role in the ontology of imitation, also plays a role in the metarepre-
sentational behaviors studied by Lewis as well.[11]

The development of a nascent sense of self that emerges during
the second year makes possible the appearance of the first self-
conscious emotions.[12] According to Lewis, these emotions include, among others, early forms of embarrassment, envy, and
empathy. Lewis at one point referred to these as *exposed emotions*

because although they involve a social interaction between the child and an observer or other actor, all that is required is that the child be aware of the interaction, but not an evaluation of some specific set of standards or rules by which the child judges his or her own behavior.[13]

For instance, Lewis provides convincing evidence linking the emergence of self-awareness and the development of embarrassment. In one investigation, Lewis and his colleagues compared children ages 9 to 24 months on the mirror self-recognition test with measures of fear or wariness when exposed to strangers as well as a measure of the presence of embarrassment.[14] Based upon prior work, there is evidence that viewing oneself in the mirror while one is observed by another causes embarrassment, indicated by such actions as a smile followed by averting the eyes from the reflection, and then fidgeting with the hair, clothing, the face, or some other part of the body. Lewis found that while there was no relationship between the fear response and self-recognition, the vast majority of children who showed the embarrassed response also had reached the stage of mirror self-recognition.

In a second study, the same group tested children aged 22 months on the rouge test and the fear assessment test, as well as on two different measures of embarrassment. These were the "over-compliment situation" in which the child was lavished with praise for trivial behaviors, and a request-to-dance situation. In this test, the experimenter gave the mother a tambourine and was asked to coax the child to dance by saying, "Let's see you dance, dance for me!" In this part of the study, once again the researchers found that embarrassment was correlated with self-recognition while fear was not.

Finally, Lewis argues that due to a child's increasing cognitive abilities during the latter half of the third year, the child begins to self-evaluate social interactions based upon an increasing grasp of social norms and standards. At this point the child is both self-aware as well as aware of others' observations of them. The child now knows how other people appraise certain actions and which actions are likely to be judged in a positive or negative light. Thus, when the child evaluates an interaction, he or she will now judge whether the behavior was good or bad by another's or his or her own standards: was the action a success or a failure, the behavior something to be proud or ashamed of.

The acquisition of these standards makes possible a higher level of emotional experience called *the self-conscious evaluative emotions*, a class that includes such complex emotions as pride, shame, and guilt, as well as more sophisticated forms of embarrassment. It is significant that during the period when the child begins to experience the emergence of the self-conscious evaluative emotions, from about 3 to 4 years of age, the child's theory of mind or mentalizing abilities are also maturing.[15] This is not surprising given that emotions such as pride, shame, or guilt depend in large part upon someone else *knowing* what you have done.

The last big leap in childhood seems to occur from about 4 years of age, the point at which Endel Tulving hypothesizes the emergence of the episodic memory system that makes possible autonoetic (self-aware) consciousness—an aspect of the cognitive hierarchy that we will consider at greater length later on.[16] This developmental period also marks the approximate end of the period of childhood amnesia, the early developmental period of life for which most persons have no autobiographical recall.[17] Daniel Povinelli, at the Center for Child Studies of the University of Southwestern Louisiana, who has done extensive research on the child's development of a self-concept, also suggests that it is at this point that the child advances from an immediately known "present self" to a "proper self" that possesses a sense of the self that endures through time and possesses a past, a present, and a future.[18]

Thus, we are able to construct a brief but coherent model of the general time frame in which the developing self is constructed in children and place these elements in a hierarchical pattern (see Figure 2-1 on page 54). Next, we'll look at how the dynamic of the developing self relates to other systems in the maturing mind of the child.

The Development of the Psychological Defenses

Along with the maturation of cognitive functions and the growth of self-awareness, the growing child is also developing *psychological defenses*. And just as the brain and the capacity for self-awareness display a hierarchical arrangement, the psychological defenses display functional characteristics that suggest they also possess a hierarchical organization.

Perhaps no one has championed the concept of the hierarchical organization of ego functions more than George Vaillant,[19] the Director of Adult Development at the Harvard University Health Service, who credits the idea of psychological defense with being the single greatest achievement of the entire Freudian enterprise:

> Perhaps Freud's most original contribution to human psychology was his inductive postulation that unconscious "defense mechanisms" protect the individual from painful emotions, ideas, and drives. In delineating the nature of ego mechanisms of defense, Freud not only established that upsetting affects, as well as ideas, underlie psychopathology, but he also established that much of what is perceived as psychopathology reflects a potentially healing process.[20]

The concept of ego defenses entails two important concepts. The first is the theoretical notion of *ego* itself. Vaillant offers this interpretation:

> The modern psychoanalytic use of the term *ego* encompasses the adaptive and executive aspects of the human brain: the ability of the mind to integrate, master, and make sense of inner and outer reality. Or, in Freud's words, "We have formed the idea that in each individual there is a coherent organization of mental processes; and we call

this his *ego*."[21] The term *ego* addresses the capacity of the integrated mind to accommodate and assimilate the world.[22]

The second theoretical concept is the idea of *ego defense*. Based upon Freud's original theories, Vaillant suggests this succinct definition:

> In more formal terms, ego mechanisms of defense describe uncon-
> scious, and *sometimes* pathological, mental processes that the ego uses
> to resolve conflict among the four lodestars of our inner life: in-
> stincts, the real world, important people, and the internalized prohi-
> bitions provided by our conscience and our culture.[23]

By Vaillant's count, Freud had identified 17 defensive operations, including the most common psychological defenses that we recognize today, such as repression, denial, projection, reaction formation, displacement, and sublimation. Although Freud suggested that the defenses followed some developmental evolution, his daughter Anna discussed this progression in children more explicitly in her book *The Ego and the Mechanisms of Defense*.[24] Phoebe Cramer, professor of psychology at Williams College in Massachusetts, later provided one of the most extensive analyses of defensive development in children, positing a hierarchy of defenses along a chronological timetable in which psychological defenses occur as a necessary and adaptive part of normal development, a view that both Sigmund and Anna Freud, among others, endorsed.[25, 26]

Cramer's research indicates that the earliest defense to develop is *psychological denial*.[27] The current psychiatric diagnostic manual, *DSM-IV-TR*, states that in adults denial is apparent when "The individual deals with emotional conflict or internal or external stressors by refusing to acknowledge some painful aspect of external reality or subjective experience that would be apparent to others."[28] In Cramer's model of the development defenses in children, denial may take many forms. The earliest and most basic is the simple ignoring of perceptual information. This mechanism may be an outgrowth of basic perceptual processes present from the first month of life onward that allow the developing nervous system to screen out unpleasant stimuli. Other forms of denial that develop later, as thought and verbal abilities improve, include ridiculing the importance of information, exaggerating information to the point that it must be denied, and reversing information into its opposite. According to Cramer, denial is the predominant defense in the preschool years, and it remains the predominant defense until about age 7.

The next defense to emerge is *projection*, a psychological mechanism that other investigators also consider an immature defense, in which the individual deals with unacceptable and unwanted emotions or thoughts by attributing them to others.[29] The use of projection markedly increases as the child develops and by about age 7, denial and projection are used about equally as often. From this point onward, projection ultimately takes the place of denial as the predominant defense.[30]

Why does the shift from denial to projection occur? According to Cramer, as the child matures, he or she is less able to use denial as a "disguise" for reality. The increasing cognitive capacity of the child enables him or her to see the self-deceptive nature of the defense, and this insight makes its less available as a self-protecting mechanism.

In one investigation, Cramer and co-worker Melissa Brilliant studied 7- and 10-year-old children's *use* of defense, and compared that with their *understanding* of defense as determined by a vignette interpretation task.[31] They found, not surprisingly, that younger children had less understanding of defense as compared to older children, and most significantly, the younger child's appreciation of the nature of defense correlated with its use, with children who better understood denial using it less. In the older group, the understanding of projection was also inversely related to its use as a defense. Among the advances that the child is making during this period is the enhanced capacity for perspective taking, so it is likely this increase is accompanied by a progressive augmentation in the child's self-awareness, causing a decline in the use of these defenses.

The Uses of Fantasy

We have thus far discussed a range of neurological and psychological functions, including the use of psychological defenses, that emerge in children from about 3 to 8 years of age. At the same time, another critical function, the development and use of fantasy, is undergoing a transformation in this period. There is an extensive literature on the role of fantasy in the development of the child's life and mind, and here I will touch upon those domains that are particularly pertinent to the adult disturbances of the self. [32]

Denial through Fantasy

Anna Freud emphasized in her work with children the manner in which the child may use fantasy as a means of denying reality,[33] and Cramer likewise describes the way that *denial through fantasy* enables the child to cope with unpleasant or unacceptable realities:

> Such fantasies serve denial in several ways. If the unreal can be made to appear true, then the real may be delegated to the realm of the untrue. In this case, the fantasies, uninfluenced by external events, acquire a salience that rivals external reality. Eventually these fantasies come to exist as an alternative reality. The denial function of this personally constructed alternative reality is manifest when it is imposed on the external world. Real events are then recognized only insofar as they conform to the fantasy. The occurence of unfounded optimism and elation in the face of objective failure may be understood as a result of the substitution of a personal fantasy for objective reality, and is a manifestation of this component of denial.[34]

Denial through fantasy, therefore, emerges in the form of a substitution, wherein an unpleasant reality is denied and replaced with a more pleasant fantasy. Psychoanalyst Theodore Dorpat, an authority on denial, views the process of denial in terms of a "cognitive arrest," where denied information is not fully cognitively processed. This process, in psychoanalytic terms, may take the form of a *screen behavior*, a mechanism that may appear in both children and adults. According to Dorpat, this process refers to "the ideas, fantasies, affects, and overt behaviors activated by the subject's need to fill in the gaps formed in the cognitive arrest phase and to support its defensive aims. From the need for this protective tactic emerge the many different masks, disguises, rationalizations, delusions, confabulations, and other forms of screen behavior."[35]

There are at least two ways that denial may be related to *wishful fantasy*. If the primary motive is denial of an external reality—for example, an unbearable traumatic event such as the loss of a loved one—the wishful substitute serves in the place of the void left by the loss, and the loss may be denied and the fantasy of the loved one as still living serves to some extent in its place.[36] In a reciprocal process, if there is the presence of an unfulfilled motive, such as a lack of love or companionship, this void may be satisfied through a pleasant, wish-fulfilling replacement.[37]

Personification and Imaginary Companions

In addition to denial through fantasy, children may also display a fantastic use of the imagination involving the adoption of *imaginary companions*. This behavior bears a striking resemblance to the behavior of patients with neurological disturbances of the self, such as in the case of SP's attitude toward her mirror image. Indeed, it was this resemblance that impelled me toward a deeper examination of the relationship between adult pathologies of the self and the imaginative and fantasy lives of children.

In a classic paper on the subject, Margaret Svendsen provided one of the earliest scholarly discussions of the phenomenon of the imaginary companion, which she describes as:

> . . . an invisible character, named and referred to in conversation with other persons or played with directly for a period of time, at least several months, having an air of reality for the child, but no apparent ob-

jective basis. This excludes that type of imaginative play in which an object is personified, or in which the child himself assumes the role of some person in his environment.[38]

Another approach to imaginary companion behaviors groups these behaviors more broadly under the general category of *role play* behaviors. According to Paul Harris, a professor of education and researcher at Harvard University who has made extensive studies of children's imaginative and play behaviors, there are three types of behaviors that fall within this group: those in which the child impersonates a target role; a second wherein the child projects a character onto an external vehicle such as a doll or a stuffed animal, and a third type in which the child creates a wholly fictitious imaginary person.[39] In all three of these cases, the child is engaging in some type of personification. Likewise, psychologist Marjorie Taylor, an expert on the subject of imaginary companions among children, includes many varieties of role play behavior as examples of "imaginary companions." Children may create an imaginary companion out of a stuffed animal or a completely invisible entity, while others see a companion in the mirror or even pretend their own hands are a companion.[40]

Imaginary companions are very common in children beginning at ages around 3 to 4 and continue to occur throughout the elementary school years. It is estimated that about 28 percent of 3- and 4-year-old children have imaginary companions and that even at 7 years of age they remained common in 31 percent of children.[41] The overall incidence of imaginary companions varies depending upon how they are defined. Some researchers include all cases of persistent impersonation, personified toys, and invisible others as examples of the behavior, while others include only the last group as typical of imaginary companions. If applied most broadly, the criteria suggest that up to the age of 7, 65 percent of children created an imaginary companion at one time or another. Even if the more conservative criteria are applied, that number was still as high as 43 percent.[42] Whatever the actual incidence, it is clear that these are among the most common fantasies in children. Imaginary companions have also been reported in adolescents and even in adults, but it is far less common in normal older individuals.

Actually the term "imaginary others" might be a more accurate name for the phenomenon since it is clear that some of the fictional beings created by children are better described as "imaginary enemies." Children have reported fearful entities that hide in the closet and scare them or want to cut off their hands, or describe them as scary monkeys in the basement. As many as 34 percent of children who had imaginary companions voiced complaints about them, such as a lack of sharing or mildly malicious acts.[43] In those childhood cases where the fear of the imaginary other centers on a monster or some persecutory presence, it seems in these cases that we are dealing with a form of *paranoia* not unlike paranoia in adults. Interestingly, the type of imaginary other was related to the child's attitude toward it. For instance, when the imaginary companion was a stuffed animal, the relationship of the child to the companion was as a caretaker, but with invisible companions, the relationship was more characteristic of a friendship. It has also been noted that older children are also more likely to create completely invisible companions.

When comparing these fantasies with the adult cases, Taylor's observations are quite pertinent to the adult cases of delusional confabulation. In the adult cases with imaginary others, I have often observed that while the other has an enduring identity, particular details about the imaginary person may change from day to to day, or even within a single interview. In a similar fashion, when the children spoke about their imaginary others their features were not always consistent:

> Even when children clearly are describing an imaginary companion that they play with on a regular basis, inconsistencies in their

descriptions suggest that they are making up details as they go along. . . . After all, although the adult's goal is to find out about the imaginary companion, for the child the interview might be just another opportunity for the child to pretend. Probably every time children think about their imaginary companion, they invent new details.[44]

Whatever shape they take, these imaginary others may serve a variety of functions. Taylor suggests that they may be used for providing fun and companionship, alleviating loneliness (hence the increased incidence in first-born and only children), to help the child achieve feelings of mastery and competence, help in conquering fears, as a way of coping with trauma, and as a vehicle for avoiding blame (scapegoating).[45] In one extensive study, the Swedish researcher Eva Hoff interviewed twenty-six 10-year-old children about their imaginary companions and found that the most common reason reported for the existence of the imaginary companion was to provide companionship and comfort to the child during moments of stress, such as feelings of loneliness or fear of darkness, as well as at times of boredom. Indeed, in Hoff's research nearly all the children gave this as the primary reason for the companion. Typical of the responses of the children she observed were the narratives of the young boy and girl, Frida and Rasmus:

Frida: *Cause, I don't know, when you've, sort of, been frozen out by other playmates or when they don't want to play with you anymore then she can, sort of, be nice to you and help you and all.*

Rasmus: *I'm usually a little sad, and sometimes when I'm having a lie-in in the mornings, I usually talk to them. Especially when I'm home alone, don't like that very much. But you feel you're not completely alone any more when they come along.*[46]

Other children stated that the imaginary companion helped them perform challenging tasks or taught them how to do things, in the process helping the child to feel more capable and confident. It was also found that some children projected their own bad and un-wanted traits upon the playmate. For example, Rasmus described the imaginary Gremlins that he played with to an interviewer:

Rasmus: *They're so chicken, because. . . .*
Interviewer: *Don't they want to go with you to school?*
Rasmus: *Yes, of course they want to come with me to school. But they're chicken.*
Interviewer: *In what way are they cowardly?*
Rasmus: *They're . . . they don't dare, well, they don't dare in that way . . . but they don't dare to take the first step.*
Interviewer: *No.*
Rasmus: *Or I don't know. They're always worrying about new things.*[47]

Another function of the companion is as a kind of "protégé" to the child. In these cases, the child considered the companion as someone who needed care and support in a way that is quite similar to the relationship that SP felt to "the other S" seen in the mirror. Compare this account reported by Hoff given by the child Saga about "Pipip" and her other imaginary companions, with that of SP about the other "S":

Saga: *Pipip was childish. He was like a small child. I was older than him. I was a bit big compared with him, but the other was more like a mother. I felt childish together with her. But I could feel a bit big too, you know when I was taking care of those two.*

Of particular relevance to patients with serious neurological injury and medical illness are those imaginary companions in children that appeared in response to severe psychological trauma or to cope with tragic events. Psychoanalyst Humberto Nagera provided a description of a 5-year-old girl named Miriam, who took on a nurturing role with an imaginary companion named "Susan," with whom she would talk for hours, after her parents' divorce, the several months long psychiatric hospitalization of her mother who suffered a mental breakdown, and a prolonged separation from her father. Nagera interpreted the relationship between Miriam and Susan as a substitute for Miriam's relationship with her psychologically withdrawn mother:

> It was obvious that Miriam mothered Susan, thus restoring in fantasy, at least to some degree, her earlier relationship to her now withdrawn, depressed, and absent mother (who was hospitalized). That Susan was created to cope with the puzzling events and the sudden absence of the mother was further confirmed by the many conversations in which Miriam asked her imaginary playmate what had happened to her mother. She was heard saying "What happened to Mummy? . . ."[48]

Selma Fraiberg, a pioneer in the study of fantasy in children, wrote in her classic book *The Magic Years* that one common pattern was for the child to attribute negative characteristics to the companion while keeping positive attributes for the self.[49] This may be regarded as an example of the well known psychological defense of *splitting*, which is considered, like denial and projection, an immature defense. The *DSM-IV-TR* defines splitting as a process in which the individual has competing feelings, and resolves this competition between positive and negative feelings by psychologically separating them:

> The individual deals with emotional conflict or internal or external stressors by compartmentalizing opposite affect states and failing to integrate the positive and negative qualities of the self or others into cohesive images. Because ambivalent affects cannot be experienced simultaneously, more balanced views and expectations of self or others are excluded from emotional awareness. Self and object images tend to alternate between polar opposites: exclusively loving, powerful, worthy, nurturing, and kind—or exclusively bad, hateful, angry, destructive, rejecting, or worthless.[50]

Taylor also found splitting at work in some children with imaginary companions. In these cases the child may actually describe the existence of two imaginary companions, one good and the other bad. In these cases the child appears to be trying to cope with conflicting aspects of the self-image. Taylor references observations made by child psychiatrist Lenore Terr who has worked with children who develop imaginary companions after experiencing extreme psychological trauma.[51] In one case, Terr describes a child named Alan Bascombe at age 8, five years after he had been kidnapped for ransom by a stranger, who had developed what Terr refers to as "post-traumatic compensatory fantasy" which in Alan's case was in the form of an imaginary companion.

Alan described that at some point after the trauma, at about the age 5, he had developed the belief in a "fake person" named "Olive," whose complexion, hair and eye color were starkly contrasting to Alan's. According to Alan he named his companion Olive after a "rotten olive" and Alan would fantasize that Olive was dead. In Terr's interpretation, Olive served the purpose of allowing Alan to split the negative and unwanted aspects of himself that resulted from his trauma. According to Terr, Alan had "demonstrated that in his imagination he has extruded the imagery of his trauma. He had split off the hurt part, the bad part, from the good . . . he had 'split off' the weak, the traumatized part of himself from the rest . . . Alan's compensatory fantasy had led him to a 'doppelganger,' to 'Olive.'"[52]

When examining these fantasy behaviors, it is worth considering the potential links between pretend play and the development of theories of mind abilities that as we have seen may be associated with the emergence of self-awareness. In one study, Taylor and collaborator Stephanie Carlson compared 3- and 4-year-old children with and without fantasy behaviors, such as whether they had an imaginary playmate or engaged in the impersonation of imagined characters.[53] The researchers then compared these ratings with their performance on a series of ToM tasks, such as the ability to judge false beliefs or imagine differing perspectives depending upon one's point of view or knowledge. In the 3-year-old group they did not find a significant relationship among the children engaged in fantasy play and performance on ToM tasks, but there was a significant relationship between these behaviors in the 4 year olds, an age in which both fantasy role play and ToM are more fully developed. In a three-year follow-up study, 100 children from the first study were reevaluated by Taylor and his colleagues and those with imaginary companions at age 4 performed better in emotional understanding tasks at age 7.[54] Although the exact reason that fantasy behaviors and performance on ToM tasks are correlated remains a matter a debate, the data indicate that the two aspects of the child's developing mind are inter-related and perhaps organized by overlapping neural systems.[55]

Finally, the shift between styles of children's fantasy and adult fantasy appears to obey a fairly consistent time frame. It appears that a cluster of fantasy behaviors in children undergo a collective rise and fall.[56] Children' fantasy play in general begins toward the end of the second year, peaks in the pre-school years and declines from ages 5 to 8. As noted previously, the incidence of imaginary companions rises until age 5 and thereafter declines significantly by age 8. Furthermore, children's beliefs in other objects of fantasy, such as the existence of Santa Claus, the Easter Bunny, monsters and ghosts, shows a similar pattern of rise and fall between ages 4 and 8.[57]

However, the existence of imaginary companions does not entirely disappear by age 12 or even beyond and these findings do not mean, as most adults can attest, that fantasy ends in adulthood. Rather the style of fantasy, and the manner in which reality is brought to bear upon fantasy, appears to undergo a change during this period.[58] Taylor observes that adults not only may maintain a personal fantasy life, but during the process of reading fiction or watching a movie also routinely suspend disbelief and partially enter a fantasy world. She concludes:

The bottom line is that, as we study the early developing capacity to pretend, we are likely to learn as much about ourselves as about our children. Although children are the ones who come to mind when we think of pretenders, the imagination is a powerful tool that is available to all of us throughout life. Even having an imaginary companion—a form of pretend play strongly associated with the preschool years—has analogs in adult behavior, both cognitively and emotionally.[59]

A Hierarchy of Defenses

The patterns of defense and denial we see in children do not simply disappear. Rather, in normal adults, they evolve and are replaced by hierarchically more mature methods of thought and emotional defense. This became apparent to Harvard psychiatrist Elvin Semrad who observed that, after an unbearable loss, the patients responded to the threat of psychological disintegration with the processes of *denial, delusional projection,* and *distortion,* which Semrad interpreted as a *regression* to pathological defenses. Further, as the patient recovered from psychosis, progressively less pathological, less psychotic, and more normal defenses were reinstituted.[60] Building upon these observations, Vaillant contructed a hierarchy of defensive operations that can be applied to adults based upon the developmental maturity of the defense.[61] (Figure 2-2). According to Vaillant's scheme, as the individual matures, increasingly more realistic and adult defenses, such as humor, altruism, and sublimation of one's drives, take the place of what we might consider more immature or neurotic defenses.

The Psychotic Defenses

In Vaillant's scenario, the three defenses of denial, delusional projection, and distortion were deemed to be the most primitive and pathological defenses and are represented at the lowest rung on the

Figure 2-2. A hierarchical/developmental arrangement of ego functions. Based upon the scheme proposed by Vaillant (1993).

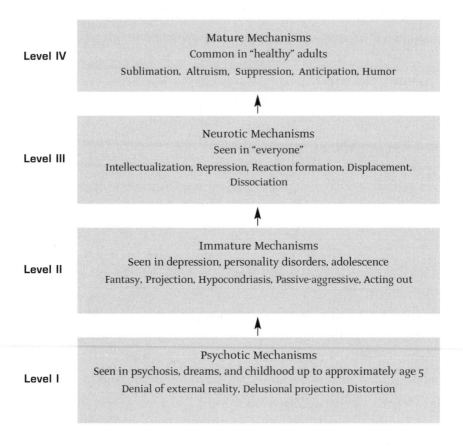

defensive hierarchy. Although Vaillant calls these defenses "psychotic" because they distort reality to the greatest degree, he points out that these defenses may also be present in normal individuals during the formation of dreams and are present in the normal development of very young children under the age of 5. Hence, both from the standpoint of degree of pathology as well as the level of developmental maturity, these defenses are considered the hierarchically lowest and the most psychologically primitive.

What characterizes these defenses as a group, and separates them from the other less pathological or more mature defenses, is the delusional nature of the mistaken belief, which may take hold for several reasons. First, the patient may not possess the requisite reality testing ability to determine that the belief cannot in fact be real. In the psychotic individual, in a dream, and to a lesser extent in childhood, the imagination is given great leeway in determining what might be possible. Second, the consequences of accepting a painful reality may be too great, in which case reality may give way to delusion. Third, in the neurological cases, the cognitive apparatus may be sufficiently impaired that the patient's belief system is altered, while under normal circumstances reality testing would correct the delusional or mistaken beliefs.

First let us consider the nearly universal defense of denial, which may be manifested in different ways. The most basic is the simple verbal denial of reality, a negation of the truth about the state of affairs in the presence of clear evidence to the contrary. There is also denial in the form of fantasy. Vaillant, for example, cites the appearance, or "return," of a deceased loved one in a daydream. This is of course a normal and common occurrence. But when denial leads a patient to set the table for the deceased spouse, the defense has become a psychotic response.

Although the distinction between the two important defenses of repression and denial is not clear-cut, when an individual must deal with troubling or unacceptable *inner drives,* such as a sexual or aggressive urges, and the psyche keeps these motives out of awareness, that process is typically referred to as *repression.*[62] When, however, distressing circumstances in the world *around us* are kept unconscious, we generally refer to that processs as an instance of *denial.* As Anna Freud describes the relation between these defenses, "Just as, in the neurotic conflict, perception of a prohibited instinctual stimulus is warded off by means of repression, so the infantile ego resorts to denial in order not to become aware of some painful impression from without."[63]

Vaillant offers another interpretation of the distinction between denial and repression. In denial, both the unpleasant reality and the affect associated with it are denied, while in repression the affect may be experienced even though the reality is unacknowledged. So the man who wipes away tears but claims he is not crying is using denial, but the man who wipes away his tears but tells us that he does not know why he is crying, is using repression.[64] Nonetheless, the distinction between denial and repression remains not as clear as we would like.

In neurological cases we are primarily interested not in repressed urges or motives, but rather in the effect that brain damage has on the ability of patients to assess their bodies, their environments, the people close to and around them, and their current life circumstances. A failure of overt accurate or realistic knowledge in these domains, as well as a failure to express the appropriate overt emotional response to present circumstances, can be seen as instances of denial.

A second psychotic defense, *delusional projection*, is recognized by two common features. First is the loss of the capacity to test reality, which renders the individual incapable of distinguishing the impossibility of the delusion or misbelief. The second concept is the process of projection itself. In psychoanalytic terms, projection is an unconscious process wherein unacceptable thoughts, feelings, or motivations are *re*jected and *pro*jected outside of the self, typically onto other persons. In this fashion, one's own thoughts and feelings do not become conscious self-attributes, but are experienced as aspects of the external world.[65] Paranoid beliefs are commonly interpreted as examples of projection; for example, where an unconscious affect ("I hate John") is attributed to the hated object ("John hates me").

The third psychotic defense is *distortion*. This is a process in which the individual grossly reshapes reality to suit his or her personal needs. In contrast to denial, in which an unpleasant reality is ignored, in distortion reality is unconsciously and unrealistically reorganized to fit the individual's desires. Examples of distortion are wish-fulfilling delusional beliefs, including grandiose and unrealistic concepts of the self.[66]

The Immature Defenses

The next hierarchical level on Vaillant's scheme, which includes among other defenses *projection, fantasy,* and *dissociation,* are termed immature defenses because they make their appearance early in development, in much the same way that Cramer, Taylor, and Harris noted the presence of these defenses in children.[67] In Vaillant's scheme, these defenses are hierarchically higher than the so-called psychotic defenses because they are less reality-distorting and require more mental and psychological development than that present in the so-called psychotic levels of defense that are seen in the severely disturbed psychiatric patient or in the contents of dreams.

In addition to the psychotic defenses identified in Vaillant's hierarchy, the three immature defenses of fantasy, projection, and dissociation appear particularly relevant to the analysis of the neuropathologies of the self. In the adult, as we have seen in the normal child, the use of fantasy—imagining wishful and fanciful circumstances for the self—in some circumstances allows the ego to escape unpleasant realities and assuage unmet needs, and under the right circumstances fantasy is, of course, a healthy adaptation to life, and plays an important part in creative thinking and art. As in the confabulations of the neurological patient, however, not all fantasies are pleasant. One can as easily imagine catastrophic outcomes as long wished for hopes in our daydreams. Projection appears again at this level in Vaillant's scheme but in non-delusional form. Here the use of projection in the adult resembles the use of this defense in the normal child. In the adult it may be counter-productive, neurotic, or immature to project our feelings on those around us, but it does not make us psychotic. Indeed, just like with fantasy, we may see the use

of projection all around us. Common forms of projection are the belief that someone you fall in love with simply must love you back, or
resentment toward the boss makes you believe he or she has it in for
you.

Finally, the individual may engage in defensive *dissociation*, a
process we have already considered that occurs in some neurological
disturbances of the self. According to the *DSM-IV-TR*, when dissociation occurs as defensive operation "The individual deals with emotional conflict or internal or external stressors with a breakdown in
the usually integrated functions of consciousness, memory, perception of self or the environment, or sensory/motor behavior."[68] Similarly, Vaillant describes dissociation as "a mechanism in which the
person sustains a temporary alteration in the integrative functions
of consciousness or identity."[69] The sense of dissociation most related to the adult neuropathologies of the self involves an alteration,
transformation, or perturbation in the way one experiences the relationship between the self to itself or to the world. As we have seen
earlier, common forms of dissociation in normal individuals are
déjà vu and jamais vu experiences and daydreaming. Induced hyp-
notic trances are also considered dissociative states.

Psychiatrist Frank Putnam, a recognized authority on the subject,
has described dissociative behaviors in children, such as make-believe play, fantasy phenomena, and imaginary companionship, on a
continuum ranging from normal dissociative-spectrum behaviors
that are commonly seen in childhood to more pathological forms.[70]
He points out that in children and adolescents the distinction between the normal and the pathological is particularly difficult to de-
tect because so many dissociative operations that are considered a
normal part of development in children could be considered signs of
pathology in adults.

At this point, I wish to emphasize that it will become evident that
there is a close relationship between the childhood behaviors and
adult pathologies of the self.[71] While denial, projection, and distor-

tion are among the immature defenses, they form a normal part of psychological maturation. At about age 7, we find both denial and projection appearing as normal aspects of the child's psychological defensive structure. In a similar way, the use of fantasy and dissociation that appear as important and adaptive operations in children may represent pathology when they excessively linger or re-emerge to an extreme degree in adulthood. Although approaches to these defenses different somewhat among researchers, it is clear that the denial of external reality, delusional projection, and distortion occur most commonly in childhood, in our dreams, and in psychosis. In the chapters that follow, we will look at how the emergence of these developmental patterns can be used to illuminate the fascinating patterns of behavior that occur in patients with damage to critical self-related brain structures.[72]

CHAPTER THREE

The Brainchild Within

AS WE HAVE SEEN, children up to age 7 or 8 most often make use of the psychological defenses of denial and projection, as well as an elaborate system of fantasy that employs personification and the development of imaginary companions. We have also seen these same patterns of behavior in the clinical cases we examined earlier. To forge the link between the child's ego system and the clinical disorders in adults, we need to find the parallels between these expressions of the childhood ego and defensive functioning in these patients. I believe a strong case can be made that the parallels are not just evident, but indeed striking, and it is this relationship that we'll turn to now.

Anosognosia and Denial

As we have seen, one of the earliest defenses in the developing child's defensive psychological armor is denial, the characteristic feature of anosognosia. Many of the original writers on the subject of anosognosia, asomatognosia, and confabulation had suspected for decades that *negative features* of these conditions such as sensory loss, hemispatial neglect, global confusional states, and memory loss, cannot fully explain the occurrence of these disorders, and these writers reasoned that *positive factors* must also be important in the creation of some of these cases. Perhaps the first person to highlight the inadequacy of purely negative neurological explanations for one of these conditions, anosognosia, was Kurt Goldstein, who in his best known work *The Organism* (1939), emphasized the need to invoke psychological factors to explain how some individuals could remain unaware of their neurological deficits:

> This lack of self-perception of a disturbance has been looked upon as a peculiarity resulting from a definite kind of damage to the cortex, and an attempt has been made to explain it, either in terms of localization, or through the assumption of faculty disturbances, such as those of attention, perception, or memory. None of these explanations has proved adequate. . . . The study of such cases, and also of a great many variously localized brain injuries, has shown me that the phenomenon which we are discussing is certainly not confined to any specific type or place of lesion in the brain; and we cannot speak simply of psychotic reactions, even in the sense of hysteria. Rather, we are facing apparently quite normal biological reactions to a very gave defect.[1]

In his work, Goldstein points out that damage to a single part of the brain, or the loss of any one faculty, cannot explain the syndrome of anosognosia. First, he did not find the same type of damage in all of these cases. But perhaps most importantly, he noted that what these patients demonstrated was not just the loss of some particular faculty, but rather a *normal reaction* to a serious neurological defect as well. He was suggesting that, rather than being due simply to neurological or psychotic disruption, the normal mechanisms of psychological defense *that remained intact* in the brain-damaged individual determined the anosognosic response. Although Goldstein was, in my opinion, on the right track, this explanation does not account for the observation that significant denial is so much more common in left as compared to right hemiplegic patients. He also appears to have unnecessarily de-emphasized the importance of negative factors, such as hemispatial neglect and sensory loss, in determining the anosognosic response.

A subsequent milestone in this research was achieved by Paul Schilder, clinical director of psychiatry at Bellevue Psychiatric Hospital in New York City, whose classic book *The Image and Appearance of the Human Body* was published in 1950. In this work, Schilder proposed that the anosognosic patient uses a defense he called "organic repression" to exclude the painful facts of his or her neurological impairments from consciousness:

> What makes these patients neglect their paralysis? What makes them disown one half of their bodies? . . . We may want to forget a defectiveness. We may want to suppress the thought that we are disabled, but the tormenting consciousness of the defect will still come back again and again. We may speak of the conscious psychic level. It is clear that in the cases mentioned this mechanism does not take place. But if we continue in our efforts, we may finally forget the difficulty, and then we shall be dealing with mechanism in which the conscious attitude has found support from the "unconscious." But then we find also a clear-cut psychic motive, which is fully understandable.[2]

In contrast to Goldstein, Schilder held that there was a significant *interaction* between negative neurological factors and other positive conscious and unconscious motivational factors in determining the anosognosic response.

The pinnacle of this line of thought was achieved in the work of Dr. Edwin A. Weinstein, a neurologist and fellow of the William Alanson White Institute of Psychoanalysis in New York City, a true pioneer in the study of the interface between neurology and psychiatry. Weinstein began his work on anosognosia in the 1940s, and over the ensuing fifty years, nearly until his death in 1998, he published innumerable papers and chapters on the subject. However, he is best remembered for his classic monograph on anosognosia, *Denial of Illness* (1955), written with one of his chief collaborators, Robert L. Kahn, Ph.D.[3]

Weinstein, more than any previous writer on the subject, pointed out the significance of motivational, defensive, and adaptive mechanisms that supported the denial response. He also explained that complete verbal denial was only one potential response in the anosognosic patient, and that these patients actually displayed a wide range of potentially defensive reactions. For example, even if patients did not display complete denial of a disability, they might minimize or attribute the disability to a more benign cause. Weinstein describes one patient who claimed his arm could move but he was too "lazy" to do it. Other patients claimed, among other excuses, that the arm was "too sore from injections" to move, or provided the explanations that "Everyone's left side is weaker than the right," "Just when you want it to do something it won't," or that it "just needs a little practice." One patient suggested that the examiner "come back some other day, you bad man," or asked "would you mind if I used my right arm instead?"[4]

Indeed, Weinstein cataloged a large number of verbal mechanisms of defense in the anosognosic patient. In addition to *explicit verbal denial* and *rationalization*, he noted the presence of other defensive operations including the use of *confabulation, delusional thinking, projection, humor* and *metaphorical language.*[5] It was Weinstein's conjecture that denial of a hemiplegic limb was more common after lesions of the right hemisphere because all these behaviors were verbally mediated and thus depended upon an intact left (verbal) hemisphere for their expression. Despite these defenses, Weinstein and his colleagues pointed out, while patients might explicitly deny their disabilities, they actually might demonstrate considerable implicit awareness of their problems:

> Actually, the term "anosogonsia" meaning "lack of the knowledge of disease" is not wholly accurate. The patient indicates knowledge of

the neglected extremities by referring to them in such expressions as a "dummy" and a "rusty piece of machinery." . . . The patient represents his disability not only in statements about, and attitudes toward, the affected side, but also in terms of other aspects of the environment, expressed in his designations of other parts of the body, of events, places, dates, people, and objects. We refer to these manifestations of the anosognosic syndrome as "metaphorical" because feelings about the self are expressed in terms of the somatic, spatial, and temporal aspects of the environment.[6]

Subsequent writers have supported the role of psychological defenses in the production of anosognosia. Theodore Dorpat, for example, provides an extensive analysis of anosognosia from a Freudian perspective, arguing that denial and other "anosognosic behaviors are subjectively meaningful and can be interpreted psychodynamically. In this respect anosognosia behaviors are no different from psychiatric symptoms in patients who do not have brain damage."[7] More recent investigators[8] have provided further evidence that psychological defenses, motivations, and wish-fulfillment play an important role in the production of anosognosia, asomatognosia, and delusions and confabulation in brain damaged subjects.

This does not mean the anosognosia is simply a result of psychological denial. Rather, my point here is that while the evidence indicates that anosognosia is in part a result of negative neurological defects such as hemispatial neglect and sensory loss, the evidence suggests that the *delusional* and *motivational* aspects of the syndrome are the result of positive factors including psychological denial. Weinstein often made the observation that a tendency to deny illness even before their neurological impairment was evident in his anosognosic patients. This factor could help explain why only certain patients develop delusional anosognosia, why neglect and anosognosia may be partly dissociated, and why the delusional beliefs in these patients cannot be corrected in spite of clear evidence that their beliefs are incorrect. Based upon these considerations, I suggest this provides the first link in our chain between childhood ego defenses and the clinical disorders of the self.

Asomatognosia, Somatoparaphrenia, and Personification

A similar pattern is apparent when we attempt to explain the sort of delusional misidentifications we witness in asomatognosia and somatoparaphrenia. One might understand on the basis of simple sensory loss, hemispatial neglect, and mental confusion why a patient may have difficulty realizing that a paralyzed arm may not be his or her own. Indeed, this explanation might even suffice in those cases where a patient mistakes the arm for the examiner's arm. But the delusional belief that the arm actually belongs to a long dead husband, for example, requires further explanation.

If various negative symptoms cannot account for the richness and complexity that we witness in the neurological disorders of the self, what other positive features might help explain these conditions? For example, one may reasonably ask to what degree the misbeliefs of these patients are motivated. How are the narratives we have reviewed influenced by the wants and needs of these patients in response to the unpleasant and painful reality that they now face, driven by the desire to replace current circumstances with a more pleasant fantasy?

With this question in mind, nearly fifty years ago Montague Ullman and his colleagues described the case of a 50-year-old Italian woman who was hospitalized at Bellevue Hospital in New York City.[9] The woman had suffered a stroke of her right hemisphere that resulted in complete paralysis of her entire left side. Her husband had died one year previously, yet the patient claimed that her left hand actually belonged to her dead husband and that he stroked her breast with it. The reports of their interviews with the woman are illuminating and poignant:

Q: *Do you remember what you said when you first told us about your arm?*
A: *Yes, I imagined that it was my husband's arm because I wished so very much he could be with me.*

Several weeks later, she tried to make sense of her confusion regarding her prior mistaken beliefs:

> *Maybe because I was wishing so much that he would come. Someone had cut my nails short like my husband's. I keep mine long and pointed, so it looked to me like my husband's hand.*

In a follow-up interview, a year after the initial stroke, she explained further:

Q: *Why do you think the thought occurred to you that it was your husband's arm?*
A: *Every night I wished he would come in like he did every night for 25 years. I always waked up when he'd come in and that night I felt he did come in.*
Q: *It really felt as though he did come in and not as if it were a dream?*
A: *No, I felt he was there and I felt his arm.*
Q: *What made you think it was his arm?*
A: *Who else would come in and do that?*

The use of personification in a motivated fantasy was also clear in one of my patients, JK, described earlier. This young man had sustained a stroke of his right hemisphere and found himself in a New York City hospital, paralyzed on his left side, and separated from his family by thousands of miles. He spoke of his loneliness and his desire to be reunited with his loved ones, desires that were expressed in his misidentification of his left arm as actually being his "brother's arm":

TEF: *What's wrong? Why are you here?*
JK: *I had some type of brain injury. Not exactly sure what happened.*
TEF: *Do you have any weakness anywhere?*
JK: *Yes. I can't move my left arm. I can feel things there but I can't move it.* [touching his left hand]
TEF: *You have told me that all your family is overseas, and that you miss them very much. How does it feel to have your brother's arm here?*
JK: [Patient begins to cry profusely. He holds his left arm in his right

hand.] *It makes me happy. It makes me very happy. It makes me feel closer to my brother. Emotionally it makes me happy.* [He remains very tearful.] *I feel sad to not be able to see my friends and family. I have to wait for them to come see me. I am learning so much. This is a sort of rebirth. It was so sad. But now I'm not sad, because I can now correct my mistakes.* [crying]

TEF: *How did it make you feel that it was your brother's?*

JK: *I thought it was a little funny . . . like a little gross.*

TEF: *A little funny and a little gross? But you also said. . . .*

JK: *But now it makes me a little comforted.*

TEF: *A little what?*

JK: *Comforted . . . because I have my brother here* [pointing to left arm, begins to cry]. *It's a little comfort for me now. . . .*

TEF: *A little comforting for you?*

JK: *But now it makes me a little comforted.*

TEF: *OK so why? You said it kept you company?*

JK: *Yes.*

TEF: *did it make you feel emotionally?*

JK: *I felt stronger. . . .*

TEF: *Because . . . you missed your family?*

JK: *Yeah. . . . I missed my brother.* [I lifted the arm toward his right side and asked him how he felt about it.]

JK: *I feel good. I feel good about this. . . . It feels good. I don't know. Just because.*

TEF: [I lifted his right hand.] *How about this?*

JK: *This is my hand . . . my right hand.*

TEF: *How do you feel about this?*

JK: *This is OK. . . .*

TEF: *This one is OK. . . . You just feel OK about this one?*

JK: *This one doesn't have a story like this one* (pointing to his left hand) *. . . it has a story. Like the one I told you . . . this hand has a background that makes me feel closer to my brother.*

When we consider such cases of asomatognosia as JK's, there are significant parallels with the personification fantasies and defenses that we see in childhood. The arm in these cases may take on an identity independent from the patient, a "companion fantasy" which for some patients provides solace in the face of cruel and difficult circumstances.

Many asomatognosic patients with specific brain lesions, especially those that involve damage to the right hemisphere, demonstrate a subtle but important alteration in the way they express their thoughts and feelings about their bodies and their personal problems and experiences. We have already noted how commonly these patients describe their arms and their paralysis metaphorically (Table 1-1, p. 10) and have referred to *metaphorical expression* to describe this shift in these patients' self-expression from the factual and the reality-based to the experiential and symbolic. When patients deny their illness, impairments, or life circumstances, in some cases their narratives are understandable as metaphorical constructs of the truth—a truth of which the patient at some deeper level may be aware. Patient LA, whom we saw earlier, for example, could not accept the idea of a brain malformation creating his current difficulties. By confabulating a horrible explosion, however, the patient devised a scenario about an event that—if it were true—might explain his current predicament in terms he could understand. Further, his idea that he might be "sleepwalking" expressed both his subjective sense that something was not right in his thinking, and at the same time the wish he might still wake up and be well.

In other cases of patients with the perturbations of the self that I have previously detailed, confabulations about illness, paralyzed limbs, and the creation of other fictitious persons, events, and narratives are understood and experienced as beliefs regarding external people, objects, and events. It is in this sense that the beliefs about the mirror people, the phantom children, asomatognosic personifications and delusions, and delusional confabulations are metaphorical and symbolic.

Due to the diversity of its forms, confabulation is most appropriately thought of as a syndrome rather than a single disorder.[10] In our work, in order to highlight the metaphorical, personal, and self-expressive aspects of confabulation, we have introduced the distinction between *neutral* and *personal confabulation* (Table 3-1).[11] In a neutral confabulation, the patient who has a neurological deficit of which he or she is unaware—for example, a memory problem or sensory defect—substitutes false for correct information. The cause of the substitution may be a retrieval defect, a self-monitoring defect, or actually any problem in which the patient cannot distinguish veridical from false information.Thus a hospitalized patient who habitually has bacon and eggs for breakfast may, when asked what he ate this morning, may reply with this answer, when in reality the hospital only serves oatmeal. Many confused patients with memory impairment may think they are at home only because they find themselves in bed in pajamas.

In contrast, in the case of personal confabulation, some disturbance in the patient's self concept and ego functions leads to a distortion in the relationship between the self and the world. The self-related and motivated misidentifications of the paralyzed arm I have described would be examples of personal confabulations.It is within the domain of the personal confabulation that metaphorical expression is most likely to occur. Although a confabulation is provided by the patient as a matter of fact account of his or her current or past circumstances, it represents in reality a symbolic representation of the patient's actual situation. In addition, personal confabulations are also more likely to express a patient's longing than represent a straightforward memory or memory retrieval defect. As we have seen in confabulations about the presence of illness in anosognosia, about the ownership of a limb in asomatognosia, and about the phantom friends in mirror companions, delusional companions and the nurturing syndrome, these delusions and confabulations often represent wish fulfillment of the patients' needs in stressful circumstances.[12]

Beyond its use as a way of expressing the patient's wishes, a further aspect of metaphorical confabulation is the manner in which it

Table 3-1. The "neutral versus personal" continuum of confabulation

Neutral confabulation	Personal Confabulation*
unimodal	multimodal
impersonal	self-referential and autobiographical
motivation not essential	motivationally driven
personality type not essential	personality may be important
non-symbolic	may be symbolic and metaphorical
non-delusional and correctable	may be delusional and impervious to correction
inconsistent/variable	may be repeated and long lasting

* Now we use the terms "personal confabulation," "delusional confabulation," or "personal delusional confabulation" somewhat interchangeably. Personal confabulations most resemble "fantastic" confabulations in the classic literature.

helps the patient adapt to his or her current distressing reality. A metaphorical confabulation may make more sense and feel more true to the patient than the actual facts of his or her illness or altered life circumstances. Hence, when an asomatognosic patient describes her arm as "dead," the reference to a paralyzed arm as lifeless may be more comprehensible than a scientific explanation that invokes the neurology of stroke and brain damage. Further, by referring to the arm as "belonging to her husband," the patient replaces the peculiar and distasteful feeling of a lifeless limb with the more conventional feeling that it belongs to her familiar husband. In some cases, patients with asomatognosia not only represent their personal feelings regarding the weakness, limpness, and lifelessness of their arms with personifications, metaphors, and nicknames, *they also treat or act upon these metaphorical expressions as reality.* Many of these patients not only misname the arm, but they actually may try to feed it, pet it, and make plans to take it home in a suitcase, expressions and behaviors we may group under a rubric of *metaphorical behaviors.*

Thus, in patients with asomatognosic cases we see a cluster of related defensive behaviors. These patients may *deny* the identity of a paralyzed arm, demonstrating the immature defense of denial. They also may *personify* the arm, and like a child with an imaginary companion, create a fantasy in which the lifeless arm is given a new and positive role in the patient's adjustment to paralysis. In addition, through the use of *metaphorical expression* to misname the arm or create a metaphorical narrative of the patient's experiences, there may be both a denial of the unpleasant circumstances as well as a *projection*—another immature defense—of personal idiosyncratic feelings or beliefs onto external referents. What was once the arm now becomes a piece of machinery, a dummy, or a piece of meat. Through the use of these immature defenses, symbolic reifications of feelings about the self, personal fears, wishes, or current concerns take precedence over what in the normal adult is consensual reality.

Delusions and Fantasies about People

In those cases where we witness a delusional misidentification of other persons, or even of one's mirror image, many theories emphasize the role that anatomical disconnection plays in the creation of these conditions. In cases of Capgras syndrome, for example, in which the patients claim someone close to them had been replaced, the behavioral neurologist Michael Alexander argues that a deep right frontal lesion could functionally disconnect temporal and limbic regions from the damaged frontal lobe.[13] This disconnection could result in a disturbance in the patient's familiarity with people and places and the presence of frontal damage could lead to an inability to resolve the cognitive conflict. Others have proposed that disconnection of the hippocampus from other parts of the brain important for memory storage could result in an inability to associate new information with previous memories, leading to reduplication[14] and others have suggested that Capgras syndrome is caused by a disconnection between visual and emotional areas of the brain.[15] Some theories propose that patients with Capgras syndrome have overt but not covert face recognition. A lesion in the dorsal system, which runs between the visual cortex and the limbic system via the inferior parietal lobule, would allow explicit but not implicit (emotional) recognition, which they suggest accounts for the occurrence of Capgras.[16] Similarly, William Hirstein and V. S. Ramachandran suggest that a disconnection between the inferotemporal cortex and the amygdala could allow the patient to correctly identify faces but not experience the appropriate emotion connected to familiar faces, leading to delusional misidentification.[17]

These explanations, which emphasize the role that negative factors play in the disorder, may indeed account for some instances of delusional misidentification. However, there are important features of the conditions we have considered that are not explained by the disconnection of all emotional processing from key regions of the brain, such as the selectivity we see in most instances of Capgras syndrome where the misidentification is often confined to specific persons, usually individuals emotionally close to the patient, or someone upon whom the patient is emotionally dependent. In all the cases of mirror misidentification I have detailed above, the patient was delusional only about his or her own mirror image. Additionally, many of the beliefs regarding imaginary companions or phantom relatives occurred without any visual misidentification of anyone. They were purely ideational and delusional fantasies about the self and the world. This suggests that other, positive factors, most likely relating to the emotional makeup or personality of the individual, must play a key role in creating the condition.

The role of motivational factors is clear in some cases of delusional friends and relatives. My patient SC found a nice companion in the mirror, someone she could share her experiences and feelings with, and she came to genuinely like the "other SC." The same is true of the patients with delusional companions described by Michael Shanks and Annalena Venerri.[18] All of these patients reported having social outlets and appear to have been isolated and lonely. The delusional companions in these cases appear to have been actually loved by the patients, and were an important source of emotional comfort. In the cases of nurturing syndrome described by Venneri and others, both patients developed the fantasy of the presence of the imaginary spouse upon a husband's death, apparently in response to the severe emotional loss.[19] In the mirror companion cases, patients who selectively misidentify themselves in the mirror not only personify their feelings about themselves in the imaginary mirror companion, they also speak to the mirror, interact with the mirror, and create a whole narrative around this fictional person.

As in the childhood cases of imaginary companions, my patients who deny their personal problems but relate them to imaginary children or imaginary best friends act as if these friends truly existed, and I have suggested that the behavioral characteristics of these two groups of children and adults are strikingly similar. First, among the types of role play behavior seen in children, those in which the child creates a wholly fictitious imaginary person and those in which the child projects a character onto an external vehicle such as a doll or stuffed toy are common in the adult cases who display personification. Second, it is clear that in both the child and adult cases there may be both imaginary friends and imaginary enemies. Third, the psychological motivations and adaptive features within the two groups are similar as well, with companions in both groups serving to provide companionship and alleviate loneliness, aid in conquering fears, and help the individual to achieve feelings of mastery and competence and to cope with trauma. Finally, there are common psychological mechanisms at work as well, including the defenses of denial, projection and paranoia, and splitting. Indeed, in the adult cases I have analyzed it is most often the case that multiple motivations and mechanisms are at work simultaneously.

Let us consider first the motivational and adaptive characteristics of the cases I have illustrated. Using some of the major functions of imaginary companions in children suggested by Marjorie Taylor[20] I have ordered what I interpret to be the major motivational and adaptive functions in selected adult cases of phantom others (Table 3-2) based either on cases that I have personally examined or reports of patients described by other investigators with sufficient detail to make judgments about the adaptive functions in these patients.

One of the most striking features of these cases is that the most common motivation in the adult patients is the manner in which the imaginary other provides companionship, also one of the most common, if not the most common of its adaptive functions in children. Across all categories, whether the patient reported mirror companions, phantom children, relatives, and friends, or in the nurturing syndrome cases, in the majority of cases the phantom provided friendship and an escape from loneliness for the patient. This clearly is a unifying bridge between the child and adult cases.

The next most common function in these cases was the role of the companion in the adaptation to a recent trauma. For example, in the case of SC, who had significant behavioral and cognitive deficits after an aneurismal rupture that also led to the breakup of his marriage, a fantasy about his plans to adopt a child provided him with the consoling delusion that he was still together with his wife. Patient CB, who suffered from delusions that both she and her niece had attempted suicide by a self-inflicted gunshot to the head, had recently experienced a prolonged hospitalization for an aneurysm, exhibited disabling memory defects, and was quite perplexed about the nature of her problems, their origin, and their consequences. The delusional narrative about the way in which she and her niece had suffered provided a convenient and more comprehensible explanation for her current situation than the abstract explanations from her doctors that included complicated and alien descriptions of ruptured blood vessels and anterograde amnesia. SA also found it more understandable that he had been injured in a friendly fraternity initiation ritual than hospitalized with a severe brain hemor-

Table 3-2. Motivational and adaptive functions in selected adult cases with imaginary others (13 cases)

Cases	Companionship	Mastery	Fears	Trauma
CASE SP Mirror companion (this volume)	+	+		
CASE RD Mirror persecutor (this volume)			+	
CASE GT Phantom persecutor (this volume)			+	
CASE AS Delusional companion Shanks & Venneri (2002)	+			
CASE AL Delusional companion Shanks & Venneri (2002)	+			
CASE ST Delusional companion Shanks & Venneri (2002)	+			
CASE LK Phantom relatives (this volume)	+	+		+
CASE SC Phantom child (this volume)	+	+		+
CASE BB Delusions about son (this volume)	+	+		+
CASE CB Delusions about niece (this volume)	+	+		+
CASE SA Delusions about friend (this volume)		+		+
CASE CS Nurturing syndrome Venneri et al. (2002)	+			+
CASE KC Nurturing syndrome Venneri et al. (2002)	+			+
Totals	10	6	2	7

rhage. In the case of the two nurturing syndrome cases, both patients developed their delusions in the context of the loss of their husbands.

In many cases, the imaginary companions also served to allow the patients to demonstrate mastery over their circumstances and neurological deficits. Patient SC, for example, was able to express his displeasure with the doctors who insisted on telling him about his cognitive impairments. When he tells the examiner that *I think there's too much pressure on the kid to really give an honest answer. I don't think a kid who is 6 or 7 years old is capable of giving you the right answer,* he is making an effort to rationalize his impairments and improve his own perception of himself as a competent individual, although his statement indicates that he *feels* like he is being treated like a child by the staff.

Similarly, the patient BB spoke often but indirectly about his feelings of being in the hospital, his loss of independence, and his inability to resume his work. He disliked being away from his job and having to engage in the hospital rehabilitation routines, but in his delusions, he was able to use his son as his proxy to discuss his displeasure about his current circumstances as well as his hopes for recovery. He stated that he had told his "son" who was "also in the hospital," *"It's like in the marines. . . . You gotta do what you gotta do, what you gotta do!"* With their imaginary companions and their delusional narratives, these patients are working out in their minds their own concerns about their current circumstances as well as attempting to restore their sense of purpose and identity.

When considering the psychological mechanisms involved in these delusions, there is again a striking overlap with the typical defenses and fantasies of children (Table 3-3). Many cases demonstrated straightforward *wishful fantasies,* as in providing a desired companion in the mirror and delusional companions and the nurturing syndrome cases. As mentioned, the fantasy of the adopted child in the case of SC provided a means for the patient to imagine reuniting

Table 3-3. Psychological mechanisms in adult cases with imaginary others (13 cases)

Cases	Denial	Projection	Paranoia	Splitting	Wishful fantasy
CASE SP Mirror companion (this volume)		+			+
CASE RD Mirror persecutor (this volume)			+	+	
CASE GT Phantom persecutor (this volume)			+		
CASE AS Delusional companion Shanks & Venneri (2002)					+
CASE AL Delusional companion Shanks & Venneri (2002)					+
CASE ST Delusional companion Shanks & Venneri (2002)					+
CASE LK Phantom relatives (this volume)	+	+			+
CASE SC Phantom child (this volume)	+	+			+
CASE BB Delusions about son (this volume)	+	+			
CASE CB Delusions about niece (this volume)	+	+			
CASE SA Delusions about friend (this volume)					+
CASE CS Nurturing syndrome Venneri et al. (2002)	+				+
CASE KC Nurturing syndrome Venneri et al. (2002)	+				+
Totals	5	5	2	1	9

with his wife, and in the case of SA, the fantasy of a being involved in fraternity initiation surely represented a better scenario than being delirious, neurologically impaired, and tied down in a hospital ward.

As in childhood, the immature defenses of *denial* and *projection* were the most common psychological defenses. In some cases this took the form of denial of neurological impairments. Cases LK, SC, BB, and CB all denied or minimized their cognitive impairments and illness, even when theses were explicitly pointed out to them. The patient with the phantom child denied his frequent hospitalizations and his separation from his wife, while the women who exhibited the nurturing syndrome denied the loss of their husbands.

In some of these cases, the patient with denial projected his or her impairments onto a phantom or a relative. LK claimed it was her nieces and an aunt who had suffered aneurysms, and that the aunt "couldn't think straight." It was the doctors who told SC that his phantom child had been hospitalized and was not making progress, while according to SC he was himself doing fine. It was not BB but his son who was hospitalized and undergoing rehab, while SP's mirror companion was the one who was "nervous" and "not too bright."

Of all the cases, the patient RD, who screamed at the whore in the mirror, and GT, who was inhabited by a malevolent amoeba, are clearly the most psychotic and paranoid in their beliefs. We must bear in mind, however, that neither patient had any psychiatric history prior to the onset of their neurological illnesses. In the case of RD, while the patient retained a positive self-image as a proper wife and mother, the other in the mirror was perceived as malevolent whore and tramp. This polarization of the self into opposite extremes, with the externalization of the negative aspects of the self, resembles the pattern of splitting as described by psychoanalysts.

The presence of *splitting* is particularly of interest from the point of view of psychodynamic defenses. In splitting, as we noted before, the patient cannot integrate ambivalent or opposing self-images, and the positive aspects of the self remain internalized while the negative aspects of the self are externalized and projected. That splitting may be seen in some neurological cases, especially with Capgras syndrome, has been noted previously.[21] In particular, some years ago Robert Berson pointed out that patients with Capgras syndrome who claim there are "good" and "bad" versions of a single person may be using the psychological defense of splitting to deal with ambivalent feelings about someone by "psychologically dividing" the person in two. This enables the individual to express dissatisfaction with the "bad" version yet still maintain an emotional relationship with the "good" one.

Some other authors, on the other hand, counter that these explanations fail because there is no reason for an individual to develop splitting or profound ambivalence toward inanimate objects such as a toothbrush or one's boots. I would argue that in the cases of misidentification of inanimate objects I have witnessed, patients are typically in the early stages of a dementia in which they are having difficulty recognizing their own property. In this context, it becomes understandable how frightening and threatening the predisposed individuals might feel as they gradually became alienated from their own clothes, furniture, or surroundings. This ambivalence leads the individual to feel that objects in the environment have become split into the originals (the good ones) and their facsimiles (the bad ones). The psychological response to the threat of "losing one's mind" may be profound, leading the Capgras patient to claim that the truth of the matter is not that he or she is crazy, but that everyone else is.

The ambivalence toward the misidentified entities may have any of a number of origins, ranging from extreme psychiatric disintegration as in the psychotic individual, to more banal loss of familiarity with the common items within one's life, as may occur in early dementia. The degree that the individual reacts with a profound and irrational response may depend upon other factors, such as the extent of suspiciousness or paranoia present and the regression to early developmental phases of defense, which may in turn reflect the patient's personality in advance of any illness or trauma.

Finally, it is also of interest, but not surprising, that in many of the cases of asomatognosia in which a limb or other object is personified (Table 1-1, p. 10), we see some of the same wishful patterns we have uncovered in the cases of the "imaginary others." For example, we see this in JK's wishful fantasy that his arm belonged to a longed for but absent brother or in the case of Ullman's patient who claimed that her arm belonged to a missing husband. Parallels between cases where patients display nurturing behaviors toward the paralyzed arm, in which it is treated like a baby, petted, fed, or sung to, and the nurturing cases of women with deceased husbands is obvious.

Thus, in summary, we have seen that adult patients with anosognosia, asomatognosia, and other delusions display patterns of defensive behavior that we recognize are typical of the 3- to 8-year-old child. The presence of denial, projection, splitting, and wishful fantasy is characteristic of this young age group, and these same defenses and behaviors are in abundant evidence in the adult cases with neurological disturbances of the self. Further, the raison d'etre for the childhood and adult cases is also similar. Why should this be so, and what are the implications of this association for our understanding of the neurobiology of the self? This is the question that we will examine next.

CHAPTER FOUR

Observing the Ego

THE CLINICAL DISORDERS that we have examined thus far, including anosognosia, asomatognosia, and the delusional "others" syndromes, are not an entirely homogeneous group of conditions. One feature that may vary considerably among individual patients, for example, is the *degree of delusional certainty* they express. As we have seen, there are many patients who appear unaware of a left hemiplegia, but when the paralysis is pointed out to them, they do not resist the truth, do not dispute the examiner, do not confabulate that the arm is actually moving, and do not rationalize the reason for lack of movement. However, others remain in denial and go to great lengths to avoid the truth about their illness. In a similar fashion, most patients do not misname the affected arm, provide it with an identity, or talk or sing to it. But there are those patients who do. And some patients with a developing dementia have difficulty identifying themselves in the mirror, but only a relatively small group create an entire new identity surrounding their misidentified mirror image. So, what do the patients who persist in their delusions have in common?

Verbal Disconnection and Confabulation

Many of the behaviors we have considered thus far are subtypes of confabulation—that is, verbal statements and beliefs that are incorrect but
nonetheless not intended to be conscious lies. Thus it is reasonable to
suggest that if one could understand confabulation as a syndrome in
general this might help explain these delusional confabulatory disorders as well. One approach to this question was suggested by the great
behavioral neurologist Norman Geschwind, who proposed that some
confabulatory responses were based upon a disconnection of perceptual regions from the language areas of the verbal (left) hemisphere of
the brain. In the case of the patient with a right hemisphere lesion who
was unaware of his or her paralysis, for example, Geschwind reasoned
that since the damaged verbal hemisphere lacks correct knowledge regarding the left side of the body, the patient "fills in" the information by
the process of perceptual completion. As Geschwind puts it:

> One most important implication is that the "introspections" of the
> patient as to his disability may be of little or no use to the examiner.
> The patient cannot "introspect" about the activities of a piece of
> brain which had no connexion to the speech area. What he tells you
> is of little value in elucidating the mechanism and may indeed be ac-
> tively misleading. Indeed, it becomes clear that many of the patient's
> responses can only be described as confabulatory, i.e. they are at-
> tempts to fill gaps in the information available to his speech area;
> phrased in more conventional terms they are attempts to explain
> what the patient cannot understand.[1]

Geschwind's theory that confabulations occur as a result of disconnection from the language areas plausibly accounts for the way
some patients with right hemisphere lesions display neutral and im-
personal confabulations about the left side of their visual and physical space and the condition of the left arm. Here the patient relies
on observations available from the intact right side of the brain to
fill in the "gap" on the impaired side.

Michael Gazzaniga offers a similar explanation for the same forms of confabulation, based upon split brain research.[2] In the split brain condition a stimulus can be presented independently to one hemisphere without the opposite hemisphere being fully aware of the nature of the stimulus. Gazzaniga argues that when the stimuli send conflicting signals, the verbal left hemisphere serves as an "interpreter" that enables the individual to "construct theories about the relationship between perceived events, actions, and feelings," acting as the final arbiter in matters of individual consciousness.[3]

An example of the left hemisphere's role as interpreter can be seen in the case of the split brain patient PS. When PS was presented with simultaneous yet different visual stimuli to each hemisphere, he could perform correct yet different responses with each hand simultaneously. Gazzaniga, who conducted the research with Joseph LeDoux, describes PS's response:

> What is of particular interest, however, is the way the subject verbally interpreted these double-field responses. When a snow scene was presented to the right hemisphere and a chicken claw was presented to the left, P.S. quickly and dutifully responded correctly by choosing a picture of a chicken from a series of four cards with his right hand and a picture of a shovel from a series of four cards with his left hand. The subject was then asked, "What did you see?" "I saw a claw and I picked the chicken, and you have to clean out the chicken shed with a shovel."
>
> In trial after trial, we saw this kind of response. The left hemisphere could easily and accurately identify why it had picked the answer, and then subsequently, and without batting an eye, it would incorporate the right hemisphere's response into the framework. While we knew exactly why the right hemisphere had made its choice, the left hemisphere could merely guess. Yet, the left did not offer its suggestion in a guessing vein but rather as a statement of fact as to why that card had been picked.[4]

The effect of the disconnection of the right hemisphere from the left in these cases is to give the left (verbal) hemisphere free reign in interpreting—and in this instance misinterpreting—the patient's actions. Like Geschwind, Gazzaniga argues that when the left hemisphere is faced with incomplete information, it tends to construct elaborate and false interpretation of events in an effort to "make sense" of actions or perceptions whose content or cause is actually unknown to the patient. Gazzaniga adds that in contrast to the left hemisphere, the right hemisphere maintains a more accurate construct of the person's actions and perceptions, and is less likely to fill in missing data or construct false beliefs.

Based on these findings, Gazzaniga interprets anosognosia and asomatognosia as the result of the destruction of the right hemisphere or its disconnection from the verbal left hemisphere:

> When a neurologist holds a patient's left hand up to the patient's face, the patient gives a reasonable response: "That's not my hand". The interpreter, which is intact and working, cannot get news from the parietal lobe, since the flow of information has been disrupted by the lesion. For the interpreter, the left hand simply does not exist any more, just as seeing behind the head is not something the interpreter is supposed to worry about. It is true, then, that the hand held in front of him cannot be his. In this light, the claims of the patient are more reasonable.[5]

According to these accounts, it is quite plausible that some aspects of confabulation could arise from the interpreter function, an idea that is consistent with theories that invoke the "gap filling" functions of neutral confabulations in which confabulations are proposed to fill in missing pieces of information.[6]

This interpretation, however, cannot fully explain certain aspects of the personal delusional varieties of confabulation on a number of accounts, some of which we have already reviewed. In many cases of personal delusional confabulation, the damage to the brain is in the frontal or right frontal region and does not necessarily entail or re-quire a disconnection of sensory representations from the language areas.[7] Further, a "filling in" or "interpreter" account fails to explain those cases of personal delusional confabulation—for example delu-sions about imaginary children—in which the confabulations are wholly fictitious and do not rely on any misperception on the pa-tient's part. The confabulations in personal delusional forms are se-lective, in that only specific and emotionally significant aspects of the patient's personal world are the topic of the confabulation, redu-plication, or misidentification. In the split brain patient, or in some patients with hemineglect, *any information* that emanates from the left hemispace, whether it is personally significant or not, may be the subject of a confabulation. The confabulations in the split brain cases are simple, rather facile, and often *logical.* The confabulations in the personal delusional forms cases are often bizarre or at least im-probable, wish fulfilling, or metaphorical.

Hierarchy, Dissolution, and Regression

I have argued that the key to understanding the delusional aspects of my patients' narratives and beliefs lies in relating these behav-iors to patterns of thought and defense that are characteristic of earlier phases in mental development. Let us consider then how there could be *re-emergence of the immature defenses* in these patients.

Thus far I have emphasized the importance—indeed the neces-sity—of modeling the nervous system and self upon hierarchical principles. Hughling Jackson's model of the nervous system and Freud's model of the psyche have in common the notion of hierar-chical development, in which the concept of evolution of brain and psychological functions is evident. A central tenet of Jackson's the-ory is that just as the brain evolved to create increasingly abstract and voluntary functions, in the presence of neurological dysfunc-tion, the nervous system may revert to earlier stages of functioning.

Jackson referred to this process as *dissolution*. The process of dissolution has certain predictable effects upon behavior and in order to describe these patterns, Jackson introduced the distinction between *negative* and *positive neurological symptoms*.[8]

A negative symptom is considered to be the result of a destructive lesion of the nervous system that creates a *loss of neurological function*, in which some aspect of behavior, such as the ability to speak or the capacity to move an arm or leg, is impaired. Under Jackson's conception of the nervous system, neurological deficit states that may accompany the disorders of the self we have discussed, such as paralysis, mental confusion, sensory loss, and hemispatial neglect, constitute negative symptoms. They represent a *loss* of faculties or other abilities due to the damage of cerebral tissue.

The negative symptom stands in contrast to the positive symptom, of which there are two varieties. In the first of these, an abnormal excitatory discharge of the nervous system, such as occurs during an epileptic seizure, may produce an over-activity within a particular brain region. When this excitation results in an over-activity of behavior, such as the shaking movements that occur during a generalized seizure, we refer to this as a positive symptom. Another type of positive symptom occurs when there is destruction of a brain region that normally regulates or inhibits another brain region. When this occurs, the destruction of the suppressing area "releases from inhibition" the normally suppressed region. A classic example of this is when a patient with a frontal lobe lesion displays disinhibited sexual or jocular behaviors, as in the famous case of Phineas Gage.[9] However, some of the positive symptoms we see in the presence of brain disease are actually the *normal functions* of the remaining but hierarchically lower systems that are released from the inhibition.

The influence that Jackson's neurological hierarchy played in Freud's thinking about the psyche is clear. In developing the notion of dissolution and applying the idea to psychoanalysis, Freud intro-

duced the concept of *regression*, as he articulated in this statement regarding the effect of a brain lesion upon language functions:

> In assessing the functions of the speech apparatus under pathologi-
> cal conditions we are adopting as a guiding principle Hughlings
> Jackson's doctrine that all these modes of reaction represent in-
> stances of functional retrogression (dis-involution) of a highly orga-
> nized apparatus, and therefore correspond to earlier states of its
> functional development. This means that under all circumstances an
> arrangement of associations which, having been acquired later, be-
> longs to a higher level of functioning, will be lost, while an earlier
> and simpler one will be preserved.[10,11]

When an individual regresses, he returns to a developmentally
earlier stage of psychological functioning. In these cases, hierarchically lower and developmentally less mature functions come to the
fore. The concept of regression has evolved since the time Freud
coined the term to convey a number of meanings. The psychoanalysts Jacob Arlow and Charles Brenner offer a useful general definition:

> Regression is the re-emergence of modes of mental functioning
> which were characteristic of the psychic activity of the individual
> during earlier periods of development. Viewed descriptively, regres-
> sion may be regarded as a primitivization of function. . . . It stresses
> the importance of maturational and developmental processes in
> shaping the form and function of the psychic apparatus.[12]

If it were true, as hypothesized by Jackson, Freud, and others, that
certain neurological systems that pertained to the self retained their
capacity to be re-established under conditions of brain dysfunction,
this mechanism could help explain why the unusual disorders of the
self that I have described in adults seem strikingly similar to childhood patterns of defense. It may be that these defenses and patterns
of thought remain dormant in adults and are only revealed in the
presence of significant damage to the brain.

The Role of Right Hemisphere Damage

Many of the negative symptoms we have discussed thus far are the predictable result of right hemisphere pathology, but these neuropsychological losses do not explain the dramatic transformation in self-related functions we have described in these cases. They also do not explain why these individuals seem to "return" to a hierarchically lower level of ego functioning. There must be other factors, profound and as yet undiscovered aspects of brain functioning that help explain what goes awry in the self-related functions of these patients.

If we are to understand how a brain lesion could create a regression or dissolution of ego functions, and what functions are lost as a result, a good place to start is to determine which areas of the brain are most commonly damaged in these patients. The damage and loss of functioning of these areas of the brain must be responsible for the *negative symptoms* in these cases that are not explained by the traditional and expected neuropsychological impairments that occur after some damage or deterioration in the brain. Do these areas make some specific contribution to the development of the self that could help explain the regression in ego functions when they are damaged?

In order to answer these anatomical questions, I and a group of co-workers analyzed a series of published cases of these conditions, a number of which I examined personally.[13] These included patients with Capgras syndrome for persons or the environment, asomatognosia, Fregoli syndrome for persons or the environment, or delusional doubling of the self or other persons. There were a total of twenty-seven cases reviewed and since two cases had more than one type of misidentification, there were twenty-nine recorded observations of misidentification reviewed. We found that all twenty-nine observations (100%) suffered right hemisphere damage, while only fifteen (51.72%) suffered from left hemisphere damage. Significantly, in twenty-eight out of twenty-nine of the observations (96.6%), right frontal damage was present. Regarding the location of the lesion, ten (34.48%) cases had exclusively frontal damage. There were no cases of any other brain region exclusively affected, suggesting that the frontal cortex is highly related to these disorders of the self and personal relatedness.

Therefore, the anatomical findings were surprisingly clear-cut. First, there was an overwhelming predominance of patients across all categories of self-disorders with damage in the right (non-dominant) hemisphere. Second, it appeared that within the right hemisphere the lesions were much more likely to be within the right frontal lobe (Figure 4-1).

Neurologist Bruce Miller and his colleagues have also provided evidence that the right hemisphere may play a significant role with reference to self-related functions. They examined patients with frontotemporal dementia (FTD), a condition that causes progressive degeneration of the frontotemporal regions of the brain, and looked for evidence of "changes in self," including alterations in the "material self," the "social self," and the "spiritual self," to use the terms articulated by the psychologist William James.[14] One woman, a formerly dynamic 54-year-old real estate agent, displayed a progressive dementia with evidence of significant bilateral and especially right frontal dysfunction. During this period, the patient developed a belief in an alter ego she named "Jenny." While the patient herself favored expensive designer fashions and jewelry, she claimed Jenny wore cheap clothes, gaudy jewelry, and ugly shoes. In contrast to herself, Jenny was also rude to strangers, aggressive, and ate too much fast food. A 67-year-old businessman, also with evidence of greater right progressive dysfunction, went from being typically self-critical, irascible, tight-fisted, and puritanical, to appearing relaxed, careless, and sexually experimental. In a number of other cases studied, those individuals with the most significant transformation in the self-related attributes, including shifts in political, religious, or

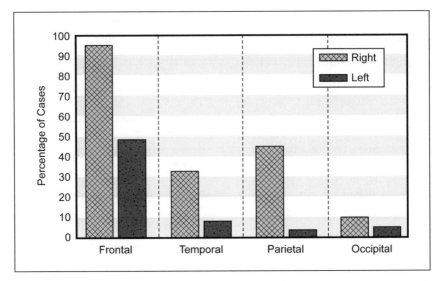

Figure 4-1. The ratio of right versus left hemisphere damage in cases with delusional confabulation/misidentification. (Adapted from Feinberg et al., 2005; Feinberg and Keenan, 2005).

philosophical beliefs, career paths, manner of dress, and sexual be-havior, and six of seven cases displayed predominantly right hemi-sphere dysfunction.

Although it has been suggested in the past that many of the misidentification syndromes are more likely to be caused by lesions within the right hemisphere, the full extent of the asymmetry, and especially the right frontal localization, came as something of a sur-prise.[15] But perhaps the evidence has been there all along. After all, if we review the cases noted in Table 1-1, every case of asomatognosia involved right hemisphere lesions. Indeed, I have never seen a case of asomatognosia with a lesion in the verbal (usually left) hemi-sphere. In addition, we found that the asomatognosic patients with the most firmly held delusions and the most confabulations had damage that included not only the right parietal and temporal lobes, but also involvement of the right *frontal* regions. Furthermore, if we

Table 4-1. Anatomical findings in adult cases with imaginary others (13 cases)

Cases	Age/sex	Etiology	Lesion location (hemisphere)	
			RIGHT	LEFT
CASE SP Mirror companion (this volume)	77/F	CVA	temporoparietal	
CASE RD Mirror persecutor (this volume)	70/F	dementia	unknown	unknown
CASE GT Phantom persecutor (this volume)	73/M	CVA	frontal, temporal, parietal	
CASE AS Delusional companion Shanks & Venneri (2002)	81/F	dementia	temporal, parietal (SPECT)	
CASE AL Delusional companion Shanks & Venneri (2002)	85/F	dementia	Parietal (SPECT)	
CASE ST Delusional companion Shanks & Venneri (2002)	74/F	dementia	frontal, parietal	
CASE LK Phantom relatives (this volume)	64/F	ACoA	frontal	frontal
CASE SC Phantom child (this volume)	64/M	ACoA	frontal	frontal
CASE BB Delusions about son (this volume)	61/M	Traumatic contusions	large right frontal	small left temporal
CASE CB Delusions about niece (this volume)	48/F	ACoA	frontal	frontal
CASE SA Delusions about friend (this volume)	36/M	traumatic brain injury	frontal	frontal
CASE CS Nurturing syndrome Venneri et al. (2002)	78/F	dementia	frontal	
CASE KC Nurturing syndrome Venneri et al. (2002)	71/F	dementia	frontal	
Totals			12	5

look at the other cases with disturbances in self-related functions I have described earlier, there is a similar pattern (Table 4-1). The damage in these cases is either bilateral or exclusively within the right hemisphere, and the frontal lobe of the right hemisphere is the most commonly involved region.

So here is the puzzle before us. There is a group of patients with brain damage who have significant and profound disturbances in their bodily, relational, or narrative selves. The disturbances they demonstrate resemble the defenses and fantasies of children in the 3- to 8-year-age range. And when we examine the sort of brain dysfunction they present, we find it occurring within the right, especially the right frontal regions.

Thus, what was initially a somewhat confusing array of findings is beginning to take shape. If we are to understand the neurobiological underpinnings of these clinical disorders of the self, and by so doing uncover something revealing about the way the brain creates the self, we need a theory that explains these findings. If we are correct in the assumption that there is in some measure a release or return of earlier defensive and adaptive functions in these patients, and this transformation is the result of right parietal and right frontal damage, what could account for this significant observation? I suggest there are several possible and interrelated explanations.

Ego Boundaries

One domain of ego functioning that undergoes transformation in the presence of right hemisphere damage, particularly when the lesion extends into the right frontal lobe, is an alteration in *ego boundaries*. In the psychoanalytic literature this term has many complex meanings, but for our purposes we can just as easily speak of the *self-boundaries*, and the way that the bodily self, the relational self, and the narrative self may be affected when the margins of the self are in flux.[16]

Many of the patients whose cases we have discussed have demonstrated pronounced disturbances within select aspects of the boundaries of the self. If the right hemisphere were dominant for certain *ego functions*, such as the self-boundaries, then right hemisphere damage could result in a disturbance in the relationship between the self and the world, both for personally significant incoming sensory information as well as for self-generated feelings and drives. We have good clinical evidence that indeed such a disturbance exists, and these patients may demonstrate *both* under- and over personal relatedness to the environment.[17]

Some clinical conditions suggest a profound under-relatedness on the part of the patient to significant aspects of the self. In these circumstances, personally significant incoming information may be disconnected from a feeling of emotional relatedness. Perhaps the most obvious transformation of the self of this type occurs in asomatognosia, when the patient mentally excises the paralyzed limb from the limits of the self. And we have also considered how patients with Capgras syndrome have undergone a transformation of the relational self in which the patient loses the personal connection between the self and either the mirror image, or some significant other or object in the environment.

There are other pathologies of the narrative self that occur in the presence of right hemisphere damage in which the patient inappropriately incorporates relatively neutral aspects of the environment into his or her self-narratives. In contrast to patients who are under-related, as in Capgras syndrome, these patients are over self-inclusive, and in certain respects seem to demonstrate the Fregoli syndrome in which the patient claims an inappropriate over-relatedness to relative strangers.

We have witnessed this type of over-personalized error while videotaping our patients during a clinical interview. We explained to our patients that we were going to videotape the interview, gained their permission, and placed the camera within plain view throughout the session. Under these conditions, some patients will incorporate topics relating to television, cameras, and film making during the course of the interview. For example, I described earlier patient LK, a 65-year-old woman with bilateral damage to her frontal lobes who produced elaborate confabulations about phantom relatives with the same types of medical and neurological problems that she had. During my first interview with her, which was videotaped, I inquired as to what she was doing in the hospital.

TEF: *And why are you here?*

LK: [looking around] *We all came down here, they said it was a good idea to come down here . . . to be exposed to . . . the lights, the camera, the action. What it would be like . . .* [at this point, a nurse caring for a patient in the next bed, can be overheard to say, "The cardiac monitor stays in place while you're in this room."] *. . . what it would like to ah . . . to get off the monitor, to get off the camera, right? So I said, "Fine with me." So that's how it started. Then I went ahead with the thing with the monitor, and they were talking to me and telling me how . . .*

TEF: *So what's your point of being here?*

LK: *To get off the camera. I'm going to get off this . . . blah. And you know what blah, blah, blah means [laughing] . . . the camera . . . and blah, blah , blah. . . .*

In a similar case, another patient with evidence of bilateral frontal damage who was hospitalized in Boston over-related to his environment when he was asked where he was:

One day he was interviewed in an office and faced a wall ornamented with a map entitled "Cuttyhunk Island, Dukes County, Massachusetts." Asked where he was, he responded: "Massachusetts." When asked to be more specific, he said: "Cuttyhunk Island."[18]

Likewise, patient BB, who, as noted above, had extensive frontal lobe lesions bilaterally but especially within his right hemisphere, spoke frequently about his son, his family, and the people from his hometown, often claiming that he was bumping into them all over the rehabilitation facility. He produced this particular confabulation while being videotaped:

BB: *There was a team down here from California doing a film . . . they were filming a type of film for TV. They said we want to do some films of you, . . . and then I was watching TV here with a couple of the fellas in here and were talking and then when I got a chance at home I put the thing on and who do I see going out and doing the fighting and all was my son . . . he had done this film for them just as a kind of like . . . he didn't realize the film was going to be on TV. Sometimes it happens that way. . . .*

And in the case of SC, who spoke of the prospect of adopting a fictional child, his projection of his personal issues into the environment of the interview took on the form of metaphor:

EXAMINER: *So what is the plan now for this child?*
SC: *Well . . . so what we would like to do is open up communications for us to go to interview some of the psychiatrists that evaluated the child and we've been working on that ever since we decided to legally adopt the child instead of just being a name on a piece of paper* [while the examiner was taking notes on the names of the patient's relatives]. . . .

A particularly dramatic example of a patient projecting her personal concerns into her environment was demonstrated by the patient LK, discussed above. During her examination, I asked LK to listen to and repeat what we call "The King Story," which is used to check not only the patient's memory but also a tendency to deny illness:

TEF: *I'm going to tell you a story, and I want you to tell it back to me as best you can. Once there was a king who was very ill and his doctors couldn't cure him. But his wisemen told him, "Oh King! You will be well, if you would wear the shirt of a happy man." So the King sent his messengers all over the kingdom, and they found a happy man, but he didn't own a shirt. Now you tell the story to me.*
LK: *There was a King who . . . had an aneurysm or something on his head* [at this point the patient lifted her left hand on top of her head feeling her own surgical scar]. *He could be cured forever if he found a man with a happy*

shirt. He went all over. The man with a happy shirt did not have a happy shirt.
So, nothing was done. He never had an operation. There was no . . . nothing done
for this unhappy man, and nothing was done for him! So, he was hanging around
the hospital unhappy.
TEF: *So, how do you feel about what's going on?*
LK: *I feel that if I'm so unhappy, I should get an operation and be happy.*

LK's version of the king story shows the permeability between her recall of the new narrative and her own self-story. She readily inserts her personal concerns, wishes, and feelings into the story, much the way that a neurologically intact adult inserts his or her personal feelings and concerns in their interpretation of a projective exam like a Rorschach test. While LK thinks she is repeating the king story accurately, what she is really relating is an idiosyncratic narrative about herself in a process that occurs without her conscious awareness. There are important features that contribute to a delusional confabulation's uniquely personalized characteristics. A perturbation in ego boundaries, in which the patient under- or over-relates to his or her circumstances could help explain the disequilibrium between reality and the patient's idiosyncratic beliefs, needs, and concerns.

Verbal Monitoring and the Reality Principle

Another feature of the delusional confabulation is its irrationality and its resistance to correction. Psychologist Marcia Johnson and her colleagues have suggested a number of frameworks to explain some of these irrational aspects of confabulation.[19] According to what she terms the "reality monitoring framework," some confabulations result from a failure to discriminate between memories and internally derived thoughts due to a "reality monitoring defect." According to another mechanism, the source monitoring framework, disturbances in the "encoding, retrieval, and evaluation" of perceptions and memories lead to a failure to distinguish veridical memory from self-generated confabulations. Confabulation in this view results from a failure of judgment processes that determine whether the perceptual information represents a true memory or is a product of the imagination, and additional judgments upon how this information conforms to previously acquired knowledge.

But while a failure of reality monitoring could help explain why some confabulations appear to be "wish-fulfilling," it does not explain why confabulations may become delusional in some patients and not others, and why delusional patients, in contrast to patients with confabulation in general, often suffer from right frontal lesions. It also does not explain why the misidentifications in these cases are so selective or why patients do not have a more generalized impairment in reality testing.

In order to account for the relationship between the brain pathology and the disorders of the self we witness in personal and delusional confabulation, I suggest what I call *ego-disequilibrium theory*.[20] This account proposes that a disturbance in *ego equilibrium* created by bifrontal or right frontal damage could also help explain these features of personal/delusional confabulation. According to this theory, the frontal pathology creates a *two-way disturbance* between the self and the environment specifically with regard to personal relatedness that could lead to disorders of *both* under and over relatedness to one's circumstances. Without the mediation of right frontal regions that subserve certain self- and ego-related functions, patterns of personally significant incoming information may be disconnected from a feeling of familiarity or personal relatedness. On the other hand, in the presence of internally derived motives, such as the desire to be home or to be physically well, without the appropriate mediation of the ego functions of the right frontal regions, the wish may appear in the patient's mind as an externalized reality. In a similar fashion, in delusional asomatognosia, when the right frontal regions fail to establish the appropriate ego boundaries, the feelings of alienation from the arm result in the unmediated projection of the arm directly into the environment.

It is within the domain of these positive features that individual differences in motivation, personality, and adaptation may come into play that may help explain why only a minority of patients with right frontal injury develop these disorders. There is some evidence from our survey that many of the patients who develop delusional confabulation after brain injury were already predisposed to abnormal ego functions prior to their brain injury. For example, in one classic case reported by behavioral neurologist Michael Alexander and his colleagues, the delusional ideation of a patient with Capgras syndrome was attributed to the presence of bilateral frontal deficits that created the inability to resolve conflicting or competing information.[21] However, in this case, the patient suffered from "grandiose and paranoid delusions, and had auditory hallucinations" *prior* to the brain injury that led to his Capgras delusions.

This observation raises the possibility that in some cases pre-morbid personality features or psychopathology, especially paranoia, perhaps subserved by brain areas left undamaged by the cortical lesions, played a positive role in the production of these symptoms. One of the striking features in our review was that five out of six cases of Capgras with delusional misidentification involving persons had either prior or current paranoia, suspiciousness, or depression. Three of seven cases with Fregoli syndrome for persons had a similar history of paranoia or other delusions, but the association was not seen to the extent evident in patients who displayed Capgras for persons. This result is supported by the finding that delusions in general have been reported to occur with increased frequency in the presence of right hemisphere pathology.[22]

Metaphorical Language

Another interesting aspect of the behavior of delusional patients is the manner in which personal feelings are expressed in terms of the external world and a tendency toward the use of metaphorical language. This language must also bear a relationship to right hemisphere pathology, since it is in this group of patients that the metaphorical tendency emerges.

A disregulation of ego boundaries could help account for the abundance of the sort of metaphors for the paralyzed limb that we have spoken of previously in cases with asomatognosia (Table 1-1, p. 10). When the lifeless feeling in the patient's limb is described as "a piece of dead meat," "this piece of dead wood," or "nothing but a bag of bones," the patient's personal feelings are reified in the form a metaphor. In a similar vein, in a patient who has delusions about a phantom child, when the fictional child serves as an alter ego for the patient, personal affects and feelings are metaphorically represented in terms of something else, in this case something external to the self in the environment.

I have often been struck by the similarity between the narratives, beliefs, and delusions of my patients and the style and content of dreams, fairy tales, and myths, or what the brilliant psychoanalyst and philosopher Erich Fromm meant when he spoke of the way the human mind expresses itself in a "forgotten language" of dreams that he called *symbolic language*.[23] As Fromm describes it:

> Symbolic language is a language in which inner experiences, feelings and thoughts are expressed as if they were sensory experiences, events in the outer world. It is a language which has a different logic from the conventional one we speak in the daytime, a logic in which not time and space are the ruling categories but intensity and association. It is the one universal language the human race has ever developed, the same for all cultures and throughout history. It is a language with its own grammar and syntax, as it were, a language one must understand if one is to understand the meaning of myths, fairy tales, and dreams. . . .[24]

Indeed, the narratives of my patients can fairly be considered personal myths in which the barriers between the self and reality are torn asunder and the individual's fantasy and emotional life is given free reign to express its needs.

When the human mind expresses itself in symbolic language, like the use of metaphor in neurological patients, the feelings of the self are expressed in terms of aspects of the external world. In Freudian terms, this quality of certain confabulations would be characterized as expressions of the *unconscious* in which the mind ignores the reality principle, and time and space lose their constraining capacities.[25] In Fromm's description of the dreaming mind:

> Most of our dreams have one characteristic in common: they do not follow the laws of logic that govern our waking thought. The categories of space and time are neglected. People who are dead, we see alive; events which we watch in the present, occurred many years ago. We dream of two events as occurring simultaneously when in reality they could not possibly occur at the same time. We pay just as little attention to the laws of space. It is simple for us to move to a distant place in an instant, to be in two places at once, to fuse two persons into one, or to have one person suddenly be changed into another. Indeed, in our dreams we are the creators of a world where time and space, which limit all the activities of our body, have no power.[26]

We are not concerned here with a purely linguistic expression of the conventional signs and symbols of everyday language, but rather a very personally constructed symbolic vocabulary, a distinction for which linguist Edwin Sapir's concepts of *experiential* and *referential* language may prove instructive.[27] According to Sapir, referential language is socially conventional language that refers to things as they generally appear to everyone without the personal connotations of individual experience and emotion. Experiential language, in contrast, is based upon one's own personal and emotional experience. Experiential symbols are therefore more often idiosyncratic and may be only meaningful to their user. I would not dream your dream, nor you mine. We also are not consciously aware of the

values within our experiential symbolic universe, and for this reason while our dreams may be filled with meaningful expression and
sometimes make sense as we dream them, when we awake and return to the world of referential meaning that characterizes our waking minds, they often make little sense.

Once again, Fromm's symbolic language leads us to this experiential expression:

> What is a symbol? A symbol is often defined as "something that
> stands for something else." This definition seems rather disappoint-
> ing. It becomes more interesting, however, if we concern ourselves
> with those symbols which are sensory expressions of seeing, hear-
> ing, smelling, touching, standing for a "something else" which is an
> inner experience, a feeling or thought. A symbol of this kind is
> something outside ourselves; that which it symbolizes is something
> inside ourselves. Symbolic language is language in which we ex-
> press inner experience as if it were a sensory experience, as if it were
> something we were doing or something that was done to us in the
> world of things. Symbolic language is language in which the world
> outside is a symbol of the world inside, a symbol for our souls and
> our minds.[28]

This does not mean that metaphorical or symbolic language is
absent in our waking minds. Far from it. We are all capable of
metaphorical expression, in the form of slang, clichés, humor, and
other forms of personal expression. The difference between normal waking ideation, however, and the symbolic language of
dreams, fairy tales, and myth expressed by my patients appears to
be in the degree that the neurological patient takes these metaphorical expressions literally. It also appears that the presence of
right hemisphere pathology disinhibits this mode of thought, and
therefore in the normal mature brain the right hemisphere, particularly the right frontal lobe, must play some role in enabling the
mature brain to put aside or keep implicit the symbolic expression
of normal experience.

You Can't Make This Stuff Up

In spite of the sometimes bizarre nature of my patients' narratives, I often think how similar their beliefs are to a dream I once had, or a movie I recall, or a book I have read. In fact, though I have focused here on the clinical literature, there are many examples from myth, literature, and film that demonstrate the widespread nature of these shared narratives, further evidence that the defensive operations and patterns of thought of the child never really "vanish" from the adult mind.

In the 1956 movie *Invasion of the Body Snatchers*, based on the novel *The Body Snatchers* by Jack Finney, Dr. Miles Bennell is confronted by several of his patients in Santa Mira, California, who report the paranoid belief that persons close to them, mothers, uncles, cousins, friends, have been replaced by imposters, "doppelgangers," who are not the "originals" they claim to be.[29] In spite of his patients' claims, however, when the alleged doubles are questioned, they appear to have complete knowledge of the originals' past history. Initially disbelieving, Dr. Bennell is convinced of the reality of the claims when he sees for himself an alien pod developing into the shape of one of his friends. When the doctor tries to alert others to the threat he is taken in by the police and deemed to be psychotic by the examining psychiatrist.

Written during the 1950s at the height of the McCarthy era, the original novel and movie are most often interpreted as a metaphor for the perceived growing threat of communism "taking over" seemingly "normal Americans" in the government, unions, education, and entertainment. Alternatively, the film can be interpreted as a reaction against the rampant paranoia created by the McCarthyism when there was widespread fear that anyone could be accused of being a communist. The characterization of the "pods" as something from outer space also reflects the growing interest in space exploration and the belief that Earth could possibly be visited by aliens

from another planet, and the theme of alien invasion was increasingly explored in other popular fiction of the time.

The relationship of the seemingly paranoid beliefs to psychiatric
disturbance is directly addressed in the movie. Dr. Bennell consults
the town's psychiatrist, Dr. Dan Kaufman, as to what possibly could
be causing the epidemic of such "delusions":

Dr. Kaufman: *A strange neurosis, evidently contagious, an epidemic mass hysteria.*
    In two weeks, it spread all over town.
Dr. Bennell: *What causes it?*
Dr. Kaufman: *Worry about what's going on in the world probably.*
Dr. Bennell: *I'd hate to wake up some morning and find out that you weren't you!*

Although the political implications of the film are clear, I am
more struck by what the film is saying about human relationships.
The similarity between the clinical form of Capgras delusions in
neuropsychiatric patients and the characterizations of the doubles
in the film is striking. Unlike their original counterparts, the clones
are described as lacking in emotion, loveless, and cold. The origin of
the Capgras delusion may also be related to the emotional alienation
that the patient feels between the supposed original and the double,
from whom the patient may report feeling alienated. The film was
made just a decade after the first use of atomic weapons and the
new technologies of robotics, automation, computers, and the threat
to personal freedom these developments might entail suggested the
theme of the dehumanization of modern society.[30]

Another enormously popular work seems to demonstrate nearly
the opposite clinical Fregoli syndrome. Unlike Capgras syndrome,
in which the familiar is seen as an imposter, the Fregoli syndrome
involves the insertion of personal familiarity and significance into
relatively less familiar persons, places, or things. The patient with
Capgras is often rejecting something in the environment, expressing ambivalence based upon prior conflicting feelings or the presence of a new neurological lesion leading to an estrangement with

a body part, such as a paralyzed arm. In contrast, some patients with the Fregoli syndrome with stroke or traumatic brain injury will claim they are in their own homes or neighborhoods in spite of clear evidence to the contrary, a scenario depicted in the film *The Wizard of Oz*.

In this classic film, the young girl Dorothy, who is an orphan, is strongly attached to her Kansas home, her beloved Auntie Em and Uncle Henry, and the three farm hands Hunk, Hickory, and Zeke. We also meet the kindly but somewhat shady Professor Marvel and the mean Miss Gulch, who threatens to take away Dorothy's dog Toto. One day a powerful tornado comes through and Dorothy is hit on the head and loses consciousness. She awakens in the extraordinary land of Oz, where many of her friends appear transformed into alter egos, but Dorothy relentlessly attempts to find her way home. Upon regaining consciousness, Dorothy recounts her adventures, surrounded by her old friends:

Uncle Henry: *Yeah. She got quite a bump on the head. We kinda thought there for a minute she was going to leave us.*

Dorothy: *But I did leave you Uncle Henry! That's just the trouble. And I tried to get back for days and days.*

Auntie Em: *There, there, lie quiet now. You just had a bad dream.*

Hunk: *Sure. Remember me? Your ol' pal Hunk.*

Hickory: *And me? Hickory.*

Zeke: *You couldn't forget my face, could you?*

Dorothy: *No . . . but it wasn't a dream. It was a place . . . and you . . . and you . . . and you . . . and you were there!* (Dorothy points to all those gathered around her. All around her laugh.) (feeling the bump on her head) *But you couldn't have been, could you?*

Auntie Em: *We dream lots of silly things when we. . . .*

Dorothy: *No Aunt Em! This was a real truly live place. And I remember that some of it wasn't very nice. But most of it was beautiful. But just the same, all I kept saying to everybody was "I want to go home!"*

In Dorothy's story, I am reminded of my patient JK, who adamantly claimed that his left arm belonged to his brother, and when he "woke up" from his initial period of disorientation he expressed to us the feelings of warmth and security that this misbelief brought to him. In a time of terrible stress, the idea that a part of his brother was close by reduced his anxiety. The women who claimed that their paralyzed left arms belonged to their husbands also found this delusion a source of comfort.

The idea of imaginary companions is also one that we see frequently in films, perhaps one of the best known examples being the film *Harvey* (1950) starring Jimmy Stewart. Based on a play of the same name, *Harvey* tells the story of Elwood P. Dowd, a name that has become synonymous with "kookiness." Elwood has a "friend" named Harvey who happens to be a six-foot, three-and-a-half-inch-tall rabbit whom Elwood claims is real, though only some people can see him. Elwood explains to those who are interested and willing to listen that Harvey is a pooka, a mysterious being from Celtic mythology. When his sister Veta tries to have Elwood committed to an asylum, she admits to the attending psychiatrist Dr. Sanderson that after living with Elwood for so many years even she has on occasion seen Harvey, an admission that leads to Elwood being released from the hospital and Vera being committed. When Elwood returns to the hospital, Dr. Sanderson plans to give him an injection that will make him stop seeing Harvey, but Veta decides that Elwood's return to normalcy is not that desirable after all and she intervenes. In the end, Elwood and Harvey leave the sanatorium and continue on their merry way.

The relationship between Elwood and Harvey is fairly typical of that between a child and an imaginary companion, though I have never seen an adult patient who harbors such a delusional belief on the basis of brain dysfunction. A more familiar story is portrayed in the film *Cast Away* (2000), where Tom Hanks plays Chuck Noland, a FedEx employee who after a horrific airline crash in the South Pa-cific is stranded alone on a deserted island. He must learn to fend for himself to survive, which he heroically does, but with only the small picture of his wife in a pocket watch to keep him company, his despondency and loneliness grows. A small number of packages have survived the crash, and in one of them Noland finds a Wilson volleyball intended as a gift to a child. After cutting his hand in frustration that he cannot make fire, he picks up and throws the ball, leaving an imprint of his bloody hand on its surface. He sees a potential face in the imprint, which he turns into a clearer likeness of a face. He names the volleyball "Wilson" and it becomes a real friend to him during his stay on the island, as he tells Wilson about the crash and the affairs of the day, and how he plans their eventual escape from the island. During that escape, Wilson is lost at sea and Noland suffers an emotional breakdown at the loss of his friend.

Some investigators claim that an imaginary companion is a totally invisible construct, like Harvey, while others stress that any personified object such as doll or stuffed animal may qualify. Surely the psychological role of Wilson in the movie is a model of the personified imaginary companion, serving as a source of friendship and solace in the way that personified objects are to patients with the nurturing syndrome.

But by far the most common literary motif with a parallel in the neurological cases is the belief in the existence of a "double" or doppelganger, which appears in the work of Jean Paul Richter, Poe, Goethe, Wilde, and Dostoyevsky, to name but a few. In one well known example, The Double,[31] Dostoyevsky portrays Petrovitch Golyadkin, an anxious and neurotic bureaucrat who, in the throes of romantic and professional failures, develops a paranoid belief in a menacing presence who insults Golyadkin's colleagues, runs up bills, and behaves in an inappropriate manner. When Petrovitch begins to see multiple versions of the double that intrude on his consciousness, he is whisked off to a sanatorium.

In Poe's short story William Wilson (1839), we have an extraordinary rendering of the psychotic aspects of the belief in a personal double.[32] The narrator William Wilson (presumably no relation to Wilson the volleyball) describes how as a boy he met another fellow who, much to William's chagrin, looked like him, was also named William Wilson, and even had the same birthday as him. The "other William" is actually the only one of his classmates who can success-fully compete with the original William and his mimicry is nearly complete:

> His cue, which was to perfect an imitation of myself, lay both in words and in ac-
> tions; and most admirably did he play his part. My dress it was an easy matter
> to copy; my gait and general manner were, without difficulty, appropriated; in
> spite of his constitutional defect, even my voice did not escape him. My louder
> tones were, of course, unattempted, but then the key, it was identical; and his sin-
> gular whisper, it grew the very echo of my own.[33]

In spite of their competitiveness in academics and sports and the frequent "quarrels" that would complicate their relationship, the original Wilson had mixed feelings toward his rival, including cer-tain feelings of affection. However, with the passage of years the double's behavior becomes untenable. William becomes increas-ingly involved in debauchery and criminal behavior, and one evening when he cheats at cards and wins a large sum from an un-suspecting patsy, the other William reveals to those assembled at the card table that William has cheated and he is forced to leave Ox-ford in disgrace. But the double follows William from country to country, tormenting him and undoing his desired and often dis-honest ends. However, William only infers his presence as he re-mains unseen for years.

The denouement for Willaim interestingly involves his mirror re-flection. William confronts the double and forces him into a room and challenges him to a duel by sword, to which the double reluc-tantly agrees. William plunges his sword repeatedly into his rival, but it is not until he sees his mirror reflection does he realize that he is bloodied and mortally wounded, as the double in the mirror informs William that by killing the double, he has killed himself.

The nature of the double in "William Wilson" is so similar to my two patients with mirror misidentification that the parallels are actually haunting. In the case of SP, the patient had a somewhat competitive attitude toward the "other" in the mirror, pointing out that the double was "not too bright" and did not communicate in sign language very well. Nonetheless, she provided companionship for SP, who seemed to enjoy their interactions. Certainly she never complained about her presence. On the other hand, in the case of RD there was extreme hatred of the mirror image as a persecutory presence, doggedly pursuing her, following her, taunting her. She even threatened to kill the mirror image, much like William Wilson actually does.

More recently, the novel *Fight Club* by Chuck Palahniuk and the film based upon it starring Ed Norton and Brad Pitt depict the experiences of an unnamed narrator (in the movie played by Norton), an alienated and troubled insomniac who works for an automobile company performing cost analyses on whether to recall their defective cars. After talking to his doctor about his complaints, the narrator begins to attend a support group for cancer survivors in order to learn about real suffering. He finds the experience helps alleviate his insomnia and he begins to fake more illnesses and attend more groups until at one he meets Markla Singer (Helena Bonham Carter) who herself is faking illness. The knowledge that Marla is also malingering ruins the beneficial effect of the group on the narrator's sleep and he detests Marla for this.

The narrator then meets Tyler Durden (Brad Pitt) and the two begin a ritual of fist fighting that evolves into a "fight club" that meets on a regular basis in the basement of a bar. Tyler and Marla become lovers but Tyler insists that the narrator never discuss with Marla their own relationship. Tyler becomes increasingly aggressive, drawing his minions into aggressive sociopathic acts against what he preaches is an emasculating commercial world of empty suits. In one vivid scene, the narrator, about to be fired, beats himself up in front of his boss and claims his boss did it. However, as Tyler's influence upon the narrator grows, the narrator becomes disenchanted with Tyler's "Project Mayhem" and its increasingly destructive trajectory, and the two part ways.

When the narrator later tries to find out what misdeeds Tyler has been up to, he finds that when he visits the fight clubs that have spread around the country, everyone refers to him as "Tyler." It eventually becomes apparent that Tyler is the narrator's alter ego, a fiction he has unconsciously created. In the end, Tyler has planned the bombing of buildings that would cripple the financial district and the narrator attempts to stop Tyler, who of course we now know is the narrator himself. The narrator is held at gunpoint by Tyler, but the narrator now has the insight that he is in fact holding the gun and shoots himself in the mouth, the narrator surviving but killing Tyler in the act.

Clinically the case of Tyler and the unnamed narrator most closely resembles the phenomenon of Dissociative Identity Disorder, although some have likened the clinical disintegration of the narrator's personality to psychosis, perhaps schizophrenia. In either case, the character Tyler serves as an expression of the narrator's need to assert his identity in a world in which he feels powerless and emasculated. As with clinical cases of doubling, the fictional character acts as an alter for the original, expressing some need or self-feeling in a fashion beyond the original's awareness. In the case of the narrator it is a wish to be powerful and self-confident.

Indeed, when I read many of these fictional stories I wonder how such similarities between fact and fiction emerge. Some depictions, such as those in *Invasion of the Body Snatchers* and William Wilson, seem so similar to clinical cases that I wonder if they were inspired by real life situations. Perhaps they were inspired by dreams. Or perhaps they spring from the well of human experience, our common fears and wishes. Clinical psychologist Richard Bentell has suggested that rather than there being a clear demarcation between delusional and normal beliefs there exists a continuum that runs from incoherent yet plausible beliefs to those that are more bizarre and fantastic.[34] Delusions also may vary in the degree of conviction with which the patient holds to the belief. Perhaps the parallels between the pathological cases and works of fiction reflect this continuum.

Some widespread cultural beliefs also resonate with my patient's idiosyncratic delusions. One that I was recently and particularly struck by are the beliefs of many Icelanders—about 10 percent of the population—who believe in "hidden people," little elves that live within the rocks and where one finds entire and fanciful little worlds. These beliefs are so firmly held that some public works projects have actually run into roadblocks because the locals became concerned that some little people would be disturbed by the projected construction of new roadways. The interesting feature to me is how common these beliefs are in normal adults, and how literally true the beliefs are thought to be. It may be one thing to read about elves in a book and wish that they might really exist (e.g., Peter Pan's clap-your-hands Tinkerbell) but it's quite another to take tea with one in your own backyard.

But of course the child's world is filled with beliefs in imaginary children as well as more culturally acceptable beliefs in angels, aliens, ghosts, and gods. In fact, when looked at from this perspective, beliefs in the unseen world of other beings is the norm, and people with a firm conviction that such beings do not exist are actually in the minority. This is especially true when as adults we are subjected to emotional stress. There is a striking relationship between the narratives of the patients I have described and the beliefs and statements of neurologically intact individuals when they are threatened with a loss of self or identity or death. Just as neurological patients deal with a difficult reality by creating metaphorical and wishful substitutes, beliefs in guardian angels, guiding spirits, and other comforting figures can be understood in part as wish fulfilling metaphors for a reality that many persons cannot fully comprehend or accept.

Summary: The Right Hemisphere and Ego Disequilibrium

I have argued that the clinical neuropsychiatric disorders of the self point to a profound relationship between the thought of the child and the adult disorders. The defenses such as denial, projection, splitting, and wishful fantasy that play such an important role in the origin of the adult delusions are also among the primitive defenses in the child. Further, the motivational and adaptive functions that imaginary others serve in adults such as the need for companionship, mastery of fears, and adaptation to trauma are among the factors that play a role in the development of imaginary companions in the child.

I believe this observation is an important clue to understanding the development of the self and its relationship to brain function. The syndromes that I have studied and described here are all disturbances of the self, but each individual patient and each group of syndromes has numerous distinctive features that make generalizations difficult. But one object of the science of neurology is to find the patterns among single observations that might help explain the origins of a condition. Our problem then is to establish what these common patterns are: How do we account for the similarity between the adult pathologies of the self and the development stages of the child, and what does that tell us about the nature of the self?

One clue pertains to the location of the brain lesions in the adult patients. The clinical cases indicate that when it comes to the self, not all regions of the brain are created equal, and that the overwhelming majority of adult neurological cases with delusional self-related disturbances have right hemisphere, especially *right frontal damage*, and I have proposed an Ego Disequilibrium Theory of personal confabulation in which the right hemisphere plays a critical role in determining the personal relatedness of the self to the world.[35] There appears to be a continuum of confabulation along a neutral-personal dimension that is determined by the degree that the confabulation is delusional, motivated and distorted by the individual's emotional needs, and influenced by pre-morbid personality. But it is a bedrock principle in neurology that you cannot explain a positive symptom by some part of the brain that is no longer there. To clarify this point, if you have a car with a broken windshield wiper, you may not be able to see clearly through it, a negative symptom of the damage. But if the car makes a loud grinding sound while you drive it with a damaged engine, the sound, the positive symptom, must be the result of the parts of the car that remain intact. In the same way, if there is a part of the brain missing, whatever behavior the patient exhibits must be affected by the parts of the brain that remain. According to this principle, the preservation and activation of the verbal defenses, such as verbal denial, projection, splitting, and fantasy must be the result of the remaining, and presumably relatively intact left verbal hemisphere. The evidence suggests that given the fact these immature defenses and fantasies are preserved in the presence of right hemisphere damage, that they may be normally lateralized to the intact left hemisphere.

These considerations have led me to propose this sequence of events. In the course of normal brain maturation, we undergo a developmental process in which there is a shift from immature defensive functions and fantasies to mature defenses and the inhibition of fantasy that critically depends upon maturational process within the right hemisphere.[36] These neural events appear to progressively develop, unbeknownst to our conscious minds, between the ages of 3 and 8. I suggest that once these brain structures are laid down, mature adult defenses are made possible, and the unbridled fantasy of the child goes underground. However, what we learn from the adult neurological cases is that in the presence of right frontal damage, there is not only a disturbance in *ego boundaries*, there is also a breakdown within the *observing ego*, the ability to take an outside perspective on one's experience. It is the inability of the ego to both experience and observe itself that facilitates the emergence in the adult of the neuropathologies of the self that represents a return to developmentally immature styles of thought and ego functioning.

It is therefore clear that the immature defenses we possess as children and the potential to create realistic fantasies never really go away. Rather there appears to be a normal balance between our hemispheres that keeps these defenses and fantasies in check, but in the damaged brain these potentialities are unmasked. On the other hand, only certain patients with damage to their right hemisphere develop a phantom child, or give their paralyzed left arm a strange nickname, or scream at their own mirror image. There must be certain personality characteristics that an individual possesses prior to any brain injury that makes him or her particularly susceptible to the development of these striking fantasies. We all know people who go through life in total denial of the bad things that happen to them. That is the person who is most likely to develop delusional denial after a stroke. And the person with the active imagination, who fantasizes, "Wouldn't it be nice if . . . ?" is more likely to nurture a photograph of a dead husband or animate a stuffed toy when these delusional beliefs bring with them relief from unbearable psychological pain. These neurological cases put a spotlight on the most extreme forms of these behaviors, but they may also suggest that the potential to express these strange and baffling behaviors may lie within us all.

CHAPTER FIVE

The Neural Structure of the Self

WHILE I HAVE thus far focused on clinical neuropathologies in order to examine the critical issue of how the brain creates the self, there are many other interesting aspects to this question that transcend the clinical conditions I have described. We will turn now to the larger model of how the brain is organized to make the creation of the self possible, and as in the hierarchical development of the self that we have examined so far, the relationship between the brain and the self can only be understood as the result of the hierarchical patterns of the growth of neural systems. In subsequent chapters we will also explore some of the most interesting yet unsolved puzzles of modern neuroscience, such as the relationship between the brain, the self, and consciousness and how the brain creates mental unity.

The human brain is the most complex structure on earth. Indeed, it is somewhat ironic that the very structure that enables us to think great thoughts is itself so difficult to understand. (How the billions of neurons within the brain coordinate their activity to create a unified self is one of the great remaining scientific mysteries—a problem I will return to later.) This complexity makes it difficult to describe in broad strokes the general patterns that make the workings of the brain comprehensible. Since the late 1980s, however, there has been enormous progress in our understanding of the neurobiology of the self. In this chapter I will examine some basic evolutionary trends and neuroanatomical principles that order the brain and attempt to integrate recent theories into a general model of the neural basis of the self.

As the human brain evolved, enabling it to accomplish its increasingly difficult tasks, the structure of the brain developed in similarly complex ways that we can observe today. In order to create a blueprint to deepen our understanding of the relationship between the brain and the self, I propose a model that approaches the nervous system from the standpoint of two organizational trends that help us understand the shape the brain takes and how that shape relates to its ability to create the self.

If we think of the central nervous system, including the brain and the spinal cord, as something like a tree, the first trend we can observe is its cross-sectional organization, as when, for example, one examines the radially arranged growth rings in the tree's trunk. In the second major pattern, a tree may also be examined from the "bottom-up," taking into consideration its hierarchical organization from its roots to its leaves. In a similar fashion, the nervous system demonstrates increasing complexity as it extends from the lower levels of the nervous system to the most evolved and highest levels. As we shall see, both of these trends, the radially arranged *medial-lateral trend*, and the longitudinally organized *caudal-rostral trend*, are essential to the development and functioning of the neural substrate of the self.

The Medial–Lateral Trend

The first important pattern, the *medial-lateral trend*, is evident at the lowest and the earliest evolved parts of the central nervous system. The lowest (or most caudal) portion of the brain is the *brainstem*, which is in closest proximity to the spinal cord (Figure 5-1) and represents its furthest upward (rostral) extension.

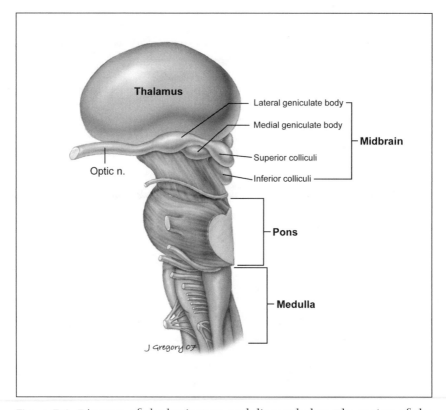

Figure 5-1. Diagram of the brainstem and diencephalon. The region of the tectum includes the superior and inferior colliculi, structures that subserve early visual and auditory processing. The diencephalon includes the thalamus (see text for more detail). The brainstem is the most caudal (lowest) part of the brain and is the region that is in closest proximity to the spinal cord and it represents its rostral (upward) extension.

If one views the brainstem in cross-section, its "center," the most medial or innermost zones, are the sectors that are situated closest to the ventricular system, which serves as a conduit for the cerebral spinal fluid throughout the brain. At this lowest level of the brainstem, the ventricular system is a long narrow tube-like section called the *aqueduct*. The neural structures immediately around and surrounding the aqueduct are therefore referred to as *periaqueductal*. The zones that extend outward from the aqueduct in a *medial-lateral trend* create progressive *concentrically* or *radially* arranged zones. The medial-lateral organization of these parts support differing functions with reference to the neural self.[1]

In one well detailed description of the medial-lateral trend, Rudolf Nieuwenhuys, a distinguished professor of neuroanatomy at the Netherlands Institute for Neuroscience in Amsterdam, and his colleagues roughly organize the brain into two domains that differ from each other both functionally and anatomically (Figure 5-2).[2] The *lateral domain* is comprised of the classical sensorimotor systems of the brain that regulate the organism's relationship to the environment. The sensory parts of the sensorimotor system are responsible for the special senses of vision, smell, sound, and taste, and for discriminative sensations from the surface of body, such as when someone needs to identify an object by touch. The motor parts of the system enable us to act upon the environment by muscular movements. The *medial domain* is associated with the maintenance of the body's homeostatic systems, the systems that regulate the internal physiological balance of the body, such as temperature, metabolism, and oxygenation, and also with what is commonly know as the limbic system, which regulates among other things emotions, motivation, and memory. Neuwenhuys had detailed these sytems in detail:

> According to this classification, the brain comprises a sensorimotor and cognitomotor domain, which occupies grossly the lateral part of the brain, and a medial domain, which may be designated as the greater limbic system. The latter differs considerably in structural, chemical and functional terms from the lateral domain. It consists of an array of highly interconnected structures, extending from the the medial wall of the telencephalon to the caudal rhombencephalon, which is concerned with specific motivated or goal-oriented behavior, directly aimed at the maintenance of homeostasis and at the survival of the individual (organism) and of the species. Both domains can be subdivided into smaller functional entities. Thus the lateral domain encompasses the great sensory systems, the association system, the pyramidal and ex-

trapyramidal motor systems and the cerebellum, whereas the medial or greater limbic domain comprises units designated as the core of the neuroaxis and the median and lateral paracores.[3]

Medial (Innermost) Zones

The *core of the neuroaxis* is located in closest proximity to the aqueduct and actually surrounds it in some parts, while the *medial and lateral paracore* regions are in direct communication with the core zone and extend from it into the more critical aspects of the brainstem. The core and paracore zones are present in all mammals and therefore represent a feature of mammalian brain organization that has persisted through millions of years of evolution. These medial core zones are dedicated to homeostatic regulation of the animal's bodily systems and serve as the neural basis for instinctual and self-protective behaviors. For example, in the rat brain lower-level core-paracore structures are concerned with breathing, swallowing, and respiratory functions, and at higher levels core-paracore structures are involved with defense, attack, and vocalization. These areas also play a role in emotional vocalization as well as sexual behaviors.

The sensory systems of the core-paracore regions are chiefly concerned with *interoceptive* stimuli (such as pain, thirst, hunger, etc.) and the feelings generated from the core regions—if they reach awareness—are self-referential in that they and are not experienced as *projected* from outside of the organism. Rather, interoceptive stimuli are experienced as originating from within the body ("I am hungry, afraid, in pain," etc.) The sensations generated from the core of the neuroaxis are intrinsically motivational; that is they make the organism *want to do something*, a feature that interoceptive feelings share with emotions in general.

Lateral (Outermost) Zones

Within the brainstem, organized in a radial ring surrounding the core-paracore zones are the systems that collectively can be referred

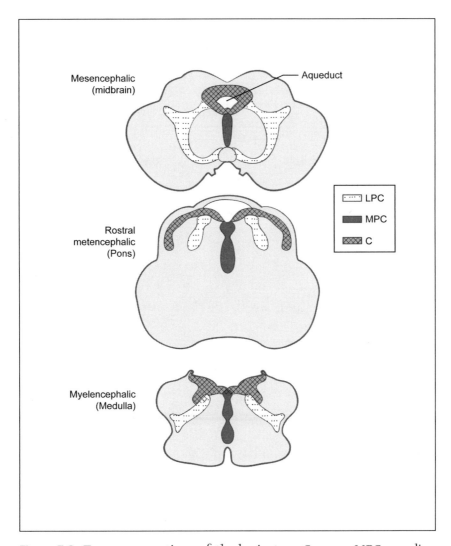

Figure 5-2. Transverse sections of the brainstem. C - core; MPC - median paracore; LPC - lateral paracore. (Based upon Nieuwenhuys, 1966, 1998, Nieuwenhuys et al., 2007). If one then views the brainstem in cross-section, its "center," the most medial or innermost zones, are the sectors that are situated closest to the aqueduct of the ventricular system, the cerebral spinal fluid filled cavities of the brain. Nieuwenhuys and co-workers describe three periaqueductal zones in the brainstem that share anatomical, neurochemical, and functional features. These areas are designated the *core*, the *medial paracore*, and the *lateral paracore of the neuroaxis*.

to as the *exterosensorimotor system*, forming the lateral or radially outermost zones of the brainstem.[4] In contrast to the core and paracore structures, these regions mediate the interaction of the animal with the external environment and represent the classical sensory and motor systems. Again, these systems inform the organism about its relationship to the external environment and enable it to create changes in the external world by movement and overt action.

The Caudal-Rostral Trend

The *caudal-rostral trend*, which co-evolved with the medial-lateral trend, is the second great organizing principle of the central nervous system. While the medial-lateral trend displays a radial organization at any given cross-section of the brain, the caudal-rostral trend displays a tendency for evolved neural systems to display progressive growth via the addition of superimposed higher cortical structures. In the process known as *encephalization*, later evolving regions of the brain appear higher on the neural axis and display a tendency to supplant or control the functions of lower regions. These regions will play an increasingly important role in the neural determination of the self.

Even as the caudal-rostral trend results in a greater complexity at upper reaches of the neuroaxis, it appears that Nieuwenhuys' medial-lateral organization is preserved at higher levels as well. For example, the lateral or outermost zones of the brainstem display a striking extension into the forebrain and project in a caudal rostral direction to regions of the cortical mantle far from the medially located cortical ventricular system. These sensory and motor systems that comprise the lateral zones within the brainstem extend as major axonal tracts that directly connect the brainstem with the higher centers of the neocortex. This arrangement ensures that sensory information is no longer processed primarily within the brainstem, but is now sent via the long sensory tracts directly to the neocortex for further processing.

As in the brainstem, the sensory aspects of these higher order systems are exteroceptive; that is, they respond to stimuli from the environment, and in the case of the special senses (vision, hearing, taste, and olfaction) the feelings or *qualia* generated by these regions display a particular phenomenal quality known as *projicience*, a term introduced by the great neurophysiologist Sir Charles Sherrington to designate the mental projection of sensations into the external environment that are characteristic of the distance receptors such as vision and audition.[5] In contrast to the interoceptive stimuli that are generated by the medial core regions and are experienced as emanating from within the organism and relating to the somatic self, the qualia experienced from the external sensory receptors relate to some space or object outside the body ("*It* looks, sounds, tastes, etc.").

Exactly what neural features of these systems account for the referral of their activity into the environment as opposed to within the interior of the organism is not known. Features of these systems that may contribute to this quality of projicience are the fact that the relay of the activity of these particular sensory systems is located in tightly organized nuclei that maintain their modality specific attributes. So, for example, visual information is organized and integrated with other visual information, touch with touch, and so on. Another possible reason is that the activity of these nuclei and the higher regions to which they project are organized into maps of the somatic surface or the sense modality they represent. When we speak of a cortical map, we are referring to the way a spatial relationship in the external world is represented in a topographical projection within the brain. Thus, in the visual system, adjacent areas in the external world are represented by adjacent areas in the retina, and in turn adjacent areas of the retina are represented by adjacent areas in the brain. In this way the organism is able to maintain a rough correlation between the external world and the brain's internal representation of that world. The tactile system that is responsive to touch on the body surface also maintains a similar internal *somatotopic* map of the surface of the body. There may be some as yet to be discovered relationship between cortical maps and mental projections of internal stimuli.

One important brain system that is critical to the construction of the internal sense of self that is organized along the caudo-rostral trend is historically referred to as the *limbic system*. The term "limbic system" originated with the neuroscientist Paul MacLean who suggested that the neuroaxis of vertebrates can be roughly divided into three nested hierarchical levels.[6] The phylogenetically oldest level of the brain he called the *reptilian brain*, comprised of the upper brainstem and including the reticular activating system, the midbrain, diencephalon, and additional structures known as the basal ganglia. Under MacLean's system, animals with a reptilian brain, such as lizards, are capable of a wide array of complex and diverse behaviors, including establishment of a territory, the making and remembering of trails, and patrolling, ritualistic displays of defense, triumph, greeting, courtship, and the formation of social groups. However, these animals perform these actions, in spite of their complexity, in an extremely rigid and stereotyped manner.

One of the great pioneers of neuroanatomy, Walle Nauta, was among the first to describe the neural hiercharchy of the brain as it extends along the caudal-rostral trend.

Walle Nauta[7] demonstrated that there were robust connections between the medial and paramedian zones within the midbrain and the higher limbic regions within the forebrain that extend along what I have referred to as the caudal-rostral trend. Nauta envisioned a *limbic fore-brain-limbic midbrain complex* consisting of interconnected structures that extended from the amygdala and hippocampal formation rostrally to the septal and preoptic regions, hypothalamus, and the mesencephalic raphé nuclei and cental gray caudally. He suggested that the medial forebrain bundle serves as the central pathway connecting these areas. Expansion of this early work on the forebrain-limbic midbrain connections led to the description of the *greatater limbic* of Nieuwenhuys *and the distributed limbic system* as described by Morgane and colleagues[8] that we will see plays a critical role in the creation of the internal sense of self.

The next hierarchical level, according to MacLean's scheme, is designated the *paleomammalian* brain, and here we witness the addition of neural structures that introduce a quantum leap in the complexity and versatility of animal behavior. This level is comprised essentially of what MacLean called the "limbic system," a group of brain structures that are nested upon the reptilian brain. It was MacLean's hypothesis that all mammals possess at least the rudiments of the paleomammalian brain and display, in addition to many of the aforementioned behaviors, more sophisticated social behaviors including maternal nurturing behaviors, separation distress calls, play behaviors, and a wider range of social displays and behaviors.

The highest level of the neuroaxis MacLean called the *neomammalian brain.* According to MacLean's schema, the reptilian brain and the paleomammalian brain are nested within the neomammalian brain, which in addition to the aforementioned neural levels includes the expanded neocortex in the brain of higher primates. The neomamallian brain is responsible for the complex, flexible, and abstract forms of thought and behavior that characterizes the mind of higher primates and humans.

MacLean points out that there are many behavioral characteristics of species with a reptilian brain that endure or have analogues in higher order behaviors in species that possess a paleomammalian brain or even a neomammalian brain. For instance, MacLean asserts that there are more than twenty-five behaviors characteristic of lizards that are also seen in mammals, and paleomammilian behaviors such as maternal nurturing, infant separation calls, and play behaviors that are of course preserved within the entire mammalian line up to humans. Therefore there must be a structural organization of the neural hierarchy that allows the lower levels to be partially operative yet permits higher regions to evolve and add to already existing functions.

As I have already noted, the limbic system displays a marked cau

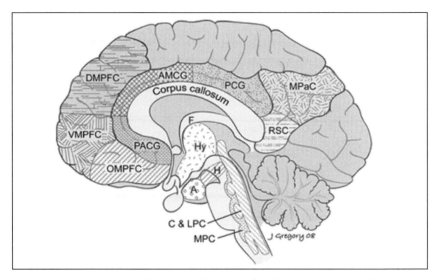

Figure 5-3. Expansion of this work on the forebrain-limbic midbrain connections led to the concept of the greater or extended limbic system. Within this system are included a large number of *medially* located structures that display many of the essential features of the core and paracore regions enumerated above. Based upon Nieuwenhuys, 1996, 1998; Nieuwenhuys et al., 2007; Morgane and Mokler, 2006; Morgane et al., 2005). There is extensive overlap between the cortical zones within this system and those cortical zones found to be critical for self-related functions (Northoff and Bermpohl, 2004). A-Amygdala; AMCG-anterior and midcingulate gyrus; C & LPC-core and lateral paracore; DMPFC-dorsomedial prefrontal cortex; F-fornix; H-hippocampus; Hy-hypothalamus; MPC-medial paracore; MPaC-medial parietal cortex; OMPFC-orbitomedial prefrontal cortex; PCG-posterior cingulate gyrus; PACC-pregenual anterior cingulate gyrus; RSC-retrosplenial cortex; VMPFC-ventromedial prefrontal cortex.

dal-rostral trend as we ascend to the higher and later evolved parts of the neuroaxis. Nieuwenhuys emphasizes the caudal-rostral extention of the core and paracore system described above into the diencephalon and forebrain (Figure 5-3), and within this system are included are a large number of *medially* located structures that display many of the essential features of the core and paracore regions that we have seen play a key role in the internal sense of self and the homeostic mechanisms that maintain the internal milieu of the organism:

> The medial part of the brain harbors a neural entity which structurally, chemically as well as functionally differs considerably from the classical systems mentioned above. This entity is designated here as the greater limbic system. It consists of an array of highly interconnected structures, extending from the medial wall of the telencephalon to the caudal rhombencephalon which is concerned with specific motivated or goal-oriented behaviors, directly aimed at the maintenance of homestasis and at the survival of the individual (organism) and of the species.[9]

Just as the medial core-paracore systems maintain their medial localization within the cortical zones of the greater limbic system, the great sensory and motor pathways that are involved with the transmission and action upon external sensory information maintain a more lateral location within the cortex. Thus the major corticospinal motor system responsible for voluntary movement, and the cortical representation for higher order aspects of touch, vision, and audition are all located on the lateral surfaces of the hemisphere.

The Neural Hierarchy

One point I have emphasized throughout this book is that there can be no self without a neural hierarchical organization. Therefore it is essential to define as specifically as possible how the neural hierarchy is organized.One of the most useful and best known ways of organizing the neural hierarchy has been proposed by Marsel Mesulam, who suggests that the cerebral cortex can be roughly organized into five hierarchically arranged subtypes: *limbic, paralimbic, heteromodal association, unimodal association,* and *primary sensorimo-*

tor regions[10] (Figure 5-4). Although Mesulam's hierarchy is based upon many variables, it utilizes to a great extent the features of brain anatomy that are felt to represent primitive versus later evolving anatomical development. Levels that are characterized as primitive cortex, such as the limbic regions, have a relatively simple neural architecture with fewer clearly defined cellular layers and less in the way of differentiated cell types when compared with zones higher on the neural hierarchy. The heirarchically highest zones show later evolving architectonic features such as an increase in the number of well differentiated cellular layers (a feature called lamination) and more highly specialized cell types. There is also an increase in cell density as ones moves from lower to higher zones.

Another feature of Mesulam's neural hierarchy is that each zone within the hierarchy has both extensive *extramural* connections with elements of other functional zones, as well as *intramural* connections within its own functional zone. It is essential to understand that the hierarchy is based upon the postulate—which Mesulam supports with very convincing arguments—that the most robust extramural connections of each zone are with the zones immediately lower or higher on the hierarchy. In this way a clear hierarchical pattern of connectivity is maintained in spite of extensive cross-talk between different regions at various hierarchical levels.

Mesulam's model nicely compliments Maclean's suggestion that the hierarchical organization of the brain parallels brain evolution, and in general the models converge. In agreement with MacLean, Mesulam considers the corticoid amygdala and the allocortical hippocampus as "limbic areas." On the other hand the cingulate gyrus, the most important limbic structure in Maclean's limbic lobe, is considered by Mesulam to show parahippocampal architectonics. If however we consider Mesulam's limbic and paralimbic structures as a single nested neural level, we roughly arrive at what MacLean re-

Figure 5-4. Mesulam proposes that the cerebral cortex can be roughly organized into five hierarchically arranged subtypes: *limbic, paralimbic, heteromodal association, unimodal association,* and *primary sensorimotor regions.* (Based on Mesulam, 2000, with permission)

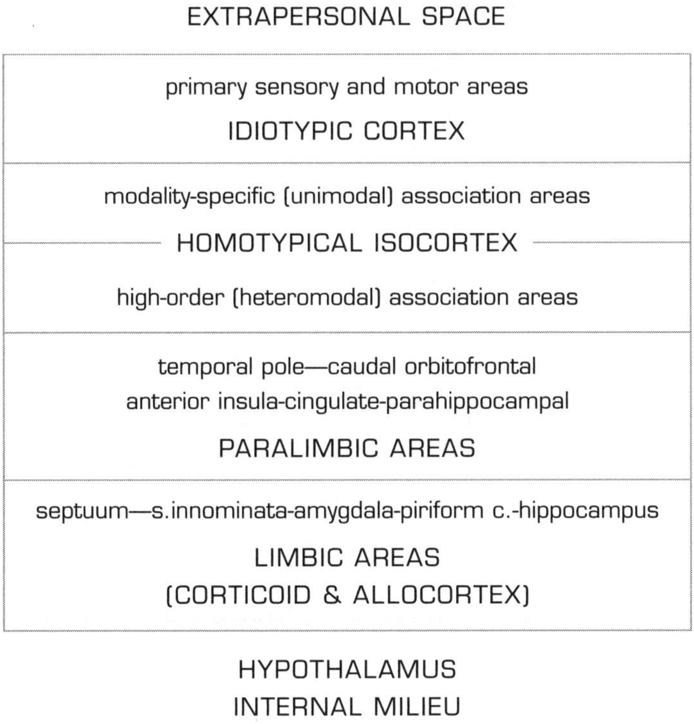

EXTRAPERSONAL SPACE

primary sensory and motor areas **IDIOTYPIC CORTEX**
modality-specific (unimodal) association areas —— **HOMOTYPICAL ISOCORTEX** —— high-order (heteromodal) association areas
temporal pole—caudal orbitofrontal anterior insula-cingulate-parahippocampal **PARALIMBIC AREAS**
septuum—s.innominata-amygdala-piriform c.-hippocampus **LIMBIC AREAS (CORTICOID & ALLOCORTEX)**

HYPOTHALAMUS
INTERNAL MILIEU

ferred to as the paleomammilian brain. The next highest level in Mesulam's scheme are the heteromodal association cortices, also known as higher order association cortices or polysensory areas because they have synaptic connections (associations) from diverse areas of the brain representing more than one type of sensory input. Among many other critical functions, these regions are essential for registering and collating information that is derived from more than one sense modality, thus enabling, for instance, the integration of visual and auditory information. In this way, these areas appear to be essential for the creation of more abstract "meaning" than primary sensory regions that register more basic information from a single sense modality—so-called unimodal information.

A somewhat paradoxical feature of Mesulam's model is that he positions the primary sensory and motor regions that serve basic sensory and motor functions at the highest level of the hierarchy and heteromodal association cortices, regions that are generally viewed as subserving advanced integrative and associative functions, are considered to be mid-level in the hierarchy (Figure 5-4). As Mesulam himself points out, however, there is controversy in regard to what cortical regions represent the most advanced hierarchical levels of the nervous system.[11] Nonetheless, it is very important for present purposes to specifically define the most advanced brain regions that create the self if an accurate model of the neural hierarchy of the self is to be achieved.

Mesulam's argument is that, based upon their advanced architectonic features such as the primary motor and sensory areas are more evolved than secondary and tertiary association regions that perform integrative functions. However, there is an alternative to view these relationships.According to principles postulated by the great neurologist John Hughlings Jackson, whose ideas have formed a bedrock for neurological theory for over a hundred years, these heteromodal regions are *functionally* the more advanced regions when one considers them in relation to self.[12] For instance, according to Jacksonian priniciples, the heteromodal regions that comprise the prefrontal cortex are the ones that are the least reflexive, the least organized (hard wired), the most voluntary, the most complex, and contribute most to the higher order thinking that we associate with higher cortical processes and the more advanced aspects of the self. Furthermore, as we shall see, there is a virtual explosion of recent data indicating that key regions within the heteromodal hierarchical levels are critically linked to the most highly developed self-related functions. Based upon these considerations, one might expect the association cortices to be highest on the neural hierarchy.

Converging lines evidence suggest that heteromodal association cortices are functionally the highest regions of the neural hierarchy.

Fuster[13] applies a hierarchical approach to his analysis of executive functions, and a hierarchical arrangement of sensory and motor systems that he refers to as the "Perception-Action Cycle." In Fuster's model, the polymodal association cortical areas also represent the hierarchically highest levels within the sensory hierarchy and the prefrontal (heteromodal) cortical areas are in the highest position within the motor hierarchy. Ramnani and Owen in a review of the anatomy and functions of the anterior prefrontal cortex (aPFC) agree that the brain possesses a hierarchical structure as a "general principle." With specific reference to the anterior prefrontal cortex (aPFC), a heteromodal domain, they point out:

> The primate cerebral cortex is hierarchically organized with information becoming increasingly abstract as it is processed at higher points in the cortical hierarchy. At the apex of each information processing stream is a supramodal (regions within the PFC and anterior temporal cortex) in which information is represented at its most abstract level.[14]

However, there is a way to resolve this intriguing paradox. Mesulam's model is based on a hierarchy of functions that runs from the structures in closest contact with internal milieu at the base of the hierarchy and located within caudal brain structures, to those structures at the top of the hierarchy that are in closest contact with the external environment and extrapersonal space. However, this pattern of organization, for completely different reasons and based upon largely different considerations, is nearly perfectly aligned with Nieuwenhuys' medial-lateral organization. In both arrangements, medial regions are most involved in the maintenance of the internal milieu, homeostasis, self-preservation, introception, and the internal needs of the organism, while the lateral domains in the brainstem and forebrain are dedicated to dealing with the sensorimotor apparatus dedicated to the out-side world. This insight points the way to a new and integrated view of the neural self.

A Model of the Neural Self

I believe it is now possible to create a unified model of the self that takes into account the critical variables of the self that we have thus considered. The medial-lateral trend deals with the organism's inter-nal needs of homeostasis and the internal milieu (medial systems) versus the the organism's relationship to the external environment (lateral systems). The caudal-rostral trend takes into account the evo-lution of the nervous sytem and the ever-increasing neural complex-ity that is possessed by more evolved neural systems that makes possible more advanced and abstract behavioral patterns and thought. With these features accounted for, I suggest that we can view the neural self as related to three hierarchically arranged and interrelated systems: the *interoself system*, the *exterosensorimotor system*, and the *integrative self system* that is interposed between the other two (Figure 5-5).

The Interoself System

Based on the predominant models examined above, the interoself system, located within either the brainstem or forebrain, contributes to the organism's relationship to the internal milieu, and serves homeostatic and self-preservative functions. The interoself system in this model is comprised in part of the core-paracore structures and the extended and distributed limbic systems of Nieuwenhuys, and Mesulam's limbic, paralimbic, and medially located hetermodal zones.The interoself system is specialized therefore for the process-ing and awareness of aspects of the self that pertain to homeostatic internal processes including self-preservation, motivational and emotional processing.

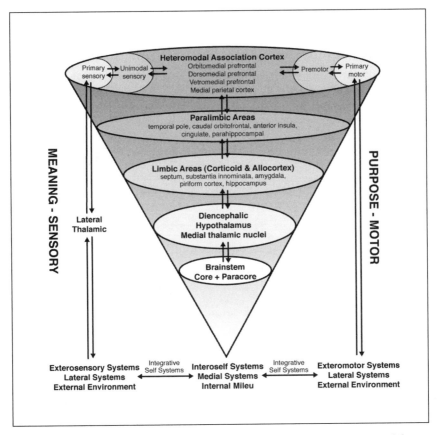

Figure 5-5. A Model of the Neural Self. In the highly schematic model presented here, the neural self is comprised of *three systems in which* lower levels of the neural hierarchy are viewed as nested within higher levels, and all levels of the neural hierarchy make a contribution to the self. Levels and their anatomy are derived and adapted primarily from Nieuwenhuys (1996, 1998), Nieuwenhuys et al. (2007) and Mesulam (2000). When these levels are considered as parts of a nested hierarchy, the sensory-perceptual systems (represented on the left side of the diagram) are constrained by the highest levels of *meaning,* and the motor-intentional systems (diagramed on the right) are constrained by the highest level of *purpose* achieved by the brain (Feinberg, 2001a). The basic sensory plan of the visual system is outlined here, but the same fundamental patterns of connectivity could apply to other sensory systems such as the auditory or descriminitve touch pathways. For the sake of simplicity and emphasis, the numerous cross-connections between ascending and descending sensory and motor pathways are not represented in the diagram.

The Exterosensorimotor System

The lateral system corresponds to the lateral brainstem and cortical regions in closest communication with and having the greatest responsiveness to the external environment. It is important to bear in mind, with reference to the controversy surrounding where on the neural hierarchy the primary sensorimotor domains should be placed, that in the higher primates and man, due to the progressive encephalization of functions, external stimuli responsible for interactions with the external environment enter the brain at the highest levels of the neural axis. Thus, although these regions are not responsible for the most evolved aspects of the self, they do represent the most evolved aspects of the lateral system.

This idea is consistent with the view of Mesulam based upon architectonic features that the lateral systems may indeed emerge latest in evolution. What this arrangement does is to (1) maintain relatively prolonged segregation of sensory inputs within each sensory modality (vision, touch, etc.) in order that they may become more differentiated from other sensory modalities; (2) allow greater higher order and abstract processing of information within each sensory modality before the different sense modalities are integrated with other higher order regions further downstream; and (3) as each level within Mesulam's hierarchy is most tightly connected with its own and adjacent levels, this arrangement allows the less differentiated regions (heteromodal association cortices) to remain connected with each other with advancing evolution.

Like the interoself system, the extero systems make a major contribution to the self. First and perhaps foremost, the highly evolved extero systems—in contrast to the interoself system—create the aforementioned quality of projicience, the mental externalization of stimuli away from body that makes self-object discrimination possible, a quality of mind that is critical for the creation of consciousness. Sherrington postulated that the development of the *distance*

receptors are the key to the development of the brain and consciousness:

> It is in the leading segments that we find the *distance-receptors.* For so
> may be called the receptors which react to *objects* at a distance. Theses
> are the same receptors which, acting as senses-organs, initiate sensa-
> tions having the psychical quality termed *projicience....* We know that
> in ourselves sensations initiated through these receptors are forth-
> with "projected" into the world outside the "material me." ... None of
> the sensations initiated in the proprio-ceptive or intero-ceptive fields
> possess this property of projicience.... The "distance-receptors" seem
> to have peculiar importance for the construction and evolution of
> the nervous system.... *The brain is always the part of the nervous system*
> *which is constructed upon and evolved upon the "distance-receptor" organs.*[15]

By this criterion, the earliest forms of consciousness and a self
may exist at the level of a reptilian brain, which can clearly respond
with appropriately directed actions "in the world" via the distance
receptors, a fact that may in itself be evidence of consciousness and
a primitive self. Here we might speculate that the reptile possesses
what Joseph LeDoux calls "implicit self"[16] or what Antonio Damasio
calls a "core self."[17] An implicit self would minimally entail, as suggested by Sherrington, appropriate perception via the distance receptors. An animal with an implicit self can also distinguish itself
from the environment and other animals. An animal with an implicit self does not respond to its own hands and tails as it does to
the same parts of another animal. According to the criteria of the
philosopher William James, an animal with an implicit self possesses both a primitive subjective "I" and objective "me."[18] The implicit sense of self in an animal lacking extensive neocortex may
correspond to a rudimentary form of consciousness that philosopher Dorothée Legrand calls *pre-reflective self-consciousness,* a form of
basic consciousness or subjective experience that does not entail
higher order self-awareness, but rather a simpler form requiring only
some level of subjective experience:

... pre-reflective self-consciousness is an intrinsic aspect of phenomenal experience. Insofar as consciousness experiences are characterized by a subjective "feel," i.e., a certain "what it is like" or what it "feels like" to have them, they also come together with a minimal form of self-consciousness.[19]

As we shall see, there are aspects of brain development that occur uniquely in higher primates that enable the creation of an "explicit self" that entails greater degrees of self-awareness that goes beyond the idea of pre-reflective self-consciousness. That said, my belief is that we are dealing here with matters of degree, without a clear discontinuity between primitive selves and later evolved forms like our own.

The Integrative Self System

Finally, an important—indeed possibly determining—role is played in the creation of the self by a third, *integrative self system* which serves to assimilate the interoself systems with the extero systems, and mediate the organism's internal needs with the external environment. Here, the cortical association regions that are not specifically consigned to the processing of the more evolved aspects of sensorimotor processing or the internal milieu take center stage. Most important for the integrative self-system are the *heteromodal cortices* that are situated between the paralimbic zones that are most allied with the limbic functions of the maintenance of homeostasis and the conditions of the internal milieu, and the unimodal zones that represent the most abstract aspects of sensorimotor processing. These regions serve as a "convergence zone" for the integration of the other two systems.[20]

Recent brain imaging studies have specifically implicated numerous medially located cortical heteromodal zones to be involved in self-related functions. Georg Northoff and his colleagues at the University of Magdeburg have provided evidence there may be a broad and fairly extensive neural network involved in the performance of self-related tasks, including a group of *cortical midline structures* (CMS) that they suggest constitute the anatomical core of more evolved aspects of the self.[21] According to this account, these midline paralimbic and heteromodal structures are critical to the implementation of a broad array of self-related functions, including judgments about self-traits, autobiographical memory, self-face recognition, and self-agency. In one large study, these researchers found that medial prefrontal heteromodal regions were activated in the broader array of self-related activation studies.[22]

Many of the CMS structures that are activated during self-related tasks may actually be viewed anatomically as the rostral extention of the interoself systems, and therefore overlap to a large extent with the greater limbic system and emotional systems in general. What may distinguish the areas most related to self-related processing is that the more the stimulus is *both* emotional and self-referential, the more likely it is to preferentially activate the medial prefrontal regions as opposed to the more caudal regions of the extended limbic hierarchy. In support of this hypothesis, K Luan Phan, now at the University of Chicago and colleagues provided evidence that some of the cortical midline structures implicated in self-related processes may be directly related to emotional processing, while others higher on the neural axis may be related to integrating emotion with its self-referential aspects.[23]

In one activation study in which subjects viewed pictures and judged the degree of the pictures regarding their emotional intensity or degree of personal relatedness, researchers found that activity in the nucleus accumbens responded to both emotional intensity and self-relatedness, and the amygdala was specifically related to emotional intensity. Thus two regions within the extended limbic system responded primarily to the degree of emotional intensity evoked by a stimulus, but not preferentially to the degree of it self-relatedness. In contrast, when subjects were required to make volitional judgments regarding the degree of personal relatedness,

heteromodal association regions including the ventral medial prefrontal cortex and dorsal medial prefrontal zones—regions that I
would include here within the integrative self-system—were activated, as was the insula. This suggests there is a hierarchical
arrangement of emotional processes with reference to the higher
aspects of self-awareness, and that medial prefrontal regions are
specifically related to self-referential material over and above its
emotional content.

Ross Buck at the University of Connecticut has also proposed a hierarchical model of emotional functions that is informative on this
point.[27] He suggests that there are roughly three levels of emotional
functioning. Emotion I is a general state of arousal that serves
homeostatic, autonomic, and self-preservative (fight-or-flight) re-

---

With regard to one heteromodal region, the dorsomedial prefrontal cortex (DMPFC), Northoff and co-workers noted many studies have provided evidence that self-consciousness may induce higher activity in
the DMPFC.[24] Allan Schore notes that the orbitomedial prefrontal cortex
(OMPFC), serves as a critical integration zone between internal (interoceptive) and external (exteroceptive) information:

> The orbital prefrontal cortex is positioned as a convergence zone where
> the cortex and subcortex meet. It is the only cortical structure with direct
> connections to the hypothalamus, the amygdala, and the reticular for-
> mation in the brain stem that regulates arousal, and through these con-
> nections it can modulate instinctual behavior and internal drives . . . due
> to its unique connections, at the orbitofrontal level cortically processed
> information concerning the external environment...is integrated with
> subcortically processed information regarding the internal visceral envi-
> ronment.[25]

Schore[26] has further suggested that specifically it is the right or-
bitofrontal region that is most critical with certain self-related functions especially with reference to attachment, an idea we will return to
later on.

sponses. Emotion II serves emotional expression and expressive displays that serve important social-signaling functions. Emotion III, the highest emotional level on this hierarchy, entails conscious awareness of emotional states including the subjective experience of feelings and affects. It may be that if a stimulus is related solely to emotion, it has only to be processed within the interoself system. However, for a stimulus or an emotion to have specific reference to the self, it needs to be processed within integrative zones where emotion is related to cognition and objective self-awareness.

Memory and the Neural Hierarchy

Up to this point I have argued that every aspect of the self, including the maintenance of the internal needs of the organism, the processing of environmental information in relationship to the self, and the integration of the two into a meaningful and emotionally relevant whole, requires hierarchical organization. There is, however, another function necessary for self-awareness that many authors have argued is absolutely critical for the creation and function of the self, which is memory. Renowned memory researcher Endel Tulving has proposed an influential model of self and consciousness that emphasizes a key role for memory in the creation of the self.[28] In Tulving's model, there are three hierarchically arranged levels of memory systems that roughly correspond to three levels of consciousness.

The lowest level he called *anoetic* (non-knowing) consciousness. Organisms with anoetic consciousness are at the very least "... capable of perceptually registering, internally representing, and behaviorally responding to aspects of the present environment, both external and internal."[29] According to Tulving, anoetic consciousness is supported by *procedural memory*, which is the simplest form of memory function and requires only the ability to acquire, retain, and retrieve cognitive, perceptual, and motor skills. Procedural memory enables one to perform actions without necessarily being able to verbally explain how one does these things, or remembering when or how the knowledge was acquired. Elements of procedural memory can be simple, such as conditioned reflexes, or complex such as the ability to ride a bike. Animals with reptilian levels of neural organization are capable of the simplest forms of anoetic consciousness.

The next hierarchical level of consciousness Tulving calls *noetic* (knowing) consciousness. Animals with noetic consciousness possess *semantic memory* that principally includes factual knowledge of the world and meanings without the memory of specifically experienced events.[30] Noetic consciousness ". . . allows an organism to be aware of, and to cognitively operate on, objects and events, in the absence of these objects and events. The organism can flexibly act upon such symbolic knowledge of the world."[31] Tulving points out that many nonhuman species, particularly mammals and birds, possess well developed semantic memory systems and these animals may therefore possess noetic consciousness. Noetic consciousness is therefore probably most characteristic of animals possessing, at a minimum, neural structures up to and including paralimbic cortices.

The highest level within Tulving's hierarchy is *autonoetic* (self-knowing) consciousness, which Tulving suggests is a singular human trait. The key to the evolution of autonoetic consciousness is the development *episodic memory*, which is, according to Tulving, the most advanced form of memory:

> Episodic memory is a recently evolved, late-developing, and early-deteriorating past-oriented memory system, more vulnerable than other memory systems to neurological dysfunction, and probably unique to humans. It makes possible mental time travel through subjective time, from the present to the past, thus allowing one to re-experience, through autonoetic awareness, one's own previous experiences. . . . The essence of episodic memory lies in the conjunction of three concepts- self, autonoetic awareness, and subjectively sensed time.[32]

In this account, the ability to "mentally time travel," to envisage one's past and in essence re-experience specific life episodes, allows the emergence of self, self-awareness, identity, autobiographical identity, and a sense of subjective time. With the capacity to envisage who one was in the past, the emerging self indeed has a past, and a self-aware present. And the development of self-aware consciousness always allows the evolution of an important new tool—the ability to imagine a potential subjective future, a capacity Tulving called *chronesthesia*. Tulving argues persuasively that the development of the "episodic memory system" and autonoetic consciousness is the key to the development of the human species:

> It took biological evolution a long time to build a time machine in the brain, and it has managed to do it only once, but the consequences have been enormous: By virtue of their mental control over time, human beings now wield powers on earth that in many ways rival or exceed those of nature itself. It is difficult to imagine a marvel of nature greater than that.[33]

As research in the episodic memory system has progressed, it is becoming apparent that this special faculty and autonoetic consciousness is critically dependent on frontal lobe structures that would be included within the integrative self-system.[34,35]

In this chapter, I have proposed a model that attempts to refine our explanation of how the brain creates a self.[36] In broad outline, the medial-lateral trend gives rise to an *interoself* system that is is concerned with the internal milieu and homeostatic needs of the organism. The products of processes generated by the interoself system are experienced as feelings coming from withing the organism itself. As a result, these sensations are not projected beyond the bounds of the organism and are experienced as belonging to the internal and personal self. The *exterosensorimotor system* is devoted to the organism's interactions with the environment, those sensations from and actions generated toward the exterior world.[37]

The caudal-rostral trend represents the nervous system's evolutionary tendency toward greater complexity of both neural organization and behavior. In the evolution of our species, as well as in our own individual development during our lifespan, the caudal-rostral trend creates an increase in brain growth and complexity that results in an enormous expansion of the *integrative self-system*. It is this system, represented for the most part by heteromodal association cortex, that is responsible for the most abstract and highest order aspects of the human self.

One of the points I have emphasized in this chapter, and throughout this book, is that all nervous systems on earth display hierarchical organization, and the more complex the nervous sytem, the greater the degree of hierarchical organization it possesses. Hierarchical organization is the bedrock of the self, the principle that makes it a reality. The human self was made possible as nature—brick by brick—built a cathedral of the mind. In the following chapters, I will try to demonstrate that an understanding of neural hierarchical processes provides a solution to the mystery of consciousness itself.

CHAPTER SIX

The Hierarchy of the Self

IN THE LAST CHAPTER we examined how the brain is organized along two critical dimensions that establish a series of continuous, connected, and hierarchically arranged neurological levels. These levels are organized to allow the creation of an increasingly complex self. There remains, however, an important question that has puzzled philosophers and scientists since the time of Descartes. If the brain is comprised of multiple zones and levels, and each of these are in turn composed of millions upon millions of individual neurons, then what are the unique qualities of brain functioning that allow the creation of our subjective feeling of a unified self and consciousness? In this chapter I will attempt to show that the solution to this hundreds-years-old mystery is related to the unique features of the neural hierarchical organization itself.

The Nature of Hierarchies

Herbert A. Simon, one of the pioneers in the study of artificial intelligence, the analysis of complex systems, and hierarchy theory, said it quite plainly: "It is a commonplace observation that nature loves hierarchies."[1] To witness the truth of that statement for yourself, simply examine any living thing. For instance, a tree displays a hierarchical progression from a single trunk to the many limbs and even more numerous leaves. This represents a basic branching hierarchy. And then take a look at a single leaf and observe how its central vein divides again and again into progressively smaller divisions. Even the human body plan is a progression from a single trunk, to four limbs, and to five fingers and toes attached to each one.

According to Simon, evolution must progress in a hierarchical fashion in order for biological advances to be preserved, and this is one reason that evolution is so conservative in many aspects of the structure of life. In order for nature to "tinker" with a later stage of evolution, the previous levels of organizations must be organized into stable subassemblies, or else every time there is a major genetic change the entire previously organized system would break down. In a now familiar parable, Simon offers an explanation for why the products of evolution are hierarchically organized:

> Two watchmakers assemble fine watches, each watch containing ten thousand parts. Each watchmaker is interrupted frequently to answer the phone. The first has organized his total assembly operation into a sequence of subassemblies; each subassembly is a stable arrangement of 100 elements, and each watch, a stable arrangement of 100 subassemblies. The second watchmaker has developed no such organization. The average interval between phone interruptions is a time long enough to assemble about 150 elements. An interruption causes any set of elements that does not yet form a stable system to fall apart completely. By the time he has answered about eleven phone calls, the first watchmaker will usually have finished assembling a watch. The second watchmaker will almost never succeed in assembling one. . . . [2]

Evolutionary biologist Leo Buss at Yale University, in his influential book *The Evolution of Individuality*, provides further explanation of why evolutionary processes are built and grow hierarchically.[3] As evolution proceeds, newer structures are built upon older and previously established biological units, with the lower units becoming contained—*nested within*—the higher units. In a moment, we will see why the principle of nestedness is so important to our understanding of the brain, but Buss points out that for biological systems in general, the result of this arrangement is that the forces of natural selection emanating from the external environment act only upon the higher biological units, while selective forces exerted upon the lower units are provided by the environment of the higher units. As Buss expresses it, *"Traits expressed in the higher unit now act as selective agents on the variation arising in the lower unit."* Therefore, lower units may evolve, but only if any change is not at the expense of the higher unit's interaction with the external environment, and evolutionary change will therefore by necessity become concentrated upon the higher units. The result is that as life evolved in this hierarchical fashion, the lower on the scale an individual unit is located, the more conservative its biological features. So, for example, the basic building blocks of all life, the genetic code of DNA, is essentially universal across all living things, and according to Buss, the essential body plan of all organisms within the animal kingdom has been fixed for a half billion years! This is one reason why the brain, at the highest level of the neuroaxis, is also by necessity at the cutting edge of evolutionary change.

There have been prior efforts to explain the problem of mental unity on the basis of neural hierarchies. One proposal—most notably argued for by the neurophysiologist Roger Sperry—is that the self and mind *emerge* in unified fashion from the diverse parts of the brain at the highest levels of the neural hierarchy. According to Sperry's account, the self is "more than the sum of the parts" of the brain that creates it, and a unified self and consciousness emerge at the topmost parts of the nervous system.[4]

The concept of emergence does not have a single meaning. John Searle asserts that there are at least two meanings of the term that he characterizes as weak and strong versions of emergence theory.[5] The weak version simply states that there are higher order properties of complex systems which are novel relative to the constituent parts which create them. An example of weak emergent property would be the fluid properties of water relative to the non-fluid properties of a single water molecule. Certainly fluidity is property of the water as an aggregate of water molecules, and it poses no particular scientific ontological mystery. If one understands all the principles of water molecules, and all the principles of fluid dynamics, the behavior of water can be understood as the result of the constituent water molecules and their interactions.

In contrast to this weak version of emergence, the most important aspect of the strong or "radical" form of emergence theory is the claim that there are emergent properties that cannot *in principle* ever be reduced to the component parts of a system. A theory of radical emergence when applied to the nervous system would claim that consciousness can never be reduced to the brain *by virtue of it being a radically emergent feature.* The emergence hypothesis is appealing for several reasons. The integrated mind and the unified self entail the "highest" and most advanced forms of cognitive processing, and the phylogenetically most advanced regions of the nervous system. For example, the prefrontal cortices, as we discussed earlier, are indeed situated "higher" or farther "downstream" on the neuroaxis when compared with regions, such as the midbrain, that are situated at the earliest stages of perceptual processing. It is also true that, due to the hierarchical arrangement of neuronal processing streams, neurons located in anatomically "higher" positions within the neuroaxis possess "higher," more abstract, and more *integrated* response characteristics than neurons positioned earlier (upstream) in perceptual pathways.

This concept is demonstrated, for example, in the work of David Hubel and Torsten Wiesel, who won the Nobel Prize for their work in the 1960s and 1970s on how the brain synthesizes and integrates visual information. They demonstrated that receptive fields of retinal cells early in the visual processing respond to simple and small points of light, but groups of these neurons converge upon single neurons downstream in the neural hierarchy in cortical area VI enabling these higher order cells to respond to lines, while even further along in the unimodal association cortex there are *complex* cortical cells that in turn converge upon single neurons to create *hypercomplex* cells, with each hierarchical level higher up the processing stream coding for increasingly integrated response properties.[6] For example some cells—referred to as "pontifical" cells (also called "grandmother," "cardinal," or "gnostic" cells) far along on the processing stream respond to the visual image of a hand or a face.[7] Some of these cells have actually been found to be selectively responsive to such unlikely stimuli as the faces of Jennifer Aniston, Halle Berry, Julia Roberts, Kobe Bryant, and Steve Carell, or specific buildings including the Tower of Pisa, the Baha'i Temple, or the Sydney Opera House.[8] If these results could be generalized to other sensory systems that contribute perceptual consciousness, one might conjecture that the "emergence" of unified consciousness might be possible because these highly specialized neurons combine to create consciousness at the highest levels of the neuroaxis

However, there are many problems with theories of mental unification that invoke this process—known as *topical convergence*—as the only explanation for the coherence, or "binding," of perceptual elements into a unified awareness.[9] For one thing, a higher order cell such as a face cell will react to the image of a face that appears almost *anywhere* in the visual field.[10] Thus, while cells early in the visual stream with small receptive fields "know" where each line of the face is, these early cells do not "know" that a given line is part of a face. Conversely, face cells "know" there is a face, but due to the process of topical convergence, these cells don't know where the face is located in space. Therefore, while it is true that cells of the brain project to successive levels in a hierarchical fashion in order to code for increasingly specific complex and abstract properties, the information coded by cells earlier in the process is not and cannot be lost in awareness and cells from early (primary sensory zones) and later (unimodal association) hierarchical zones all must make a contribution to awareness. Furthermore when we perceive a stimulus that has a combination of sensory qualities, such as color, sound, and smell, it is clear that an enormous number of brain regions at a vast range of hierarchical levels must be involved, and it cannot be the case that cells that represent all these different qualities ultimately converge on any single neuron. There simply are too many perceptual qualities and too few neurons. This strategy may work for early stages of integration and highly specialized perceptual functions such as vision, but it cannot apply as a generalized mechanism for all instances of binding in consciousness.[11]

In fact, most neurons in these higher perceptual regions actually do not display the specificity of pontifical neurons. By some estimates, out of one billion medial temporal lobe neurons that could potentially demonstrate such specific response properties, fewer than two million actually do so, and some of the neurons that do show some degree of specificity do not show complete response exclusivity. For instance in one experiment, one hippocampal neuron within the temporal lobe responded to the faces of *both* Jennifer Aniston and Lisa Kudrow, but not to other individuals, making this a sort of *Friends* neuron. Therefore, some researchers of these neurons estimate that individual cells in the medial temporal lobe probably actually respond to a range of 50 to 150 distinct individuals or objects. Thus, although these cells are "grandmother-ish" they are not nearly as specific as the term might suggest if strictly applied.[12]

What is true of the unification of sensory perception also applies to the synthesis of intended actions, which poses an equally important problem for a theory of mental unity. When we act, we subjectively feel there is a single self that is the source of what we do. In spite of this subjective sense of unity, neuroanatomical analysis reveals that the *motor system* is composed of millions of individual neurons that act in unified fashion to achieve specific goals. The control of action is not entirely at the highest, most explicitly conscious, levels of the neural hierarchy but is distributed across multiple hierarchical levels. While these neurons are organized to produce exquisitely integrated and unified actions, as with the visual system, there is no single region or point in space at the top of the motor hierarchy to explain this unity.

The brilliant scientist, philosopher, and prolific author Arthur Koestler, who was one of the forefathers of hierarchy theory, devised a prescient image of this very same neurological design problem in his apt use of the metaphor of an army as a hierarchical system.[13] Koestler points out that in an army, when the general who is situated at the top of the hierarchy issues an order to his subordinates, the command contains only in broad outlines the plan of action for the entire army. A command such as "Take that hill!" doesn't necessarily specify how, when, and where the mission is to be accomplished. However, as the order moves down the chain of command from commanders, to lieutenants, and so on, at each level of the hierarchy the exact action of each soldier becomes increasingly specified. In reverse order, information about the enemy is collected at the lowest of the hierarchy by individual soldiers who may be eye witnesses to a particular enemy movement, position, or feature of the battlefield. As information moves up the hierarchy it is condensed, filtered, and integrated with the information from other troops as it flows up converging lines of command until it reaches the general. Therefore, the general knows the overall aspects of the plan but does not specify the particular actions of the troops. The troops know how they are to take the hill but not necessarily its importance to winning the overall battle. The troops also know—unbeknownst to the general—that there is a division of snipers immediately in their path, but the general knows—unbeknownst to the troops—that there is a mile-long front forming in the region. The general has only the "big picture" while the troops on the ground have the specifics.

Remarkably, Koestler was writing about this hierarchical design problem at about the same time that Hubel and Wiesel were making their initial discoveries about the hierarchical arrangement of the visual system. And though he doesn't mention their research in his famous work *The Ghost in the Machine*, his theories parallel their discoveries to a remarkable degree:

> Here we have a very simplified model of the working of the sensory-motor nervous system. On the motor side, we had a series of "triggers." On the perceptual side we have instead a series of "filters" or "scanners," through which the vital input traffic must pass on its ascent from sense-organ to cerebral cortex. Their function is to analyse, de-code, classify and abstract the information that the stream carries, until the chaotic multitude of sensations, which constantly bombard the senses, is transformed into meaningful messages.[14]

Thus, the problem before us is this: in order to explain how the neural hierarchy operates, an adequate model must explain how the brain could *simultaneously* (1) be physically distributed across multiple connected but anatomically discrete levels; (2) allow for the creation of higher order integrated (whole) and abstract conscious awareness; and (3) ensure that *both* lower and higher levels of the hierarchy make a contribution to the entire mental experience. Furthermore, ideally our explanation should lead us to the answers for, or at least be consistent with, the other fundamental questions we have discussed, such as the nature of qualia and the projection of conscious states. In order to work our way through these thorny problems, we need take a closer look at the different types of hierarchies and their operational principles.

General Parameters of Hierarchies

Nestedness

In order to better understand how biological hierarchies actually operate, and how those operational features could create a self, let us begin with some of the general principles of hierarchical design as they pertain to different types of hierarchies. There are two basic

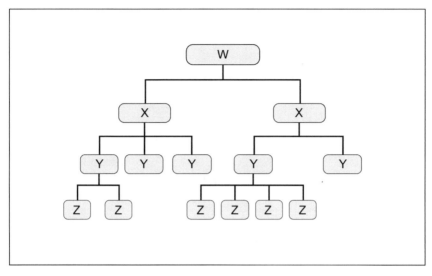

Figure 6-1. A non-nested hierarchy. In a non-nested hierarchy the entities or holons at the higher levels of the hierarchy are physically independent from the entities at lower levels. The control or constraint of the hierarchy comes from the higher to lower levels ("downward" or "top-down" constraint).

types of hierarchies, *non-nested* or *control hierarchies* and *nested* or *compositional hierarchies.*[15] A non-nested hierarchy has a pyramidal structure in which higher levels within the hierarchy are not physically composed of the lower levels as, for example, in our metaphor of military command with a general at the top and successively lower levels of command below. In an army, a general directs and controls the operations of the lower levels of the hierarchy; however, the general is not physically *composed* of his lieutenants, nor are the lieutenants composed of the troops under their command (Figure 6-1). Non-nested hierarchies are also called control hierarchies because the ordering of levels is based upon the pattern of constraint of higher upon lower levels.

The other type of hierarchy is known as a *nested* or *compositional hierarchy* (Figure 6-2). In a nested hierarchy any given level of the organization is entirely composed of its constituent parts. All living

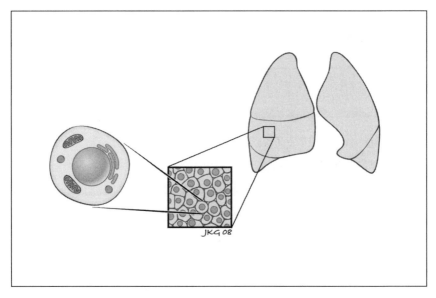

Figure 6-2. Nested hierarchy. In a nested hierarchy the entities or holons at the higher levels of the hierarchy are physically composed of the entities at lower levels. Although higher levels of the system constrain lower levels, constraint does not emanate from any unified or centralized holon.

organisms are nested hierarchies. In a nested hierarchy such an organism, the elements comprising the lower levels of the hierarchy are physically combined or *nested* within higher levels to create increasingly complex wholes (also known as "holons").[16] For example, an organ of the body such as a lung is entirely comprised of its constituent cells, and the entire body, the highest level of the hierarchy of a living organism, is entirely composed of the constituent organs of which it is comprised. Professors T. F. H Allen and Thomas Starr, who have written extensively on hierarchy theory in biological systems, distinguish nested from non-nested hierarchies:

> A nested hierarchy is one where the holon at the apex of the hierarchy contains and is composed of all lower holons. The apical holon consists of the sum of the substance and the interactions of all its daughter holons and is, in that sense, derivable from them. Individu-

als are nested within populations, organs within organisms, tissues within organs, and tissues are composed of cells. . . . Non-nested hierarchies relax the requirement for containment of lower by higher holons and also do not insist that higher holons are derivable from collected lower holons.[17]

Constraint

In addition to the compositional differences between nested and non-nested hierarchies, non-nested and nested hierarchies differ in the control that higher levels impose upon lower levels, referred to as *constraint*.[18] In an army, or a "control hierarchy," a general issues orders that are communicated down the chain of command until the orders are executed. In a non-nested hierarchy, the constraint of the hierarchy likewise comes from the top. In a nested hierarchy, in contrast, the constraint of the system is embodied within the hierarchical system itself. In organisms, individual cells constrain the organelles to perform cellular metabolism, the organs of the body constrain the cells so that they, for example, secrete enzymes, and at the highest level the entire organism constrains the individual organs to perform all the functions necessary for its survival. Therefore, there is no "general" within the organism directing its operation; rather the constraint of the organism's operation is generated from within the entire nested system of the organism. In the nested hierarchy of a living organism, all parts make a contribution to the life and activity of the organism, and in the nested hierarchy of the individual, many parts of its living brain make a contribution to the self.

Centralization

In a non-nested or control hierarchy, such as an army, the number of constituent parts tends to decrease as one moves up the hierarchy from lower to higher levels. Thus in a control hierarchy, constraint emanates from the top of the hierarchy, which is centralized relative to lower levels. In a nested hierarchy, although parts are organized into greater wholes, the number of constituent parts tends to increase, and there is in theory no centralized control of the system, and the entire system considered as a whole exerts downward constraint on lower levels.

Rates

Some living hierarchical systems, such as trees, have slow rates of operation, whereas others such as nervous systems have extremely rapid rates of operation. Whatever the speed of operation of the overall system, higher levels of a nested hierarchy are characterized by slower time constants than those of lower levels. Indeed, one of the defining features of a hierarchy is as a system of communication, where holons with slow behavior are at the topmost echelons of the hierarchy, while entities with faster behavior are at lower levels.[19] Because higher level entities function at slower frequencies than lower, they serve as the *relatively invariant context*, or the functional higher order background, for lower level entities. It takes a long time for the state of the entire organism to affect a single cell of the body. When you are hungry, you may immediately begin rummaging through the fridge, but your liver cells won't react for a long time to this change in state. In this way, in a nested hierarchy, the relative invariance of higher levels is one way that higher levels constrain lower levels over relatively long time frames.

Volume and Number

In a non-nested hierarchy, the number of holons decreases at higher levels while in a nested hierarchy, since lower level entities combine to create higher level entities, the higher levels will have greater volume and more holons than lower levels. However, looked at another way, since the highest holon represents a single integrated entity, one could also say that the highest levels of a nested hierarchy has the fewest integrated or complex holons, while the lowest levels have the greatest number of primitive or basic entities.

Bond Strength

In one dimension, nested and non-nested hierarchies are similar. In both types of hierarchy lower order entities are more tightly bound to one another than to the entities at higher level. This is another factor, in addition to frequency, that gives various levels integrity. In a non-nested hierarchy, the troops are more tightly bound to each than to the general; in a nested hierarchy the cells within a tissue are more tightly bound by physical forces to one another than to the entire organ. In this way as the hierarchy is built up, the weak forces that bind entitites at a lower level of a nested hierarchy are the strong forces that bind the entity at the next highest level of analysis.[20]

In summary, as we ascend from lower to higher levels of a hierarchy, in a control hierarchy the number of parts decreases, while in a nested hierarchy the number of contained holons increases but they are organized into a smaller number of higher holons of greater volume and increased integration. The forces holding together the parts of lower levels are stronger than the forces holding together parts at higher levels, and the rates of operation decrease at higher levels of the hierarchy, with the longest time scales associated with the weakest forces and the largest structures. With these parameters in mind, how can we relate the neural hierarchy to the creation of the consciousness and the self?

The Hierarchies of the Self

In order to demonstrate just how the unique features of the neural hierarchy are able to create consciousness and a self in a way that the other types of hierarchical systems do not, I have compared the parameters of non-nested and nested hierarchies with four biological hierarchies of increasing complexity. These include Level 1: organisms without a nervous system; Level 2: neural systems that operate reflexively without any consciousness; Level 3: non-reflexive perceptions and actions that require participation of the central nervous system and consciousness but do not require self-awareness; and Level 4: the highest levels of consciousness that require both consciousness and self-awareness.

In Table 6-1, each of these levels of hierarchical complexity is analyzed according to eight selected features that helps distinguishes each level from the next higher level of complexity. My aim is to demonstrate how the nature of these hierarchies hold important keys to understanding the nature of the neural self.

Non-nested Hierarchies

The first two columns in Table 6-1 summarize the general features of the two basic forms of hierarchy. As we have already discussed, the sine qua non of non-nested hierarchies is that higher levels within the system are not composed of lower levels. However, the interactions of lower level entities contribute to emergent properties that are realized at higher levels, and these properties contribute to the constraint of higher upon lower levels. The hierarchy is centralized in the sense that lower levels converge upon higher levels and the highest levels tend to constrain all lower levels. Although the relative speed of reactions decreases at higher levels of the hierarchy, the absolute speed of interaction depends upon the constituents of the actual hierarchy. In the case of our army, for example, the speed of communication between the troops and commander will determine the speed with which upward properties emerge and downward constraint is imposed. In another example, among a group of primates with a dominance hierarchy there may be the rapid imposition of constraint, such as when the troop must follow the leader when moving from a threat, or the slower manifestation of hierarchical patterns, as when individuals select mating partners according to dominance rules.

Nested Hierarchies

In nested hierarchies constituent parts not only contribute to higher levels, parts at any level of the hierarchy comprise those levels. In-

Table 6-1. Comparison of hierarchical patterns of body, brain, and self/consciousness.

	Non-nested hierarchies	Nested hierarchies	**Level 1** Soma*	**Level 2** Reflexes without consciousness	**Level 3** CNS with con-sciousness	**Level 4** Brain with consciousness and self awareness
Lower levels physically nested within higher levels	–	+	+	–	–	–
Lower levels functionally nested within higher levels	–	+	+	+	++	+++
Rapid (millisecond) communication between levels	+/–	+/–	–	+	+	+
Higher and lower levels contribute to the system	+	+	+	+	++	+++
Interaction at lower levels contribute to higher levels (emergent properties)	+	+	+	+	++	+++
Upper levels constrain lower levels (downward constraint)	+	+	+	+	++	+++
Centralization and convergence of levels	+	–	–	–	+	++
Representation (modeling)	+/–	+/–	–	–	+	++

*Soma refers here to the body not including a nervous system. CNS = central nervous system.

teractions between parts create emergent properties at higher levels of organization and the holons created at higher levels constrain individual entities at lower levels. There is no centralization in the sense that a single holon controls all others, but rather the entire collective system considered as the highest level of organization imposes self-constraint upon its parts. Rates of interaction, as in non-nested hierarchies, are left undetermined, and dependent on the specific hierarchy.

Using these basic properties of hierarchies, how are the several natural hierarchies of living things, and especially conscious living things, organized along these dimensions?

Level 1: The Soma Minus the Brain

The simplest natural hierarchy that can be analyzed in a straightforward way is an organism comprised of a single cell or a collection of cells lacking a nervous system. Entities of this kind can vary, for example, from an amoeba or paramecium to a single liver cell within the human body to an entire organ like a lung or kidney. These are all are examples of nested hierarchies. In each of these entities, all the sub-cellular and cellular constituents of the cell contribute to the various life-sustaining processes of the organism, but the "life" of the entire organism is a collective or "emergent" property of the entire system.

In a simple organism without a nervous system, there is no collective top-down constraint, nor is there a centralization of the action of all the parts. This does not mean the parts do not interact, nor does it mean there is no constraint of the entire system upon its parts, but rather that there is no single, unified, or overall controlling entity at the top of the hierarchy. I would call this *constraint without convergence*, and without convergence, there can be no central representation, self, or consciousness. Finally, as with any nested hierarchy, the parts within different levels interact but the rates of interaction may be over relatively long intervals. For instance, the effect of a blood cell on the spleen is very slow, measured in minutes, hours, or even days, while operations in the brain take place in milliseconds. This is another limitation that makes this sort of system, although capable of life, incapable of creating consciousness.

LEVEL 2: REFLEXES WITHOUT CONSCIOUSNESS

Just as the digestive system is physically composed of the organs within it, the neural cortex is physically composed of its constituent neurons, and like other less complex systems in the body, these neural systems can operate reflexively but nonetheless lack consciousness. Consider, for example, the pupillary light reflex. When a bright light is shined into the eye, the light stimulus reaches the retina and stimulates the retinal ganglian cells that project via the optic nerve to centers in the midbrain. These centers then activate a cranial nerve that connects to a muscle in the iris of the eye causing it to constrict. This mechanism allows the person's vision to adjust to the degree of light present and protect the eye from excessive and potentially harmful light rays. This reflex will operate if the individual is asleep, in some degrees of coma, and even if there is considerable brain damage that spares these midbrain centers and nerves. In other words, while this is a nervous system function, it is one that does not require consciousness.

When the reflex and the pathways and centers that create it are considered as a system, we see that while the lower order elements in the reflex—retina, optic nerve, midbrain nuclei, and cranial nerve—are not physically nested within each other, they are functionally nested within the overall reflexive system. Further, while higher and lower levels of the neuroaxis operate in conjunction to create the overall reflex, one critical distinction of this level hierarchy is that centralization of levels is not necessary for the reflexes to operate. Hence, while upper levels may constrain, control, and influence lower levels, they are *not necessary* for the reflex to run its course, and the reflex may operate in a serial fashion—like a series of dominoes falling one after another—all within one level of the neuroaxis. For example, while higher level brain damage may influence the force of a lower level knee jerk reflex, even in the total absence of the brain these lower level spinal reflexes can operate. This is, of course, not true of consciousness which requires the centralization of neural activity for its very existence. Therefore, while the parts of the reflex may display functionally nested properties, there is no centralization of levels, and therefore there can be no central representation of levels, and hence no consciousness or self.

LEVEL 3: CENTRAL NERVOUS SYSTEM FUNCTIONS WITH CONSCIOUSNESS

It is at this level that things begin to get complicated. We have seen how, in a purely somatic system (Level 1), entities at any given level of the hierarchy provide mutual constraint upon each other. For example, when we consider the functions of the human body, within the cardiopulmonary system, as blood oxygen levels decline, our respiratory rate will demonstrate a compensatory increase. But within the system of an organ or organism without a nervous system, there is no overall centralized hierarchical control of the entire system. One might say at the level of the entire organism the hierarchy in this instance is functionally flat, with no central command functions at the higher levels of the system and no convergence of lower levels upon higher levels that create higher level properties. Thus, although lower levels contribute to the operations of the whole, the system as a whole has no unified central control, as one would see in a non-nested hierarchy such as Koestler's army. The system as a whole provides the constraint of the entire hierarchy. The same is true of simple reflexes like a knee jerk or the light reflex (Level 2), which can operate without centralized control.

In contrast, when we analyze the functions of the nervous system during behaviors that entail consciousness, we have seen that there is a pattern of centralization of the activity of the entire system that is a characteristic of a non-nested hierarchy. As lower level information is conveyed ultimately to the highest levels of the organization, as illustrated in Figure 6-1, the highest levels of the hierarchy have more abstract and integrated responses characteristics relative to lower levels, which have more specific and narrow information and more abstract response characteristics than neurons positioned earlier (upstream) in perceptual pathways. As we have seen, this process of topical convergence can produce "higher order" cells that possess amazingly abstract and specific response properties. This arrangement appears more typical of a non-nested hierarchy, where a "grandmother" cell is activated by a given higher level property of a stimulus, such as a face.

However, this same system also demonstrates *at the same time* patterns that are characteristic of nested hierarchies. We have already seen that the conscious representation of a face requires contributions from diverse and widely separated brain regions at upper and lower levels of the system. In the same way that an individual organelle makes a contribution to the life of a entire cell in a nested hierarchy, in the hierarchy of a mind and a self, all the lower order elements that make up total awareness of the face make a contribution to consciousness. Therefore, in terms of the parameters outlined in Table 6-1, lower order features combine in consciousness as "part of"—or *nested* within—higher order features.

For another illustration of the principle of nestedness in perception, consider watching an apple fall from a tree. The overall shape of the apple is composed of tens of thousands of individual line segments. A lower order feature, for instance, the stem, emerges in awareness as "part of"—or *nested* within—something else, in this case the overall shape of the apple. Short line segments are bound to longer line segments to create the outline of the apple, just as a small patch of red of the apple is bound to a larger red patch that is part of the redness of the entire image. Further downstream as the consciousness representation evolves, the redness of the apple is bound to its shape, which is bound to its movement as it falls from the tree, which is eventually bound to the "thud" it makes when it hits the ground. All of these various and anatomically distributed representations are bound together to create the entire conscious experience. Therefore, to say an element is "bound" to another is simply another way of saying that they are represented in awareness *dependently* and are *nested* together. Further, the more bound one element is to another is a reflection of their degree of mutual restedness. And as noted above, consistent with hierarchical principles, lower order elements are more tightly bound to each other than higher order elements. Finally, at the highest levels of the hierarchy, color, shape, and movement are nested together within the image of the apple and this image in turn is nested within the entire scene.

The nested quality of awareness is manifest as well when one considers the interactions between the intero- and extero aspects of the self described in chapter 5. If we are stuck by a pin on the finger, we feel the pain in the finger as "coming from" the pin. The quality of pain ascends the neural hierarchy within the interoself system up and beyond to the insular cortex. But at the same time, the extero system aspects of seeing the pin prick the surface of the skin is integrated with the experience of pain. What enters into awareness ultimately is the *entire nested experience* of feeling a sharp pinprick on the tip of the finger. All aspects of the experience are nested within consciousness in spite of the widely distributed neural substrate of the experience. If consciousness were not organized as a nested hierarchy, the unified aspects of awareness would not be possible.

Therefore, where any conscious and voluntary system is concerned, the hierarchy displays features of *both* non-nested and nested hierarchies, and in this regard appears to be unique among biological and non-biological systems. Only the nervous system operates such that it *simultaneously* functions in both a nested and non-nested fashion at both the neurocellular and global levels. How is this remarkable aspect of neurological functioning achieved?

This problem was addressed early on by the great neurophysiologist Sir Charles Sherrington, who pondered the question of mental unity as well. Like Descartes before him, Sherrington wondered how was it possible that there is a "singleness" of normal binocular vision when either eye alone is able to generate a separate mental image? Sherrington noted that normally:

Our binocular visual field is shown by analysis, to presuppose out-
look from the body by a single eye centered at a point in the mid-
vertical of the forehead at the level of the root of his nose. It,
unconsciously, takes for granted that its seeing is done by a cyclopean eye having a center of rotation at the point of intersection just
mentioned.[21]

Therefore, when we use both eyes to see, simply put, the mind
seems to observe with a virtual single eye, a point of visual synthesis located somewhere between our eyes and behind the top of our
nose. Our subjective experience is as though there were a single *cyclopean eye* looking out from this point on the forehead, and it is from
this central—and single—vantage point that we visually experience
the world as a coherent entity. The enigmatic feature of this subjective experience of unification is that we do not have an eye physically located in the middle of the forehead, nor do we have a point of
convergence within the brain where the information of the two eyes
can be united. Rather, the brain works in a fashion such that we *seem*
to have a central, cyclopean eye.

In terms of the hierarchy theory outlined above, we may say that
the lower order elements, in this case the information about the visual field that comes from each eye, is *constrained* to combine into a
single unified visual percept. This constraint or control of the whole
upon the parts does not suggest the elimination of these individual
parts from the mind because the image from each eye continues to
make a contribution to the unified cyclopean eye.

In the case of the cyclopean eye, top down constraint serves two
purposes. First, it allows us to see a single visual percept instead of
two independent—and not terribly useful—images. Second, by integrating the information generated by each eye independently the
brain creates an additional—emergent—feature of the visual scene,
depth perception, a feature of visual awareness that is only possible
by the integration of visual information emanating from both eyes.
In order to create cyclopean perception, the brain does not "physi-

cally" merge the two visual images, one from each eye. Rather, the two images create a mental condition where their meanings are conjointly represented in awareness to produce a higher level of meaning. In the cyclopean eye, the higher level of meaning is that of a single image now seen in depth. It is the higher meaning of the combined images that produces the "top-down" constraint upon the individual elements. Constraint leads to the elimination of the *independence* of each part from each other when operating within the framework of the nested hierarchy of consciousness. By saying that these parts are represented dependently we are also saying that they are represented meaningfully in consciousness.

In the hierarchy of our conscious awareness, it is *meaning* that provides the constraint that "pulls" the mind together to form the "inner I" of the self. When the control of action is considered as a nested hierarchy, it is *purpose* that provides the constraint and guiding force of the self, the "ghost in the machine."[22] The actions of the neurons at these lower levels of the hierarchy are nested within the higher levels of the hierarchy and the purpose of the act provides the *constraint* of higher levels upon lower levels of the motor hierarchy. A single muscle fiber in your tongue may fire exactly the same way whether you are delivering a soliloquy from *Hamlet* or licking a crumb from your upper lip. At the lowest level of the hierarchy the individual cells do not care or know why they do what they do. It is only through the constraint of the higher order purpose of the act that the cells are bound into meaningful unified action. And the greater the degree of constraint over nested parts within a hierarchy, the greater a behavior is purposive and therefore conscious.

How Does the Brain Do It?

The actual manner in which the microstructure of the brain physically provides the constraint that creates this nested structure is an interesting question. One plausible way to explain binding in the visual system is that the brain uses synchronized oscillations to unify perception.[23] The idea here is that perceptual binding occurs by co-ordination in time, rather than by convergence in space, and there is increasing experimental evidence that indeed widely spatially distributed neural networks integrate—in systems terminology, *entify*—a stimulus by temporally synchronizing the firing of neurons or groups of neurons representing the same stimulus. Thus, neurons that are responding to the same object are able to represent that object in consciousness as an integrated percept because they are firing their response to that object in temporal synchrony. It may be that a similar cross-modal synchrony could also be responsible for binding elements from different sensory modalities into single and unified percepts.[24]

One notable finding speaks to the relationship between synchrony and hierarchical arrangement in the cyclopean eye we have just considered. In most cases, we have the subjective experience of cyclopean vision when the two eyes are properly aligned when viewing one visual field or stimulus. If the two eyes are misaligned, or do not see the same visual scene entirely, one experiences *binocular rivalry*. In this circumstance, only the information from one or the other eye will reach consciousness, and the brain will switch back and forth between seeing from one eye or the other. It is as if the brain demands that experience be unified. But in the clinical condition known as *strabismus* (lazy eye), the axes of the two eyes are misaligned and visual fusion does not occur. Under these conditions, with both eyes open the patient may "see double" if the information from both eyes is active in the brain, or may see a single image from one or the other eye if one image is suppressed within the brain.

In one study, Professor Pascal Fries of the Netherlands and his colleagues studied cats with strabismus and binocular rivalry and indeed found that when one or the other eye was responsible for the information that reached awareness (the dominant eye) the neurons in the early stages of visual awareness fired in synchrony.[25] At the same time, the neurons responsive to the suppressed eye that did not reach awareness showed no temporal correlated firing. This correlation between synchronized temporal firing and conscious awareness has been demonstrated in numerous investigations across various species and in motor and memory systems in addition to all sensory systems. These researchers do not claim that synchrony is the *only* mechanism for creating consciousness, and clearly the sort of convergent pathways described above for the visual system must contribute to consciousness. But these data indicate that temporal synchrony plays an important—perhaps necessary—role in access to consciousness.[26] With the nested model I propose, temporal synchrony could provide the constraint necessary for perceptual binding and serve as an essential mechanism for structuring the hierarchical arrangements of consciousness and the self.

What is true in the case of visual perception may be true for more complex neural operations as well. Professors Andreas Engel and Wolf Singer, two of the pioneers in synchrony research suggest that temporal synchrony could play an essential role in the creation of higher order consciousness:

> Consciousness may require the embedding of contents into progressively higher-order contexts, both in space and time. This recursive embedding might be mediated by hierarchical binding of assemblies into higher-order arrangements, which could be achieved, for instance, by multiplexing of interactions in different frequency bands. Such higher-order bindings could form the basis for "meta-representations" necessary to incorporate low-level contents into global world-and self-models. [27,28]

Thus, a combination of convergent hierarchical pathways and higher level temporal oscillation could provide sufficient integration of neural activity to enable the binding across hierarchical levels to provide for a nested hierarchical consciousness.[29] It may be that in the earliest stages of processing, bottom-up feature detection cells are critical, while as processing progresses, top down temporal synchrony is necessary for the organization of higher order analysis and hence final awareness. It is likely, therefore, that the brain uses many mechanisms to perceptually bind objects in awareness, including convergence as well as synchronized oscillations. Nonetheless, whatever mechanisms the brain uses to bind objects, it seems clear that these various mechanisms operate within the hierarchical parameters I've proposed.

A singularly important factor that contributes to these differences between general functions of the body and functions of the nervous system, but one that does not get sufficient attention, is the speed of interaction between the parts and levels of the systems. The snail's pace of interaction evident in general somatic functions becomes in the nervous system the nearly instantaneous communication with the brain. The importance of this variable cannot be overemphasized. The rapid communication between levels that the nervous system possesses, as compared to the relatively sluggish speed of communication between the hierarchical levels of a tree, a liver, or even an entire human body, makes all the other properties we have considered—emergence, constraint, and centralization—possible. Without the speed provided by neurochemical-electrical transmission of nerve impulses, consciousness most likely would never have evolved.

REPRESENTATION, MODELING, AND MAPS

A final essential difference between a nervous system with and without consciousness is the role of maps, representation, or modeling. The modeling functions of the brain are surely one of its most obvious features and one that must necessarily be emphasized, and the subject of much speculation regarding this function for a philosophy of consciousness and the self.[30] One thing is certain—the brain is literally filled with neural maps, some of which encode aspects of the external environment, while others represent aspects of the self. Many of these maps in the brain maintain a rough spatial relationship to what is being mapped in the external environment or the body. For example, in the somatic sensory system there are four complete cortical maps in the primary sensory region in the parietal lobe, each one responsive to a different type of somatic stimulus. These neural maps represent multiple, somewhat distorted, but fairly complete representations of the body's surface, and are referred to as *somatotopic* maps. In the visual system, the spatial relations of visual field are preserved in multiple visual regions in the brain that are referred to as *retinotopic*. However, not all cortical maps are spatially organized in correspondence to a physical dimension of external space or the body, and these cortical arrangements are more appropriately referred to generally as *neural representations*. For instance, the auditory system is arranged such that neurons responsive to tones close in frequency are arranged in a *tonotopic* map.[31]

In the visual system we have seen how the modeling functions of the world are built upon hierarchical principles, and the same is true of other sensory systems. The point I wish to emphasize here is that whatever maps or representations we are considering, and which are all uniquely neurological and a necessary property of mind and self, they are only made possible by the brain's hierarchical structure. The auditory system operates within a tonotopic hierarchy and there are hierarchical principles at work in the olfactory and gustatory systems as well. For example, the olfactory system displays a *chemotopic* organization that is present in the olfactory bulb and may have some preservation within the olfactory projection regions in the cortex.[32] Whatever system we consider, without hierarchy there could be no somatotopic maps.

Level 4: Brain with Consciousness and Self-Awareness

Having thus viewed in some detail how neural hierarchies operate at Levels 1 to 3, I believe the idea of self-awareness can now be demystified. When viewed within the perspective of biological hierarchical organization, the self, and the process of self-awareness, are simply the result of the greatest number of constituent parts, the highest degree of centralization, and the highest degree of constraint achieved by the nervous system. Indeed, when viewed within this model, there appears to be a natural progression in complexity that leads from consciousness in, for example, a rat or dog, to the self-consciousness present in some higher primates and humans. Rather than there being anything "special" about human self-aware-ness compared to other primates, it is merely a matter of degree as the more evolved and advanced human nervous system begins to take the self into consideration as an object with reference to other objects and other selves.[33] The achievement of the human self, of Tulving's autonoetic awareness, is the outcome of an increasingly complex but ontologically necessary hierarchical arrangement of the nervous system.

It is my belief that, once hierarchical Level 3 has been achieved, the fundamental parameters of consciousness change in degree but do not change in kind. Rather, I have argued that the highest level of the self attained—the self that we think of as the human self—is char-acterized by the higher degrees of *meaning* and *purpose* that can only be achieved by the increasingly complex hierarchy of the human nervous system. In perception, the highest level of meaning provides the hierarchical constraint for the billions of neurons involved in human perception, and the highest levels of purpose provide the constraint for the most complex human actions. These two ele-ments—meaning and purpose—are the artist of the mind and the en-gine of the soul, and both are made possible—indeed may only be possible—by the hierarchical organization of the brain.

In the preceding chapters I have laid out the parameters of the neu-ral hierarchy that contribute to the creation of the self, first high-lighting the physical composition of the nervous system that might embody the self, and then demonstrating how the functional fea-tures of the neural hierarchy are in a unique position to contribute to mental synthesis. In the next chapter I will tackle the remaining question surrounding the most profound and still unexplained as-pects of the self and consciousness: the relationship between brain, mind, and the self.

CHAPTER SEVEN

The Self and Consciousness

To UNDERSTAND the most advanced hierarchical levels of the self presented in the last chapter is to understand that self and consciousness are intimately—indeed indissociably—related. However the fact remains that the relationship between the self, consciousness, and the brain remains largely unexplored. In this chapter I will explore how the self relates to consciousness, and in so doing unlock some of the mysteries surrounding the as yet unexplained basis of consciousness itself.

It may seem surprising that an argument about whether or not the self even exists continues to this day. The philosopher William James likened the self to a "cheap and nasty edition of the soul" and argued that while the idea of a self may have a place in religion, the concept had no place in scientific discourse.[1] Daniel Dennett, in his book *Consciousness Explained*, sums up nicely why the belief in the self remains so controversial and why great minds can come to such diametrically opposed points of view:

> Since the dawn of modern science in the seventeenth century, there
> has been nearly unanimous agreement that the self, whatever it is,

would be invisible under a microscope, and invisible to introspection, too. For some, this has suggested that the self was a nonphysical soul, a ghost in the machine. For others, it has suggested that the self was nothing at all, a figment of metaphysically fevered imaginations. And for still others, it has suggested only that a self was in one way or another a sort of abstraction, something whose existence was not in the slightest impugned by its invisibility. After all, one might say, a center of gravity is just as invisible—and just as real. Is that real enough? The question of whether there really are selves can be made to look ridiculously easy to answer, in either direction. . . ."[2]

Philosopher David Chalmers has simply framed the "neurophilosophical" problem of the nature of consciousness into so-called "easy" and "hard" problems. Easy problems, those that are already understood or theoretically can be solved unproblematically in the future, include questions such as how the brain controls attention, how the retina responds to a light stimulus, or how synapses of the brain communicate with one other. These problems can be examined objectively and make no reference to subjective experience. The hard problem of consciousness, however, is why do certain neurological states feel the particular way that they do? As Chalmers put it:

> The really hard problem of consciousness is the problem of *experience*. When we think and perceive, there is a whir of information-processing, but there is also a subjective aspect. . . . This subjective aspect is experience. When we see, for example, we *experience* visual sensations: the felt quality of redness, the experience of dark and light, the quality of depth in a visual field. Other experiences go along with perception in different modalities: the sound of a clarinet, the smell of mothballs. Then there are bodily sensations, from pains to orgasms; mental images that are conjured up internally; the felt quality of emotion, and the experience of a stream of conscious thought. What unites all of these states is that there is something it is like to be in them. All of them are states of experience.[3]

I am sure there are many questions about consciousness, the mind, and the self that are of concern to philosophers, neurobiologists, social scientists, and certainly theologians, but these questions are not within my purview, which is understanding the nature of the self and its relationship to the brain. And the "hard problem" for a neurological understanding of the brain and consciousness is that there appear to be features of subjective experience *that are not reducible* to neurons when they are objectively observed and analyzed.

Chalmer's view that consciousness—and therefore the self—cannot be fully reduced to brain functions has been most firmly and coherently affirmed in the writings of the philosopher John Searle, who first introduced the concept of *ontological subjectivity*. The idea here is that conscious states have features that are irreducibly first-person which cannot simply be reduced to the nervous system:

> Because conscious states are subjective in this sense, they have what I call a first-person ontology, as opposed to the third-person ontology of mountains and molecules, which can exist even if no living creatures exist. Subjective conscious states have a first-person ontology ("ontology" here means mode of existence) because they exist only when they are experienced by some human or animal agent. They are experienced by some "I" that has the experience, and it is in that sense that they have a first-person ontology.[4]

Searle claimed that it was impossible to reduce consciousness—and I would add the self—to the physiological functions of the nervous system in the way that, for instance, we can explain diabetes by a lack of sufficient production of insulin by the pancreas or the pumping of blood to the contractions of heart muscle. And surely, when we try to reduce consciousness and self to the workings of axons of the brain, we find there are some fundamental features of consciousness that are not readily reducible.

Although there are many thorny and hotly debated issues regarding the nature of why we experience the world the way we do, in order to simplify this complex issue, I have condensed the "hard problem" of ontological subjectivity to three major concerns:

Table 7-1. Ontologically subjective features of consciousness. There are at least three features of consciousness that are not entirely reducible to brain states (*ontological subjectivity*). These non-reducible features are the result of and explained by the *nested neural hierarchy*.

Lower order systems (nonconscious)	Higher order systems (conscious)
Objectively distributed	Subjectively unified
No qualia	Qualia
No Intentionality	Intentionality–(meaning, purpose)

First, while we experience a unified consciousness, there appears to be an ontological difference between the unified mind—that is, the sense of the self or "I"—and the component parts of the divisible brain. This is known as the *grain problem*, or the problem of *mental unity*.[5] Second, it appears that any explanation of the working of the brain "leaves something out," namely how something feels. This is the *explanatory gap* or the *qualia problem*.[6] Third, there is the problem of *intentionality* of neural states, that is, why the activity of our own brains are subjectively experienced not as the axons and dendrites that create them but rather as "things" outside of them or beyond them, such as the knowledge of objects in the world. These fundamental problems of consciousness, I believe, can only be explained with reference to the neural hierarchy of the self that I have delineated in the previous chapter, or what I call the *Neural Hierarchy Theory of Consciousness (NHTC)*.[7]

Mental Unity

The first of these problems, the problem of mental unity, is only a problem, of course, if we consider the self a unified entity in the first place, and there actually is considerable controversy on this point.

The philosopher Emanuel Kant, in his monumental work *Critique of Pure Reason*, argued that not only was the self a real and integrated entity, but the unity of consciousness and therefore a unified self was an *a priori* fact of all knowledge of the world:

> There cannot be any knowledge within us nor can knowledge be connected and unified within itself without unity of consciousness preceding all empirical data and serving to make possible all representation of objects. This pure, original, and unchangeable consciousness I call 'transcendental apperception'.[8]

In his wonderfully insightful book *Philosophy, Psychiatry, and Neuroscience*, the psychiatrist Edward M. Hundert reiterates the Kantian philosophy that an integrated self comes before all other meaningful experiences. Indeed it makes all meaningful experience possible:

> . . . personal identity is not some product of my experiences, to be found by searching through my experiences for a common theme or set of themes. Personal identity, in the Kantian view, is a *condition* not a *product* of human experience: the "self" must already be involved in actively connecting or uniting my experiences or I would not have a continuing self-consciousness through which to begin searching.[9]

Perhaps the most personally compelling reason we intuitively feel that the unified self must exist is our subjective feeling of our own unified existence. For my part, I awake each morning with the feeling that the various parts of my body and my mind pretty much work together. I do not have the sense that I need to gather up my arms and legs to get to work. When I look out my window, I do not have to slowly piece together the scene into a unified whole and add on "I must be seeing this." Rather my brain integrates fairly automatically and swiftly the visual experience into a unified and subjectively personal whole.

But in addition to our subjective feeling that we exist in a normally integrated state, there are several good scientific arguments that support the proposition that the self is real and unified. For example, if an integrated subjective self exists, and it depends upon a physically integrated brain, then it follows that by disturbing the brain's integrity, the self should also become disunited. Indeed, this is what in certain cases and in certain ways occurs.

Indeed, as we have seen in early chapters, there are numerous neurological conditions in which the patient's sense of self has been seriously disturbed. Another neurological condition that demonstrates the potential frailty of the self is known as the *alien hand syndrome* or *anarchic hand syndrome*, in which patients who have sustained certain types of brain damage appear to possess a hand that seems to have a "mind of its own" and behaves in a way that is in conflict with the patient's stated intentions. The first reported instance of alien hand syndrome was described by the renowned German neurologist Kurt Goldstein, who in 1908 recounted the now famous case of a 57-year-old woman who claimed that her left hand acted in a seemingly purposeful manner of its own accord.

> On one occasion the hand grabbed her own neck and tried to throttle her, and could only be pulled off by force. Similarly, it tore off the bed covers against the patient's will. . . . She soon is complaining about her hand; that it is a law unto itself, an organ without will [willen-loses Werkzeug]; when once it has got hold of something, it refuses to let go: "I myself can do nothing with it; if I'm having a drink and it gets hold of the glass, it won't let go and spills [the drink] out. Then I hit it and say: Behave yourself, hand [literally, mein Händchen]" (Smiling,) "I suppose there must be an evil spirit in it."[10]

Although there are different forms of the alien hand syndrome, the most clear-cut examples are caused by a pure *disconnection* of the right and left hemispheres, known as the *split-brain* syndrome.[11,12] For instance, the condition is known to occur in patients who have had their corpus callosum—the main white matter pathway connecting

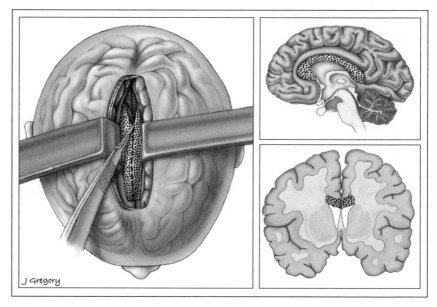

Figure 7-1. The corpus callosum as seen from top (left side of figure) saggital (right top) and coronal (right bottom) views. The corpus callosum is shown in blue. In the diagram on the left the patient is shown undergoing a corpus callosotomy in which the corpus callosum is cut, surgically disconnecting the hemispheres. After this operation the patient may have a left alien hand that performs actions that are in opposition to the patient's conscious intentions.

the two hemispheres—surgically cut for the control of epileptic seizures or as a result of a stroke (Figure 7-1). In the alien hand cases due to callosal lesions, the anarchic hand is typically if not always on the left side.

Under these conditions certain functions that are normally united across the two hemispheres may be disconnected. For instance, if an image is flashed briefly in the left visual field, because the visual fields are largely crossed in the brain, the stimulus will be initially received in the opposite—in this case the right—hemisphere. Under normal circumstances in the intact brain that information would then cross the corpus callosum and be registered in the left (typically verbal) hemisphere and the patient would then be able to verbally report what the stimulus was. However, if the corpus callosum is cut, the information that is received in the right hemisphere is disconnected from the left hemisphere, and the patient may not even know that the right hemisphere saw anything, much less be able to report on what it was.

For a similar reason, the patient's hands may not always work in a coordinated fashion, as if one hand literally did not know what the other hand was doing. At other times, the hands may actually work toward opposite goals, fight with one other, or attack the patient. Some of the reported examples of the behavior of patients with alien syndrome are astonishing:

> You should have seen RY yesterday—one hand was buttoning up his shirt and the other hand was coming along right behind it undoing the buttons![13]

> . . . while doing the block design test unimanually with his right hand, his left hand came up from beneath the table and was reaching for the blocks when he slapped it with his right hand and said, "That will keep it quiet for a while."[13]

> . . . putting his glasses on his nose with the right hand and removing them with the left.[14]

> . . . while the patient was trying to open a case with his right hand, the left prevented him . . . when asked to write with his left hand, his right one took the sheet of paper and dropped it to the floor; when asked why he had done that, he denied having performed such an act.[14]

> She awoke several times with her left hand choking her, and while she was awake her left hand would unbutton her gown, crunch cups on her tray, and fight with the right hand while she was answering the phone. . . . She described this unpleasant sensation as if someone "from the moon" were controlling her hand.[15]

... she could not tie a rope by herself as the left hand would not help the right and at times even tried to inhibit the action. When she held a piece of paper with both hands, each hand would pull against each other . . . the left hand would not release the telephone when she wanted to use it with her right hand . . . she felt as if the left hand was under someone else's control.[16]

It woke me up one night, it [the left hand] was around my neck . . . I had to take it down before it did any damage . . . it gets into the most wierdest places. Sometimes it will actually hunt for my other hand . . . sometimes when I'm trying to eat it will grab my right and it just won't let me get a fork or a spoon full of food. . . . It is always looking at destruction because it will always work against me . . . it's times like that when I think it doesn't like me. That's the child in it I think.[17]

My hand [the patient's left hand after a split brain procedure] had a mind of its own, right from the beginning. From the moment I woke My hand, it was right there. It did whatever it wanted to do. I would light a cigarette and my hand would put it out. . . . It was sitting in an ash tray it would put it out. . . . Or it would light another cigarette. I would be on the phone and it would actually disconnect the phone. . . . I did not understand what was going on. I would be trying to eat and it would take the fork out of my hand . . . doing the dishes . . . if my hand doesn't want to do the dishes it shuts the water off. . . . it must do those things I don't allow myself to do. . . . you have to be watching it all the time! [With drawers] If I try to open it, it will shut it, if I try to shut it will open it. Basically it does the opposite of what I'm trying to do. [When playing cars] My hand tries to change the plays my right hand makes [I ask: It could be a better move?] Yes! Yes! My hand tries to fix them so I just let it go. Let it do whatever it has to do. Usually it makes it better. Its absolutely incredible. . . . Its amazing. Its amazing.[18]

Finally, in Stanley Kubrick's Cold War classic, *Dr. Strangelove or: How I Learned to Stop Worrying and Love the Bomb* (1964) a crazed Air Force

General initiates a nuclear attack on Russia with B-52 bombers.   As
the planes make their way to Russia, some of the hawks in the Pen-
tagon actually try to convince the President to see the attack
through, but it turns out that even if the President warns the Sovi-
ets of the attack—which he does—total mutual annihilation is still as-
sured because of a Doomsday Device that the Russians had installed
in case of a nuclear strike. In one of the most memorable scenes in
the movie, the President summons "Dr. Strangelove," a former Nazi
portrayed by Peter Sellers in one of his signature roles, to seek his ad-
vice on how to manage the crisis. Strangelove is clearly neurologically impaired and confined to a wheelchair, but the most prominent
odd behavior he displays is that his leather-gloved right hand invol-
untarily gives the Nazi salute or goes for Strangelove's own throat in
an apparent effort to strangle him. The similarity between Strangelove's behavior and the alien hand syndrome is so striking that in
fact, the syndrome is sometimes known as the "Dr. Strangelove Syndrome."

Thus, if you cut the pathways between brain regions, you can *partially* sever the wholeness of the self. However the split brain patients do not become "two people in one head." There are remaining
inter-hemispheric connections that can provide cross-communica-
tion between the hemispheres, and most importantly, the singular
brainstem of the split-brain patient remains undivided. In most respects mental unity and the unified self is preserved. However, what
the alien hand cases do demonstrate is that complete mental integrity depends upon anatomical continuity of brain regions, and
under normal circumstances, with the brain intact, the self function
as a whole.

I believe that the key to mental unity lies within the unique nature of the neural hierarchy and its relationship to consciousness
that I have previously described (Table 6-1). As we've seen, lower levels of the neural hierarchy, in contrast to the body in general, are *not*

physically nested within higher levels. Thus the thalamus, which appears at a higher level, although it is reciprocally connected to the
lower levels of the midbrain, is not physically composed of the midbrain in the same way that say the liver, a higher level, is composed
of liver cells at a lower level of organization. And the cortex, although it is reciprocally connected to the thalamus is not physically
composed of the thalamus, any more than the thalamus is physically
composed of the midbrain. These hierarchically arranged levels are
physically distinct and not physically nested within each other. In
contrast, when we consider the higher levels of the nested hierarchy
of the self (Table 6-1, Levels 3 and 4) we witness a remarkable—and
neurologically unique—functional feature of the process of consciousness and the self. At higher levels of the neural hierarchy, consciousness is unified since lower elements in the neural hierarchy
are *functionally* nested, bound, and unified within higher levels on the
hierarchy.

Further, here we can unpack an essential aspect of ontological
subjectivity of mental unity (Table 7-1). The structure of the nervous
system, unlike the form of the body in general, when objectively examined is not *physically* a nested hierarchy; however, like the body,
the brain's functions—its process—globally operates in a *hierarchically
nested* and unified fashion. From the standpoint of the neuroscientist, the separable parts of my brain, the individual cells of which it
is comprised, are organized into a hierarchically arranged non-
nested hierarchy with lower order elements physically independent
of higher order elements. However as the possessor of that brain, I
experience the very same brain—its process—in a *hierarchically nested*
and unified fashion. Hence the ontological realities of these two
viewpoints upon *the same organ at the same time* are ontologically non-
reducible. These two views are scientifically compatible, but they are
mutually irreducible. As far as I can tell, this is a feature of the brain
that is entirely unique within nature.

Qualia

If this account of mental unity provides an adequate explanation for the non-reducibility of mental states when viewed objectively as opposed to when they are experienced subjectively, what about the other two non-reducible aspects, qualia and intentionality?

Qualia, the way things subjectively feel—such as why red feels different from blue, and why blue feels different from cold—are *par excellence* ontologically subjective. As the proverbial tree does not make a sound when it falls in the forest if there is no one to hear it, there are no sounds, smells, tastes, or pain "in the world" if there are no neural systems to experience them. No sensation from an objective standpoint has the same ontological status as when it is subjectively experienced, and indeed qualia would not exist were it not for brains. This much is obvious, but this simple observation has led some to claim that qualia do not "exist" or that they are ineffable, mysterious, and beyond human understanding.

Let me suggest that qualia are simply the products of the interactions of neural levels we have previously described, and are therefore uniquely biological, hierarchical, and ontologically subjective. Qualitative experiences reflect and can only be related to the neurobiological hierarchy that creates them. Consider, for example, the sensation of pain as it would be modeled along the lines of Figure 5-5 where I outlined the neural hierarchy of the self. Pain begins with select neurons that are responsive to a particular constellation of tissue-damaging stimuli. But these lower level neurons are not themselves capable of feeling "pain." What is required is for these primitive responses to ascend the neural hierarchy to create the *experience* of pain. According to one hierarchy of pain pathways, pain is ultimately elaborated in the insular and cingulate cortices that are interacting with the lower and the higher levels of the neural hierarchy.[19] Without these structures and the physiological interactions between levels, there is no pain. Therefore pain, or any quale for the matter, is a uniquely biological product of the interactions between hierarchically arranged neural levels.

From the standpoint of ontological subjectivity, the critical point here is that any sensation is uniquely related to the neural systems that create it, not to the stimuli in the environment to which it responds. There is no mandatory relationship between the particular wavelengths of light in the world and certain ontologically subjective experiences. A nervous system made up of some other type of neural tissue—or on some other planet—would have a very different experience of the physical properties of light that create "red" in our minds. But there is a mandatory relationship in our world between certain neural pathways in the human brain and certain conscious experiences. In our brains, the visual occipital lobe can feel color but cannot feel pain, and the insular cortex cannot see a tree but can embody pain.

Therefore, qualia are ontologically subjective for two reasons. First the neural systems that create sensations are only relative to neural levels and their interactions themselves, and not to anything outside or beyond these neural levels including the world to which these neural systems respond or the standpoint of the outside observer. There are things that exist in the world outside of our brains, but the quality of the experience of these things only exists within the mind. So certain wavelengths of light cannot be reduced to our experiences of them, and the "outside" observations of neurons cannot be reduced to one's "inside" experience of them.

Second, since all experiences are the result of the interactions between neural levels, they represent a process, not an observable thing, such as rock, or a pancreas, or even the brain itself. Thus, just as "life" is an abstraction based upon physiological actions, *consciousness is the process that the brain does.* We will return to this point at greater length in the final chapter.

Intentionality

I have grouped the last set of ontologically subjective features of the brain under the term "intentionality," a quality that philosophers have for centuries argued is one of the essential characteristics of the mind. The use of the word "intentionality" dates to medieval times and is derived from the Latin verb *intendo*, which means "to point at" or "extend toward." The seventeenth century German philosopher and psychologist Franz Brentano argued that intentionality is the defining feature of mental processes, and only mental phenomena possess the characteristic of intentionality.

Searle describes intentionality, "the second intractable feature of the mind," as "the feature by which our mental states are directed at, or about, or refer to, or are of objects and states of affairs in the world other than themselves."[20] For example, beliefs are considered intentional because they are maintained *about* a state of affairs. A fear is considered an intentional state because it is a fear *of* something. Perceptual states are considered intentional because if I experience an object in the world, whether I see, hear, touch or smell it, then I have a perception *of* an object. In a similar way, action states are considered intentional when they are *directed at* something in the world.

The neurobiological basis of intentionality, the final pillar of ontological subjectivity, can be described as having at minimum two interrelated features that leads to the non-reducibility of its subjective aspects. First, when we compare neural states as they are externally observed to these same states when subjectively experienced, we can see that the brain has no sensation "of itself." It has been known since the time of Aristotle that the brain is insensate, so that for instance sticking a pin, or the surgeon's knife, into the cortex evokes no pain that is referable to the brain itself.[21] As Gordon

Globus, Professor Emeritus of Psychiatry and Philosophy, University of California, Irvine puts it, the brain does not "represent in any way its own structure to the subject."[22] Brain activity is never "about itself" and there is no way that someone can become objectively aware of the activity of his own neurons, "from the inside." They can be known only objectively from the "outside." So, for example, when I test a patient's sensitivity by applying a pinprick to the hand and asking where the pain is located, even though pain is registered in the brain I have never had a single patient point to his or her head. Conscious neural activity refers to external objects, not to the brain itself, and this relationship is at the heart of the notion of intentionality. This is the first reason why objectively observed brain states cannot be reduced to subjectively experienced conscious states.

Second, we saw in chapters five and six how neurons create ontologically subjective "meanings" and "purposes" and that these two aspects of the subjectively experienced self are generated within the nested neural hierarchy. In the context of the neurological model presented here, meanings are always "about something" with reference to the experiencing self. Whether I experience a red apple as "out there in the world" a few feet to my left, or a pain on the left side of my Adam's apple, these experiences always occur in the context of my experience of myself. In a similar way, reflexes and involuntary actions, for example the knee jerk or the constriction of the pupil to light, or even the withdrawal of the leg from a noxious stimulus, do not require purposiveness or consciousness. Purposeful actions that are experienced as "willful" and conscious are experienced as such with reference to the self performing the action.[23]

Thus a crucial defining feature of a meaningful perception and a purposeful action is *how it feels in relation to the self.* There is a clear-cut and undeniable subjective qualitative difference between having my pupil constrict from a ray of light while I am asleep and seeing the sun, and there is a subjective qualitative difference between a knee jerk and a willful kick of the leg. The former do not necessarily involve qualia, the latter by definition do. Thus, by the criteria of non-reducibility of qualia defined above, the subjective qualitative aspects of intentional neurological states will always remain non-reducible to the objectively observed brain states that create them because the subjective experience of these states occur in relation to the subjective sense of the self.

Thus, the problem of consciousness is very much related to the problem of the hierarchical nature of the nervous system and the self. The chief problem of the nature of consciousness—ontological subjectivity—can be understood as actually based upon three irreducible features of consciousness: mental unity, qualia, and intentionality. Further, these three features of consciousness are, within the constraints of our biologies, based upon the hierarchical arrangements of neurons. It is only within the parameters of the nested neural hierarchy that consciousness and intentionality are realized, and this physiology may indeed be ontologically necessary.

The relationships between the hierarchical systems of the brain, the higher aspects of consciousness, and the self are apparent. All three features of higher awareness—mental unity, qualia, and intentionality—only exist in relationship to more complex selves. The higher up this neural hierarchy a brain is functioning, the greater the differentiation and demarcation between the exterosensorimotor systems and the interoself, the self and the world, and the more that consciousness is present and the self unfolds. A simple primitive reflex such as a pupil's constriction in response to a beam of light has no mental unity, requires no feeling, and displays no conscious meaning or purpose. But it is the higher self that achieves and experiences the wholeness of being, feels the warmth of the sun and the pain of the flame, and appreciates the underlying meaning of a Picasso. As human brains matured through evolution, and our individual being develops along with our brains, so do the self, and hence consciousness, grow from axons to identity.

CHAPTER EIGHT

The Process of the Self

The Astonishing Hypothesis is that "You," your joys and your sorrows, your memories and your ambitions, your sense of personal identity and free will, are in fact no more than the behavior of a vast assembly of nerve cells and their associated molecules. As Lewis Carroll's Alice might have phrased it: You're nothing but a pack of neurons.

—FRANCIS CRICK[1]

... consciousness was conceived to be a dynamic emergent of brain activity, neither identical with, nor reducible to, the neural events of which it is mainly composed. Further, consciousness was not conceived as an epiphenomenon, inner aspect, or other passive correlate of brain processing, but rather to be an active integral part of the cerebral process itself, exerting potent causal effects in the interplay of cerebral operations. In a position of top command at the highest levels in the hierarchy of brain organization, the subjective properties were seen to exert control over the biophysical and chemical activities at subordinate levels. It was described initially as a brain model that puts "conscious mind back into the brain of objective science in a position of top command...a brain model in which conscious, mental, psychic forces are recognized to be the crowning achievement ... of evolution."

—ROGER SPERRY[2]

WHICH NOBEL LAUREATE is correct? Are we really just assembled in ways so that we have experiences, but are in actuality no more nor less than the sum and substance of the brain's parts? Or, as Sperry would have us believe, is there something more, something beyond the material brain, that gets to the heart of who we are as selves?

Francis Crick's "Astonishing Hypothesis" was that everything we are, our loves and fears, our minds and our identities are "nothing but a pack of neurons." To put it another way, there is no difference between our axons and our identities. I would like to present a different "astonishing hypothesis" that runs 180 degrees in the opposite direction. I propose that the view of the self as "just axons" is an impoverished perspective that simply misses the point of what it is to be human. A brain may be nothing more than a pack of neurons, but a person is surely more so. In this chapter I will look, finally, at the essence of the self as a process of the brain.

The Process of the Self

In the nineteenth century, Charles Darwin observed the structure of living things and deduced the *process* of evolution. In the twentieth century James Watson and Francis Crick observed the process of life and elucidated the *structure* of DNA. Today, one of the missions of neuroscience is to explain both the structure of the brain as well as the process of consciousness and the self. I believe that the greatest obstacle we face in this regard is that although Watson and Crick's discovery proved to be among the most significant discoveries of the twentieth century, we should follow Darwin's lead when it comes to understanding the self. The great nineteenth-century philosopher and psychologist William James already understood that consciousness must be viewed as process rather than structure when he wrote:

> To deny plumply that "consciousness" exists seems so absurd on the face of it—for undeniably "thoughts" do exist—that I fear some readers will follow me no farther. Let me then immediately explain that I mean only to deny that the word stands for an entity, but to insist most emphatically that it does stand for a function. There is, I mean, no aboriginal stuff or quality of being contrasted with that of which material objects are made, out of which our thoughts of them are made; but there is a function in experience which thoughts perform, and for the performance of which this quality of being is invoked. That function is *knowing*. "Consciousness" is supposed necessary to explain the fact that things not only are, but get reported, are known. Whoever blots out the notion of consciousness from his list of first principles must still provide in some way for that function's being carried on.[3]

Given that the brain is an object, as much an object as a tree or a hamburger, it is easy to see why it is so difficult to comprehend ourselves, our consciousness, and our consciousness of our selves, as process. On the one hand, the plain fact is that there is no scientific evidence that a self, an individual mind, could exist without a physical brain. However, there are persisting reasons why the self and the mind do not appear to be identical with, or entirely reducible to, the brain. The subject that represents the "I" in the statement "I think therefore I am" cannot be directly observed, weighed, or measured. And the experiences of that self, its pains and pleasures, sights and sounds, possess an objective reality only to the one who experiences them. In other words, as the philosopher Searle puts it, the mind is "irreducibly first-person."

However, the transparency of the self, mind, and consciousness had not stopped some scientists from seeking to locate the material self. In one famous example, in 1907, Massachusetts physician Dr. Duncan MacDougall and his colleagues set out to determine the measure of the soul by weighing patients before and after death, presumably after the soul had left the body. MacDougall simply could not conceive of consciousness, the personality, the soul not being a "thing" like any other.

> It is unthinkable that personality and consciousness continuing personal identity should exist, and having being, and yet not occupy space. It is impossible to represent in thought that which is not space-occupying, as having personality; for that would be equivalent to thinking that nothing had become or was something, that emptiness had personality, that space itself was more than space, all of which are contradictions and absurd.[4]

To conduct his experiments, MacDougall placed patients on the brink of death upon specially designed platforms that served as scales, which he counter-balanced carefully. The result of MacDougall's experiments were described by him in an article in the *New York Times:*

Four other physicians under my direction made the first test upon a
patient dying with tuberculosis. This man was one of the ordinary
type of the usual American temperament neither particularly high
strung nor of marked phlegmatic disposition. We placed him a few
hours preceding death upon a scale platform which I had constructed and which was accurately balanced. Four hours later with
five doctors in attendance he died. The instant life ceased the opposite scale pan fell with a suddenness that was astonishing—as if
something had been suddenly lifted from the body.[5]

MacDougall conducted a second experiment with the same remarkable result, but a subsequent test proved somewhat problematic.
Like the other two men, this subject was also dying from tuberculosis, but he was a larger and physically slower individual than the
first two men, and MacDougall described to the *Times* the surprising
observation upon this gentleman's death:

The subject was that of a man of larger physical build, with a pronounced sluggish temperament. When life ceased, as the body lay in
bed upon the scales, for a full minute there appeared to be no change
in weight. The physicians waiting in the room look into each other's
faces silently, shaking their heads in the conviction that our test had
failed. Then suddenly the same thing happened that had occurred in
the other cases. There appeared a sudden diminution in the weight,
which was soon found to be the same as that of the preceding experiments. I believe that in this case, that of a phlegmatic man slow
of thought and action, that the soul remained suspended in the
body after death, during the minute that elapsed before it came to
the consciousness of its freedom. There is no other way of accounting for it . . .[6]

I suppose one can hardly blame the soul for its "delayed release"
under these difficult circumstances. After all, it had lived inside this
"phlegmatic" man his entire life. But Dr. MacDougall did not stop
there. He sought further confirmation of his hypothesis that he had
indeed captured the human soul leaving the mortal coil by repeating

his experiments with a series of fifteen dogs that, for the purposes of the research, were "vitiated" by the use of fatal drugs. On this point, MacDougall notes he would have preferred to use dogs that were dying of natural causes, but, "It was not my fortune to get dogs dying from such sickness." Since dogs do not have souls, he was pleased to find that no such loss of weight was observed at the time of passing of the dog's life. MacDougall summarized his findings this way:

> Is it the soul substance? It would seem to me to be so. According to our hypothesis such a substance is necessary to the assumption of continuing or persisting personality after bodily death, and here we have experimental demonstration that a substance capable of being weighed does leave the human body at death.[7]

Based on his experiments, MacDougall fixed the weight of the average human soul at about 21 grams. Unfortunately, his methodology has subsequently been questioned and his findings have never been reproduced. But the problem of the concreteness of the self remains.

While the brain can be readily understood as a "thing," on the order of a rock or a plant or an amoeba, concepts like the mind and the self do not lend themselves to any such easy explanation. To some extent all "things" are abstractions; however, most scientists do not claim that rocks or brains do not exist on this account. But even if all things in the universe are abstractions, the self and the mind appear even more suspect as "things." So what can we say about the ultimate nature—the ontology—of the unique system we call "ourselves"?

Without the processes of the constituent atoms of things, which are in constant flux, there would be no "things." The English philosopher Alfred North Whitehead took up William James's emphatic assertion that consciousness is a process and argued that the shortcomings of Cartesian dualism—the fundamental distinction between matter and soul—can be traced to the failure to adequately discriminate form from process.[8] The Cartesian notion of *res extensa* held that observable objects such as bodies and brains are extended in physical space and can be identified with form. Descartes identified the *res cogitans*, that which thinks, also as a "substance" as well, albeit of a different sort. Whitehead argued instead that the mind should be identified with the process of the brain, not with any as yet to be discovered or more adequately defined form, or as he put it, "consciousness will be the function of knowing."[9]

Searle places a similar emphasis on consciousness as process in his brilliant work *The Rediscovery of the Mind*:

> The famous mind-body problem, the source of so much controversy over the past two millennia, has a simple solution. This solution has been available to any educated person since serious work began on the brain nearly a century ago, and, in a sense, we all know it to be true. Here it is: Mental phenomena are caused by neurophysiological processes in the brain and are themselves features of the brain. To distinguish this view from the many others in the field, I call it "biological naturalism." Mental events and process are as much part of our biological natural history as digestion, mitosis, meiosis, or enzyme secretion.[10]

What is essential here is that consciousness, like the other functions Searle cites, is a physiological process. In Searle's words, echoing James, "Consciousness is not 'stuff,' it is a *feature* or *property* of the brain in the sense, for example, that liquidity is a feature of water."[11]

It is obvious that if we freeze the brain, for example, consciousness would cease to exist even though we would not disturb the brain's physiological arrangement. What we would eliminate is the product of its functions. Therefore the only intelligible way to understand consciousness is from the standpoint of a physiological process. Consciousness is what the brain *does*.

The emphasis herein placed on process when dealing with hierarchical systems, and particularly consciousness, is critical. Only by considering process, as opposed to physical structure, can the brain's functionality, and subjectivity, be understood. This does not mean what the brain does is independent of what it is made of, and especially of how it is put together. I do not subscribe to the school of philosophy that argues that all that matters is function, and that a conscious entity could be made out of anything. Indeed, I believe the evidence points entirely in the opposite direction, that consciousness as we know it is *ontologically neurobiological*. All indications are that, at least among carbon-based life forms on Earth, all conscious things have the same structural hierarchical design and physiological function, that all things with this structure-function appear to possess consciousness, and that no things without this structure-function are conscious.

This view of mind and self is consistent with our current view of life in general. Just as life is not localized within any particular cell in the structure of an organism, consciousness is not localized in any particular zone or structure of the nervous system; rather, it is embodied within the physiological functions of the brain. Is a calcium molecule within your femur alive? Is a single atom located within your heart muscle alive? Well, yes and no, I suppose. The same is true of the individual elements of the brain. No single neuron is "conscious," nor is even a more complex neurological structure like the spinal cord. Sever its relationship to the living brain and the essence of the biological self remains intact. Nor will the spinal cord display any consciousness on its own beyond the primitive sensorimotor reflexes of a snail. Yet all these elements, in what I term the *Neural Hierarchy Theory of Consciousness (NHTC)*, can be considered as a part of the ascending nested hierarchy of the nervous system that contributes to what we call the mind and self. [12]

Is it really astonishing that the self is best conceived of as a "process"? I find this conception of the self the only reasonable explanation for the seeming transparency and apparent immateriality of what we are. I've always assumed Crick's materialistic conjecture about the nature of consciousness to be the correct one. I do not believe there is a mind that is separable from the brain, no magical essence that leaps upon angels' wings from dendrites and synapse to create the self. And yet, in spite of this conviction, there still appeared to be this unbridgeable gap between the self, the mind, and the brain.

However, once I changed my perspective from one of investigation of the effect of trauma on the material brain to begin to see the self as a process of the brain, many of the mysterious problems of the mind-brain relationship were resolved. The reification of different aspects of the self, sub-entities of the self introduced by Freud such as *ego, id, superego*, are useful metaphors when describing psychological functions; indeed, I freely use the term "ego functions" in lieu of other terms such as "self functions" because these terms have a certain psychodynamic connotation that I wish to exploit. However, the ego, id, and superego do not exist any more than the self. We may refer to ourselves as particular entities—I am, you are, we are—but in fact the self is a function, evanescent and in a constant flux of whirling change. Although we experience ourselves as things, as fixed entities occupying a physical space in the world, we are in reality a process, a continuous unfolding in time, constantly becoming.

Science has confronted similar issues when faced with the perplexing problem of life itself. The biologist Ernst Mayr points out that, lacking a complete knowledge of biology and especially without the discovery of DNA and the mechanisms of molecular biology, for most of human history naturalists assumed by default that there must be more to "life" than mere mechanism:

> . . . They were convinced that in a living organism certain forces are active that do not exist in inanimate nature. They concluded that,

just as the motion of planets and stars is controlled by an occult, invisible force called gravitation by Newton, the movements and other
manifestations of life in organisms are controlled by an invisible
force, Lebenskraft or *vis vitalis*.[13]

What led these early naturalists to the position of vitalism was
their ignorance regarding certain processes essential to life. The
process of evolution had yet to be discovered. One could further
argue that Watson and Crick's discovery of the double helical structure of DNA was so remarkable because it immediately suggested
how genetic material could lead to the process of self replication, or
as the authors rather coyly imply in their initial report, "It has not
escaped our notice that the specific pairing we have postulated immediately suggests a possible copying mechanism for the genetic
material."[14] With these developments in the biological sciences, the
vitalist school was exhausted. As Mayr explains:

> The end of vitalism came when it no longer could find any support-
> ers. Two causes were largely responsible for this: first, the failure of
> literally thousands of unsuccessful experiments conducted to demon-
> strate the existence of a Lebenskraft; second, the realization that the
> new biology, with the methods of genetics and molecular biology,
> was able to solve all the problems for which scientists traditionally
> had invoked the Lebenskraft. In other words, the proposal of a Leben-
> skraft had simply become unnecessary.[15]

How close are we today to that point of resolution in the neuroscience of the self? I propose that we are there now. There simply is
no evidence—nor do I believe any will be found—that there is some
"missing ingredient" to consciousness. As I have tried to show, I believe that the nature of consciousness is based upon a particular hierarchical system of organization that makes the creation of mind
and self possible. And it is the nature of this system itself that can
explain the remaining most perplexing issue in consciousness—ontological subjectivity. This problem will never be explained away by

some as yet undiscovered brain substance or function. Rather it can be fully understood as the outcome of the brain's known organization and processes.

Your life is not a pack of cells; your life is what your particular pack of cells collectively do, though I cannot observe such a thing as your life, touch it, put it under a microscope, or keep it in a bottle on a shelf. In exactly the same way, you are not a pack of neurons; you are what your own pack of neurons collectively do. And if I want to touch your "self," I must do so by word and deed that, once they leave me, become a part of you.

NOTES

Introduction: From Axons to Identity

1. Strawson, 2000, p. 39.

2. Leary and Tangney, 2003.

3. Searle, 2000, p.559.

4. For excellent reviews of the concept of the "narrative self " see the work of Shaun Gallagher (2000, 2003).

5. Freud, 1930, p. 66.

6. For this volume, whenever possible, I have tried to introduce new clinical material to illustrate the mechanisms behind the clinical syndromes. Some descriptions are extended or reanalyzed versions of previously described cases. In the latter case I have found that new insights into the underlying basis of a particular syndrome have led me to a new form of analysis.

Chapter One: Damaged Brains, Damaged Selves

1. For other versions of the sense of the body or the bodily self see Damasio, 1999; Craig, 2002, 2003a, 2003b, 2003c; For a discussion of the narrative self with reference to schizophrenia, see Phillips, 2003. For philosophical views on the narrative self, see Gallagher, 2000.

2. See the edited volume Kircher and David, 2003.

3. Anton, 1899; Babinski, 1914, 1918.

4. Berlyne, 1972; Moskovitch and Mello 1997; see also DeLuca, 2000; Hirstein, 2005.

5. Korsakoff, 1889; Bonhoeffer, 1901, 1904; Van der Horst, 1932; Williams and Rupp, 1938; Talland, 1961, 1965.

6. For reviews see De Luca, 2000; Feinberg and Giacino, 2003; Johnson et al., 2000.

7. For additional description of PM see patient "Patsy" in Feinberg, 2001a.

8. Gerstman, 1942; Schilder, 1950; Critchley, 1953; Weinstein and Friedland, 1977; Cutting, 1978; Levine, Calvanio, and Rinn, 1991; Feinberg and Roane, 2003.

9. Weinstein and Friedland, 1977; Feinberg et al., 1994; Feinberg, Haber, and Leeds, 1990.

10. Cappa et al., 1987; Bisiach et al., 1991.

11. Feinberg, 2001a; Feinberg, Haber, and Leeds, 1990.

12. Weinstein and Kahn, 1955; Feinberg et al., 1994; Feinberg, 1997a; Feinberg and Roane, 1997; Ramachandran and Blakeslee, 1998.

13. Anton, 1899; McGlynn and Schacter, 1989. Weinstein et al., 1964; Lebrun, 1987; Feinberg and Roane, 2003; Shenker et al., 2004.

14. Critchley, 1953, 1955, 1974; Feinberg, 1997a; Feinberg, Haber, and Leeds, 1990; Feinberg et al., 2000; Feinberg, 2001a.

15. Gerstman, 1942; Critchley, 1953; Vallar and Ronchi, 2009, provide an excellent review of this syndrome.

16. Feinberg, 2001a.

17. Bisiach et al., 1991.

18. Ullman, 1960.

19. Critchley, 1953

20. Brock and Merwarth, 1957.

21. Halligan, Marshall, and Wade, 1995.

22. Weinstein and Kahn, 1955.

23. Halligan, Marshall, and Wade, 1993.

24. Critchley, 1974.

25. Weinstein and Friedland, 1977.

26. CM this volume.

27. JK this volume.

28. GS this volume.

29. PG this volume.

30. Lackoff and Johnson, 1980, p. 5.

31. This patient was designated as "Mirna" in Feinberg, 2001a.

32. This patient was designated as "Shirley" in Feinberg, 2001a.

33. Capgras and Reboul-Lachaux, 1923.

34. Courbon and Fail, 1927.

35. Vié, 1930; Christodoulou, 1977.

36. Feinberg and Roane 1997.

37. Anderson, 1988; Anderson and Williams, 1994.

38. Rubin, 1988; Hwang, Yang, and Tsai, 2003.

39. Breen and co-workers (2001) described two cases of this syndrome in men, but neither case had the extreme paranoid reactions that have been described in women. Their case TH also appears to have had a generalized disturbance in dealing with reflective surfaces that was not present in the cases I have reported.

40. Gluckman, 1968, p. 40.

41. Cummings, 1985.

42. Mendez, 1992, p. 415.

43. Molchan, 1990.

44. Spangenberg, Wagner, and Bachman, 1998, p. 152.

45. Rowan, 1984; Jenkins et al., 1997; Hwang, Yang, and Tsai, 2003; Kasahara et al., 2005.

46. Hwang, Yang, and Tsai, 2003.

47. Phillips et al., 1996, p. 156.

48. Shanks and Venneri, 2002.

49. Weinstein, Kahn, and Morris, 1956.

50. Baddeley and Wilson, 1986.

51. This case was designated as "Linda" in Feinberg, 2001a.

52. This case was designated as "Sam" in Feinberg, 2001a.

53. This case was originally reported in Feinberg, Eaton, Roane, and Giacino 1999, and was designated as "Bart" in Feinberg, 2001a.

54. Venneri et al., 2000.

55. Weinstein, Kahn, and Malitz, 1956.

56. Weinstein, 1996.

57. Weinstein and Lyerly, 1968.

58. American Psychiatric Association, 2000, p. 822.

59. Kihlstrom, 1994.

60. Cardeña, 1994.

61. Cardeña, 1994, p. 19.

62. Janet, 1889, 1904, 1907.

63. This case was designated "Rosamond" in Feinberg 2001a.

64. Cardeña, 1994, p. 24.

65. McGeown et al., 2008.

66. "Marriane" in Feinberg, 2001a.

Chapter Two: The Growth of the Ego and Psychological Defense

1. This case was designated as "Susan" in Feinberg, 2001a.

2. For research and reviews on the early cognitive and social development of the self in the infant and child, the reader may refer to Amsterdam, 1972; Courage and Howe, 2002; Happé, 2003; Howe and Courage, 1997; Leslie, 1987; Leslie et al., 2004; Lewis, 1992, 1995, 1997, 2003; Lewis and Brooks-Gunn, 1979; Lewis and Ramsey, 2004; Povinelli and Simon,1998; Rochat, 1995, 2001, 2003; Stern, 1985; Welch-Ross, 1995.

3. Lewis et al., 1989; Lewis, 1992, 1997. An additional thread of research relevant to the hierarchical neuroanatomy of self-related functions has emerged from research on the theory of mind (ToM). The term "theory of mind" (ToM) was coined by pioneering primate researchers David Premack and Guy Woodruff (1978) who used the concept to describe what they saw as the ability of one animal to sense what another animal was thinking, or to "read the mind" of others. The application of ToM theory to humans and brain research received its greatest impetus from the work of Simon Baron-Cohen and others who suggested that the underlying basis for childhood autism was the failure of these children to develop a normally functioning ToM (Baron-Cohen, Leslie, and Frith, 1985; Baron-Cohen, 1995).

4. See Lewis, 1992 for a discussion of the rational for controversies around the primary emotions.

5. Lewis et al., 1989.

6. Lewis and Ramsay, 2004. p. 1821.

7. Gallup, 1970, 1979; De Veer et al., 2003.

8. Lewis and Brooks-Gunn, 1979.

9. Lewis and Ramsay, 2004.

10. Asendorpf, 2002.

11. Rizzolatti and Craighero, 2004.

12. Lewis et al., 1989.

13. Lewis, 1992.

14. Lewis et al., 1989.

15. Wimmer and Perner, 1983; Hogrefe, Wimmer, and Perner, 1986; Keenan,

Gallup, and Falk, 2003, Happé, 2003; Leslie, Friedman, and German, 2004.

16. Tulving, 2002a, 2002b.

17. Nelson, 1992, 1993; Welch-Ross, 1995.

18. Povinelli, 1995; Povinelli and Simon,1998; Skouteris and Robson (2006) however, have suggested a somewhat earlier age, about age 3, for this critical transition.

19. Vaillant, 1977, 1992, 1993.

20. Vaillant, 1992, p. 3.

21. S Freud, 1923, 1962.

22. Vaillant, 1993, p. 3

23. Vaillant, 1977, p. 9.

24. A Freud, 1936. According to Vaillant, the book was an eightieth birthday present from Anna to her father.

25. Cramer, 1991.

26. A. Freud, 1936; S. Freud, 1937; see Cramer, 1991 for review of these theories.

27. For a review on the defense of denial see Breznitz, 1983; Dorpat, 1985.

28. American Psychiatric Association, 2000.

29. American Psychiatric Association, 2000.

30. Cramer, 2006.

31. Cramer and Brilliant, 2001.

32. For excellent sources, see, Fraiberg, 1959; Piaget, 1962; Singer and Singer, 1990; Harris, 2000; Goncu and Gaskins, 2007.

33. A Freud, 1936.

34. Cramer, 1991, p. 38.

35. Dorpat, 1958, p. 14.

36. Lindemann, 1945.

37. Breznitz 1983; Dorpat 1985; Feinberg et al., 2005.

38. Svendsen, 1934, p. 988.

39. Harris, 2000.

40. Taylor, 1999.

41. Taylor and Mannering, 2007.

42. Gleason et al., 2000.

43. Taylor, 1999.

44. Taylor, 1999, p. 24.

45. Taylor, 1999.

46. Hoff, 2004-2005, p. 162.

47. Hoff, 2004-2005, p. 166.

48. Nagera, 1969, p. 190.

49. Fraiberg, 1959.

50. American Psychiatric Association, 2000.

51. Terr, 1990.

52. Terr, 1990, p. 204.

53. Taylor and Carlson, 1997.

54. Taylor et al., 2004.

55. See Harris, 2000; Taylor and Carlson, 1997, for some of the controversies on the reasons behind the relationship between fantasy and ToM behaviors.

56. Woolley, 1997.

57. Prentice et al., 1978; Taylor 1999.

58. Woolley, 1997, provides an analysis of the adult and childhood styles of fantasy

59. Taylor, 1999, p. 163

60. Semrad, 1967; see also Vaillant, 1971.

61. Vaillant, 1971, 1977, 1992, 1993.

62. Brenner, 1974.

63. A Freud, 1936, p. 89.

64. Vaillant, 1977. For excellent reviews of denial, see also Dorpat, 1985; Breznitz, 1983.

65. Vaillant, 1992.

66. Vaillant, 1971, 1977, 1992, 1993; Perry and Bond, 2005.

67. Vaillant's model of denial and projection as early and immature defenses fits with Cramer's developmental model of defense development in children. They differ in that according to Vaillant's model, the "psychotic" use of denial and projection are characteristic of children under the age of 5, but we do not see in Cramer's work any notion of a delusional aspect in the child's thought.

68. American Psychiatric Association, 2000, p. 811.

69. Vaillant 1992, p. 238.

70. Putnam, 1994.

71. The relationship between the childhood defenses and the adult pathologies is also supported by the evidence that the dissociative behaviors in children may be linked to the development of the pathological forms displayed by adults. For instance, there is evidence that adults with dissociative disorders, such as Dissociative Identity Disorder, in which individuals alternate between several different personalities, had imaginary compan-

ions as children that were more vivid than the norm. Also, children who are subject to abuse or other trauma in childhood are more likely to develop both imaginary companions and other dissociative syndromes including Dissociative Identity Disorder (Putnam, 1989). In some cases of Dissociative Identity Disorder, one of the "alter personalities" can be related to an earlier imaginary companion that the adult patient had developed as a child in response to abuse or other psychological trauma (Sanders, 1992).

72. There are other hierarchical approaches to understanding the defenses, in addition to the immature-mature continuum of Vaillant. These hierarchical models are based upon such variables such as the degree of pathology, the level of complexity of the defense, or the degree of reality distortion (Gill, 1963; Schafer, 1968; Wallerstein, 1985; Willick, 1985). Most of theses constructs have in common the placement of denial and projection among the more "immature" defenses. Both the Defensive Functioning Scale in DSM-IV-TR (American Psychiatric Association, 2000) and Defense Mechanism Rating Scale (Perry, 1990; Perry and Bond, 2005) hierarchies include among the immature or psychotic defenses distortion, psychotic denial, and delusional projection.

Chapter Three: The Brainchild Within

1. Goldstein, 1939, p. 39.

2. Schilder, 1950, p. 29.

3. See, for example, Weinstein and Kahn, 1955; Weinstein and Friedland,1977; Weinstein, 1991.

4. Weinstein and Kahn, 1955.

5. Weinstein and Friedland, 1977.

6. Weinstein et al., 1964, p. 384.

7. Dorpat, 1985, p. 257.

8. Ullman et al., 1960; R. Joseph, 1986; McGlynn and Schacter, 1989; Lewis, 1991; Feinberg, 1997a, 2001a; Feinberg and Roane, 1997; Conway and Tacchi, 1996; Kaplan-Solms and Solms, 2002; Turnbull, Berry, and Evans, 2004; Fotopoulou et al., 2004, 2007a, 2007b.

9. Ullman et al., 1960.

10. As early as the first decades of the twentieth century, Kraeplin (1904, 1907, 1919) distinguished two subtypes of confabulation: one he termed "simple confabulation," and suggested that it was caused in part by errors in the temporal ordering of real memories; the other he termed "fantastic confabulations," which he observed were more likely to be bizarre and patently impossible statements that were not or could not be derived from

true, or veridical memories. Later, Berlyne (1972) affirmed the validity of this distinction and further noted that momentary confabulation typically was provoked by questions from the examiner and that the content of such confabulations usually consisted of actual memories that were temporally displaced. Other researchers, including Van der Horst (1932) and Williams and Rupp (1938) also noted that many confabulations were derived from preserved past memories, observations that support the viewpoint that confabulation results from *temporal context confusion* due to frontal-executive dysfunction (Schnider, von Daniken et al., 1996a; Schnider, Gutbrod et al., 1996b; Schnider and Ptak 1999; Schnider, Ptak et al., 2000; Schnider, 2003). Finally, Koppleman (1980) reframed the definitions of two major categories of confabulation as *provoked confabulations* that were elicited specifically in response to questions that probed the patient's memory, and *spontaneous confabulations* that were more grandiose, florid, and occurred without provocation. The personal confabulations described in this book most resemble "fantastic confabulations."

11. Feinberg (1997a), Feinberg and Roane (1997), Coltheart (2002), and McKay, Langdon, and Coltheart (2005, 2007) offer a cognitive neuropsychiatric model of delusions that involves a "two-deficit" account; a perceptual disorder plus a deficit in belief formation. Motivational factors are posited in this model to be active. These accounts are consistent with the neutral-personal dichotomy here proposed, the difference being that I propose that a much larger number of potential variables should be considered.

12. Conway and Tacchi, 1996; Turnbull, Berry, and Evans, 2004; Fotopoulou, Solms, and Turnbull, 2004.

13. Alexander, Stuss, and Benson, 1979.

14. Staton, Brumback, and Wilson, 1982.

15. Ellis and Young, 1990.

16. Bauer, 1984, 1986.

17. Hirstein and Ramachandran, 1997; Hirstein, 2005.

18. Shanks and Venneri, 2002.

19. Venneri et al., 2000.

20. Taylor, 1999, Taylor et al., 2004; Taylor and Mannering, 2006.

21. Berson, 1983; Moskowitz, 1972.

Chapter Four: Observing the Ego

1. Geschwind, 1965, p. 590.

2. See, for example, Gazzaniga, 1985, 2000.

3. Gazzaniga, 2000, p. 1293.

4. Gazzaniga and LeDoux, 1978, p. 148-149.

5. Gazziniga, 2000, p. 1319.

6. Bonhoeffer, 1901, 1904.

7. Feinberg et al., 2005.

8. Jackson, 1884.

9. Harlow, 1868.

10. Freud, 1891.

11. Freud, 1891/1953, p. 87.

12. Arlow and Brenner, 1963, p. 71.

13. Feinberg et al., 2005.

14. Miller, 2001.

15. Alexander, 1979; Joseph, 1986; Feinberg and Shapiro, 1989.

16. Federn, 1952; Fenichel, 1945.

17. Feinberg et al., 2005.

18. Stuss et al., 1978, p. 1167.

19. Johnson, 1991; Johnson, Hayes et al., 2000.

20. Feinberg (in press).

21. Alexander et al., 1979.

22. Levine and Grek (1984). Malloy and Richardson (1994). Malloy and Richardson (1994) in a literature review of a wide variety of content-specific delusions, including delusional misidentification, sexual delusions, and somatic delusions, found a high incidence of lesions of the frontal lobes and right hemisphere, and Kumral and Özturk (2003) found delusional ideation in 15 of 360 stroke patients that was associated with right posterior temporoparietal lesions.

23. Fromm was a co-founder of the William Alanson White Institute of Psychiatry, Psychoanalysis, and Psychology in New York City in the 1940s. As noted previously Weinstein was a training analyst at the Institute and was probably influenced by Fromm's ideas on dreams, thought, and symbolism.

24. Fromm, 1951, p. 7.

25. Arlow and Brenner, 1963; Brenner, 1974; Solms, 2000.

26. Fromm, 1951, p. 4.

27. See Weinstein and Kahn, 1959, for a discussion of Sapir's work.

28. Fromm, 1951, p.12.

29. Finney, 1955.

30. Richard Gid Powers, "Introduction" in Jack Finney, *The Body Snatchers* (Gregg Press, 1976; Steven King's Danse Macabre, 2001.

31. Dostoyevsky, 1976.

32. Poe, 1839.

33. Poe, 1839.

34. Bentall, 2003.

35. Feinberg, in press.

36. Neurosychologist and expert on Freud, Mark Solms (Kaplan-Solms and Solms, 2000; Feinberg et al., 2005) suggests that the right hemisphere, because of its dominance for spatial cognition, plays a greater role in the creation of ego boundaries in the early developing infant when the self/non-self boundary is initially forged. He considers the right perisylvian region to be critical in this regard. This could set the stage for later self/non-self confusion in the adult with right hemisphere disease, although our findings suggest that it is the right frontal regions that are critical.The central role for the right hemisphere in early infant attachment and the self-maternal bond as outlined by the work of psychiatrist Allan Schore (2000, 2003a, 2003b, 2005) fits nicely with this hypothesis.

Chapter Five: The Neural Structure of the Self

1. Niewenhuys, 1996; 1998; Nieuwenhuys et al., 1988-1989; Merker, 2007; Panksepp, 2007.

2. Niewenhuys, 1996, 1998; Nieuwenhuys et al., 1988-1989; Nieuwenhuys et al., 2007.

3. Niewenhuys, 1998, p. 2024.

4. Panksepp, 1998, 2007; Merker, 2007.

5. Sherrington, 1947.

6. See, for example, MacLean, 1973, 1990; also Panksepp, 1998, for an excellent review and elaboration of this theory. See LeDoux, 1996, 2002 and Cory and Gardner, 2002 for some of the controversies around the theory.

7. Nauta 1958, 1973; Nauta and Haymaker, 1969.

8. Morgane and colleagues (Morgane et al., 2005; Morgane and Mokler, 2006) proposed a similar complex of connected structures that they call the *distributed limbic system* that includes the aforementioned medial and paramedial structures as well as paralimbic and heteromodal forebrain regions to which the brainstem system is highly connected. These latter telencephalic structures include paralimbic and heteromodal regions including the cingulate, parahippocampal gyrus, insula, and medial prefrontal cortex (mPFC). These systems and pathways provide the basis for the greater complexity of the homeostatic and self-preservative behaviors that are built

upon the reptilian brain. There is a general correspondence between the sensory-afferent input to the core-paracore system and its rostral extension within the greater limbic system as envisioned by Nieuwenhuys and another recently described homeostatic-interoceptive system elucidated by A. D. Craig (Craig, 2002, 2003a, 2003b, 2003c; in press.). Craig has described a hierarchically arranged system that he suggests, like Nieuwenhuy's core-paracore systems, subserves primarily homeostatic and emotional functions. Craig argues that this system involves the elaboration of *homeostatic emotions* and informs the organism about the internal state of the entire body. In this scenario, Aδ and C-type primary afferent fibers are received by lamina I neurons in the spinal cord and relay information regarding the homeostatic conditions (e.g., pain, temperature, itch, tissue metabolism, hypoxis, etc.) of all the tissues of the body. This information is projected at intermediate levels along the brainstem and culminates in a complete representation of the homeostatic state of the entire organism within the dorsal posterior insular cortex, a region that is considered limbic sensory cortex. The anterior cingulate cortex (ACC), considered by Craig a limbic motor region, provides the element of motivation, and the combination of feeling generated by the insula and motivation provided by ACC constitutes the emotion. In agreement with this model, Nieuwenhuys considers lamina I cells of the dorsal horn as part of what he called the greater limbic system. Thus, the greater limbic system and Craig's interceptive-homeostatic system therefore share many anatomical and functional features.

9. Nieuwenhuys, 1998, p. 2040.

10. Mesulam, 2000.

11. Mesulam points out (2000, p. 11), "There are two divergent opinions about the primary areas. One is to consider them as the most elementary (even rudimentary) component of the cerebral cortex; the other is to consider them as its most advanced and highly differentiated component" (Sanides, 1970). The latter point of view can be supported from the vantage point of cytoarchitectonics. Thus, the primary visual, somatosensory, and auditory cortices display a "koniocortical" architecture representing the highest level of development with respect to granualization and lamination, whereas primary motor cortex displays a unique "macropyramidal" architecture characterized by highly specialized giant pyramidal neurons known as betz cells.

12. As noted by Meares (1999) ". . . Jackson conceived of the CNS as having a hierarchical organization that reflects evolutionary history. . . . Ascending levels show increasing integration and coordination of sensorimotor rep-

resentations. The highest-level coordination, which allows the greatest voluntary control, depends on prefrontal activity. Self is a manifestation of this highest level of consciousness . . ." (Meares, 1999, p. 1851).

13. See, for example, Fuster, 2003.

14. Ramnini and Owen, 2004, p. 186.

15. Sherrington, 1947, p. 324.

16. LeDoux, 2002.

17. Damasio, 1999.

18. William James, 1983, 1985.

19. Legrand, 2007, p. 585.

20. Damasio, 1999, p. 219. Jon Kaas points out that evolutionary patterns indicate that these association brain regions, in addition to being interposed between the interceptive self and the exteroceptive systems, are also intercalated between sensory and motor functions, and according to his account are the areas that display the greatest development in evolution. Development of these "middle stages" of sensory processing allows a greater amount of sensory processing prior to a motor response:

> The simple hierarchies of visual areas, with little more than beginning and end stations, that characterize the brains of mice and hedgehogs become complex hierarchies, like those of monkeys and cats, by the addition of new visual areas in the middle stages of processing. As a result, a change occurs from the situation where the first cortical station, area 17, directly accesses some of the end or near end cortical stations in frontal and limbic cortex, as in rats and mice . . . to where area 17 relates to only early stages of a lengthy hierarchy, as in monkeys. (Kaas, 1989, p. 130)

21. Northoff and Bermpohl, 2004; Northoff et al., 2006; Northoff et al., 2007.

22. Northoff et al., 2006.

23. Phan et al., 2004.

24. Northoff et al., 2007.

25. Schore, 2003a, p. 42.

26. Schore, 2000, 2003a, 2003b, 2005. Schmitz et al. (2004) found right hemisphere dorsolateral prefrontal activation on fMRI when subjects were making self versus other judgments. This raises the question whether there is a special role for the non-dominant (typically right) hemisphere in self-related functions. Northoff and co-workers (2006) peformed a meta-analysis of imaging during self-related tasks laterality effects did not emerge. That is, it did not appear that one hemisphere had an advantage over the other when it came to processing self-related material. There is

other evidence that the right (non-dominant) hemisphere may, however, play a dominant role in some self-related processes. Donald Stuss and co-workers (2001) provided additional evidence in brain injured subjects that the medial frontal regions, especially within the right hemisphere, supported theory of mind (ToM) tasks. Nonetheless, a domain in which laterality effects appear to be present is in *self-face recognition*, the act of recognizing the image of one's own face. It was established many years ago that either hemisphere of a person's brain can independently recognize his or her own face (Sperry et al., 1979). However, there is some evidence that the right hemisphere may have an advantage for self-face recognition (Uddin et al., 2005, 2007; Keenan, Wheeler et al., 2000; Keenan, Nelson et al., 2001; Keenan, Gallup, and Falk, 2003; Keenan, Wheeler, and Ewers, 2003; Keenan, Wheeler, Platek et al., 2003; Platek et al., 2004; Devue et al., 2007) although others have found evidence for a shared or left hemisphere representation (Kircher et al., 2001; Turk et al., 2002; Brady et al., 2004; Platek et al., 2006; Sugiura et al. 2005, 2006). It is of interest that the regions that are activated when viewing the self-face partially overlap the paralimbic and heteromodal association cortices that are activated in other self-related tasks.

27. Buck, 1999.

28. Tulving, 1985, 1987, 2002a, 2002b; Wheeler, Stuss, and Tulving, 1997. For the purposes of this discussion, I will utilize Tulving's original conception of the levels of memory functioning, although controversy exists regarding how exact these divisions may be drawn. For a detailed examination of the levels of memory and consciousness according to this model, see Wheeler, Stuss, and Tulving (1997). For another hierarchical analysis related to Tulving, see Fujiwara and Markowitsch (2005).

29. Tulving, 1985, p. 3.

30. Tulving, 1985, 2002a, 2002b.

31. Tulving, 1985, p. 3.

32. Tulving, 2002a, p. 5.

33. Tulving, 2002a, p. 20.

34. Wheeler, Stuss, and Tulving, 1997; Stuss, Picton, and Alexander, 2001. Markowitsch, 2003; Keenan et al., 2003a; Keenan et al., 2003b; Stuss et al., 2005.

35. Recent fMRI imaging studies have provided convincing evidence that the medial prefrontal cortex, a heteromodal association region, is activated (along with the temporal poles, and posterior superior temporal sulcus) during theory of mind tasks (Frith and Frith, 1999, 2003).

36. Antonio Damasio (1999) posits three hierarchically arranged levels of the self.

The *proto-self* is an unconscious neural representation of the current state of an organism; *the core-self* is a conscious second order but non-verbal realization of the self that emerges when the *proto-self* interacts with an external object; and an *autobiographical-self* is based on autobiographical memory and anticipated future events. These three levels appear roughly similar to MacLean's levels of the triune brain and very similar to Tulving's three levels of *anoetic*, *noetic*, and *autonoetic* consciousness. Gerald Edelman (1989, 1992, 2004) proposes a complex and subtle dichotomous hierarchical distinction between *primary consciousness* and *higher-order consciousness*. Primary consciousness requires perceptual categorization and "value-catagory memory," learning and a "biological self-nonself distinction." Higher-order consciousness is "the capability to be conscious of being conscious." Higher-order consciousness requires an increasingly complex nervous system that allows the connection of an emerging sense of self, memories of the past, and imagined future events with primary consciousness creates the emergence of higher-order consciousness. According to this account, semantic or linguistic abilities are minimally required and the most advanced forms of higher order consciousness require a social self and concepts of a personal past and present. First and foremost, the model I present in this chapter pertains to the creation of the self, not specifically the architecture of consciousness, which is certainly the emphasis in Edelman's work, and to a certain extent in Damasio's as well. While the self and consciousness are surely intertwined, and each of these two aspects of mind entails the other, the way the two relate to brain architecture and the questions and problems they pose differ. In the next chapter I will consider some of these. In addition, the model I propose incorporates both the medial-lateral trend in the organization of brain functions, along with the causal-rostral trend that is emphasized by the aforementioned authors. These aspects of neural organization do not represent separate selves, or separate consciousnesses, however. This medial-lateral trend organizes the self according to its interceptive and exteroceptive aspects along the entire length of the brain. It follows from this that I have scrupulously avoided *reifying* any horizontal organization of the neural self. By this I mean that I do not believe, for example, that there is a "core self" or there is a "primary consciousness." These terms suggest that the self or consciousness can be envisioned as comprised of discrete or discontinuous levels that can be anatomically or functionally defined and that actually exist. I believe this is a mistake, and I argue that a better approach is to understand that consciousness and the self are based on a continuum of hierarchically organized functions without any discrete levels. Therefore I do not assign to any given hierarchical level a name or separate identity, or identify it with any neural specific organization. Rather, I envision consciousness and the self as the product of hierarchically organized neural systems in which all levels make a contribution to the self.

37. There are some philosophical issues regarding whether one is dealing with aspects of the self or the world that I think are clarified by this model. For instance when one is cut by a blade, some aspects of the experience are referred to the knife—"Its sharp!"—and some to the self—"I am in pain." Presumably these two aspects of the entire experience are created by the simultaneous activation of the different self systems I have described. The important point is the interoself system cannot appreciate the knife as it exists as an object in the world, and the exterosensorimotor motor system cannot experience the pain of being cut.

Chapter Six: The Nested Hierarchy of Self and Consciousness

1. Simon, 1973, p. 5.

2. Simon, 1973, p. 7. For a beautiful analysis of the mathematics of branching hierarchies, see Wolfram, 2002.

3. Buss, 1987. For other theories of emergence see; Kim, 1992, 1995, 1998; Beckermann, Flohr, and Kim, 1992; Johnson, 2001; Morowitz, 2002; Searle, 1992.

4. Sperry, 1966, 1984, 1990.

5. Searle, 1992.

6. Hubel and Wiesel, 1977, 1979; Hubel, 1988; Zeki, 1993.

7. Barlow, 1995; Fried et al., 1997; Gross et al., 1969, 1972, 2002, 2008; Krieman et al., 2000; Quiroga et al., 2005, 2008.

8. Quiroga et al., 2005, 2008.Theories that emphasize the view that large and distributed populations of neurons code for complex stimuli, are called "distributed population coding theories." Those that emphasize the selectivity of smaller groups of neurons to specific stimuli are called "sparse coding" theories.

9. For commentary on and analysis of the "binding problem" see, for example, Albright et al., 2001; Singer, 2001; Koch, 2004; Revonsuo, 2006.

10. Movshon and co-workers, 1985; Zeki, 1993; Beckers and Zeki, 1995.

11. Albright et al., 2001.

12. Quiroga et al., 2007; Jennifer Aniston and Lisa Kudrow appeared together on the television series *Friends*.

13. Koestler, 1967, 1978.

14. Koestler, 1967, p. 77.

15. Ahl and Allen, 1996; Allan and Starr, 1982; Pattee, 1973; Salthe, 1985.

16. Koestler (1967, 1978) referred to the parts of hierarchical systems as "holons." The word is derived from the Greek "holos" meaning whole, to which he added the "on" to suggest a particle or part. He wished to designate the entity as simultaneously a part and a whole.

17. Allan and Starr, 1982, p. 38. See also Salthe, 1985.

18. Ahl and Allen, 1996; Allan and Starr, 1982; Pattee, 1973; Salthe, 1985.

19. Allan and Starr, 1982.

20. Ahl and Allen, 1996; Pattee, 1973.

21. Sherrington, 1947, p. xiv.

22. Ryle, 1949.

23. Crick, 1994; Crick and Koch, 1990; Edelman, 1989; Engel, Fries et al. 1999; Engel, Fries, and Singer, 2001; Engel and Singer, 2001; Singer, 1999; Singer, Engel et al., 1997; von der Malsberg, 1981.

24. Melloni et al., 2007.

25. Fries et al., 1997.

26. Engel and Singer, 2001; Engel et al., 2001.

27. Engel and Singer, 2001, p. 24.

28. It is important to note that an important role in neural synchrony does not negate the hierarchical patterning in anatomical relationships between brain regions. As noted by Engel et al. in a review, these two major processes seem to work in harmony to create the necessary factors for consciousness:

> In contrast to the top-down models discussed above, the patterns relevant to the dynamic selection of input signals would be generated not only by assemblies in association cortices that carry more abstract, invariant representations, but as the result of continuous large-scale interactions between higher- and lower-order cortical areas. The pattern of coherent activity emanating from such large-scale interactions could bias the synchronization of input signals, leading to a selective enhancement of temporal correlations in subsets of the activated populations. This would result in enhanced saliency and a competitive advantage for the selected populations of neurons. (Engel et al., 2001, p. 706)

29. A model that incorporates both temporal patterning and a neuroanatomical-functional hierarchy has been proposed by vision researcher Semir Zeki (2008) who offers three hierarchical levels consciousness. The first is *micro-consciousness*, which functions primarily *within* a specialized brain region, for instance the color region V4, and binds perceptually alike fea-

tures. At a later (and hierarchically higher stage), binding occurs between attributes, and he refers to this as the *macro-consciousness* stage. At this level, different sets of features are bound; for example color and motion. Finally, the level of *unified consciousness* corresponds to the Kantian "I," the transcendentally unified experience of the unified self.

30. Damasio, 1999; Edelman, 1989.

31. Kandel and Schwartz, 2000; Mesulam, 2000.

32. Gottfried, 2006.

33. Craig (2002) argues that the interoceptive lamina I afferent pathway that culminates in the insula is unique to primates, and this distinguishes subprimate from primate consciousness. He proposes that the insular cortex (Figure 2-5) possesses a higher order map of the interceptive self that represents the unified internal homunculus of the pain and other homeostatic systems that could form the basis of the conscious awareness of the internal self. Craig's model is also explicitly hierarchical with lower regions in a hierarchically nested within and contributing to more integrated zones. Other authors point to the presence of so-called Von Economo neurons that are found in the anterior cingulate and frontoinsular cortices especially in higher primates and man (but recently found in whales) accounts for the diffences between human and primate consciousness and the rest of the animal kingdom (for discussion of Von Economo neurons see Allman et al., 2001, 2002; Nimchinsky et al., 1999; Seeley and Miller, 2005; Seeley et al., 2006)

Chapter Seven: The Self and Consciousness

1. William James, 1890/1983, p. 345.

2. Dennett, 1991, pp. 412-413.

3. Chalmers, 1995, p. 201; see also 1996.

4. Searle, 2000, p. 561.

5. Sellars, 1963; Meehl, 1966; Teller, 1992.

6. Chalmers, 1996; Dennett, 1991; Flanagan, 1993; Metzinger, 2003; Nagel, 1986; Revonsuo, 2006; Searle, 1992; Tye, 1997.

7. Feinberg, 2008. See also Feinberg 1997b; 2000.

8. Kant, Critique, A106.

9. Hundert, p 19.

10. Goldstein 1908, pp. 169-70; cited by Harrington, 1987.

11. Feinberg et al., 1992.

12. Baynes and Gazzaniga, 2003;Gazzaniga, 1985. Zaidel et al., 2003.

13. Zaidel et al., 2003, p. 357.

14. Leiguarda et al., 1989, p. 1028.

15. Geschwind, 1995, p. 803.

16. Suwanwela and Leelacheavasit, 2002, p. 533.

17. *Alien Hand* on Science Frontiers, The Learning Channel, 1996.

18. Personally examined case.

19. Craig, 2002, 2003a, 2003b, 2003c.

20. Searle, 1984, p. 16.

21. Clarke and O'Malley, 1996, p. 9.

22. Globus, 1973, p.1129; See also Globus, 1976.

23. I wish to emphasize that this argument is not about whether we have absolute "free will" or any free will at all. Only that our *experience* of willful actions is clearly different from reflexive actions.

Chapter Eight: The Process of the Self

1. Crick, 1994, p. 3.

2. Sperry, R. W. (1977).

3. William James, 1904, p. 478.

4. MacDougall, 1907, p. 240.

5. *The New York Times*, "Soul Has Weight, Physician Thinks" March 11, 1907.

6. *New York Times*, 1907.

7. MacDougall, 1907, p. 242.

8. Whitehead, 1925.

9. Whitehead, 1925, p. 151.

10. Searle, 1992, p. 1.

11. Searle, 1992, p. 105.

12. Feinberg, 2008.

13. Mayr, 2004, p. 22.

14. Watson and Crick, 1953.

15. Mayr, 2004, p. 2.

GLOSSARY
OF KEY TERMS AND CONCEPTS

Consciousness The concept of consciousness endorsed here is one of a continuum of hierarchically organized states of awareness, in contrast to theories that advocate a categorization based upon discrete levels of consciousness, such as "core," "primary," "secondary," and so on, varieties of consciousness. This organization of consciousness requires that a neural hierarchy that creates consciousness must be subjectively experienced in a nested as opposed to a non-nested fashion according to the dictates of the *Neural Hierarchy Theory of Consciousness (NHTC)*. Consciousness is a prerequisite for self and in spite of the role that neurons play in the creation of consciousness, it is conceived as a process as opposed to a substance.

Constraint via *meaning* and *purpose* Constraint is the control that higher levels of a hierarchy exert upon lower levels. Hierarchies require constraint to operate in a collective fashion. Constraint can be focal and local as when in a non-nested hierarchy a general controls an army, or generalized as an emergent property within the entire collective operations of a nested hierarchical system. In the nested hierarchy of consciousness, constraint in sensory consciousness is provided by the highest level of subjective meaning, and in the motor system constraint is provided by the highest level of purpose.

Delusional Misidentification Syndrome (DMS) In a DMS a patient consistently misidentifies persons, places, objects, or events. In the Capgras syndrome, the patient harbors the delusional belief that a person or persons have been replaced by "doubles" or imposters. In the Fregoli syndrome, the patient believes that a person who is well known to her is really impersonating, and hence taking on the appearance of a stranger in the patient's environment. There are many other variants of DMS and these conditions may be seen in association with neurological or psychiatric disorders. When a DMS occurs in neurological patients, the condition is selective and delusional in that only certain persons or objects are misidentified, usually those of personal significance for the patient, and the patient clings to misbelief in spite of evidence to the contrary. My position is that these features add an emotional and motivational element to the etiology of the condition.

Ego Disequilibrium Theory (EDT) of Personal/Delusional Confabulation The *Ego Disequilibrium Theory (EDT)* proposes that there is under most circumstances an ego equilibrium created by a balance between right and left hemisphere functions with reference to personal relatedness and psycholgoical defense. According to this theory, frontal and especially right (non-dominant) frontal pathology creates a *two -way disturbance* between the self and the environment specifically with regard to personal relatedness that could lead to disorders of *both* under- and over-relatedness between the self and the world. In the presence of right frontal damage, without the mediation of right frontal regions, patterns of personally significant incoming information may be disconnected from a sense of personal relatedness or an internally derived motive may appear in the patient's mind as an externalized reality. This also may lead to the unbridled activation and expression of primitive psychological defenses lateralized to the *dominant* hemisphere.

Neural Hierarchy of Theory of Consciousness (NHTC) The NHTC proposes that the brain is subjectively experienced as a global nested hierarchy in which lower order features combine in consciousness as "part of" or nested within higher order features. Elements that are bound together in consciousness are nested together, which allows neurons at both lower and higher hierarchical levels to contribute to consciousness. Robustly interconnected nested neural levels create qualia (how things subjectively feel) via the interaction of hierarchical levels. The NHTC proposes that all conscious things have this structure and function, all things with this structure/function possess consciousness, and no things without this structure/function are conscious. The NHTC model helps explain some enigmatic features of consciousness such as ontological subjectivity and the "hard problems" encountered by conventional scientific reduction.

Neutral versus Personal Confabulation According to this account, *neutral confabulation* may occur in any sensory or cognitive domain, such as in memory or vision, but it most circumstances the confabulatory tendency is confined to that domain. The content of neutral confabulations is nondelusional and does not entail the creation of fantastic or imaginary persons, places, or events. Neutral confabulations stand in contrast to *personal confabulation* in which the patient misconstrues an actual event in his or her life or creates a wholly fictitious and distorted narrative about themselves or persons close to them. Patients who display personal confabulation represent themselves, their personal experiences, and their problems and preoccupations in a story. Unlike neutral confabulations, personal confabulations are much more delusional and certain details may be stated with every retelling. We currently use the terms "delusional confabulation" and "personal delusional confabulation" for essentially the same subtype of confabulation. The more general term "personal confabulation" entails more features than just delusions. Personal confabulations resemble "fantastic" confabulations in the classical terminology.

Ontological Subjectivity Ontological subjectivity refers to the idea that there is something fundamentally and irreducibly subjective about consciousness. It is related to the "hard problem" of consciousness and I believe the position has most clearly expressed by philosopher John Searle who first introduced the term. He asserts that it is axiomatic but non-problematic from the standpoint of philosophy that conscious states are characterized by a "first-person ontology." The position I defend in this book is that when the mind is considered in relationship to the brain, there appear to be features of conscious mental processes *that are not reducible to* neurons when they are objectively observed and analyzed. The solution to the problem of ontology is to recognize that mind is a process and that when the the nervous system is objectively observed it appears to operate as a non-nested hierarchy, but when it is subjectively experienced it functions as a nested hierarchy.

Self The model of the self proposed here is neurological. The proposal is
that the self is organized according to two major trends. The *medial-
ateral trend* is inspired by the studies of Nieuwenhuys and is represented
by the outward progression of *concentrically* or *radially* arranged zones
from the center of the neuraxis to the periphery. The medial zones are
chiefly concerned with *interoceptive stimuli* and are experienced as originating from within the body. In a radial ring outside of the medial
zones are the *exterosensory* and *exteromotor* systems that collectively can
be referred to as the *exterosensorimotor system* that mediates the interaction of an organism with the external environment. The other trend is
the *caudal-rostral trend* in which evolved neural systems display progressive growth via the addition of superimposed higher cortical structures,
a process known as *encephalization*. The caudal-rostral trend preserves
the radial organization of the medial-lateral trend and results in the *interoself system*, the *exterosensorimotor system*, and the *integrative self system*
that is interposed between the other two.

REFERENCES

Ahl V, and Allen TFH (1996). *Hierarchy Theory.* Columbia University Press, New York.

Albright TD, Jessell TM, Kandel ER, and Poner MI (2001). Progress in the neural sciences in the century after Cajal (and the mysteries that remain). In PC Marijuán ed., Cajal and Consciousness: Scientific Approaches to Consciousness on the Centennial of Ramón y Cajal's Textura. *Annals of New York Academy of Sciences, 929,* 11-40.

Alexander MP, Stuss DT, and Benson DF (1979). Capgras syndrome: A reduplicative phenomenon. *Neurology, 29,* 334-339.

Allen, TFH, and TB Starr (1982). *Hierarchy. Perspectives for Ecological Complexity.* University of Chicago Press, Chicago.

Allman JM, Hakeem A, Erwin JM, Nimchinsky E, and Hof P (2001). The anterior cingulate cortex. The evolution of an interface between emotion and cognition. *Annals of the New York Academy of Science, 935,* 107-117.

Allman J, Hakeem A, and Watson K (2002). Two phylogenetic specializations in the human brain. *The Neuroscientist, 8,* 335-346.

American Psychiatric Association (2000). *Diagnostic and Statistical Manual of Mental Disorders,* 4th edition (Text Rev.) American Psychiatric Association, Washington, D.C.

Amsterdam, B (1972). Mirror self-image reactions before age two. *Developmental Psychobiology, 5,* 297-305.

Anderson DN (1988). The delusions of inanimate doubles: Implications for understanding the Capgras phenomenon. *British Journal of Psychiatry, 153,* 694-699.

Anderson, DN, and Williams E (1994). The delusions of inanimate doubles. *Psychopathology*, *27*, 220-225.

Anton G (1899). Über die Selbstwahrnehmung der Herderkrankugen des Gehirns durch den Kranken bein Rindenblindheit und Rindentaubheit. *Archives Psychiatrie*, *32*, 86-127.

Arlow JA, and Brenner C (1964). *Psychoanalytic Concepts and the Structural Theory*. International Universities Press, New York.

Asendorpf JB (2002). Self-awareness, other-awareness, and secondary representation. In AN Meltzoff, and W Prinz, eds., *The Imitative Mind: Development, Evolution, and Brain Bases* (Cambridge Studies in Cognitive Perceptual Development, pp. 63-73). Cambridge University Press, New York.

Babinski J (1914). Contribution à l'étude des troubles mantaux dans l'hémiplégie organique cérébrale (anosognosie). *Review Neurolique (Paris)*, *27*, 845-848.

Babinski J (1918). Anosognosie. *Review Neurologique (Paris)*, *31*, 365-367.

Baddeley AD, and Wilson B (1986). Amnesia, autobiographical memory, and confabulation. In DC Rubin, ed., *Autobiographical Memory*. Cambridge University Press, UK. pp. 225-252.

Barlow H (1995).The neuron doctrine in perception. In MS Gazzaniga, ed., *The Cognitive Neurosciences*, pp. 415-435. MIT Press, Cambridge, MA.

Baron-Cohen S (1995). *Mindblindness*. MIT Press, Cambridge, MA.

Baron-Cohen S, Leslie AM, and Frith U (1985). Does the autistic child have a theory of mind? *Cognition*, *21*, 37-46.

Bauer R (1984). Autonomic recognition of names and faces: A neuropsychological application of the Guilty Knowledge Test. *Neuropsychologia*, *22*, 457-469.

Bauer R. (1986). The cognitive psychophysiology of prosopagnosia. In H Ellis, M Jeeves, F Newcombe, and A Young, eds., *Aspects of Face Processing*. Martinus Nijhoff, Dordrecht. pp. 253-267.

Baynes K, and Gazzaniga MS (2003). Callosal disconnection. In TE Feinberg and M Farah, eds., *Behavioral Neurology and Neuropsychology*, 2nd Ed., pp. 401-409. McGraw-Hill, New York.

Beckermann A, Flohr H, and Kim J, eds. (1992). *Emergence or Reduction? Essays on the Prospects of Nonreductive Physicalism*. New York: Walter de Gruyter.

Beckers G, and Zeki S (1995). The consequences of inactivating areas V1 and V5 on visual motion perception. *Brain*, *118*, 49-60.

Bentall R (2003). The paranoid self. In T Kircher and A David, eds., *The self in neuroscience and psychiatry*, pp. 293-318.Cambridge University Press, New York.

Berlyne N (1972). Confabulation. *British Journal of Psychiatry*, *120*, 31-39.

Berson RJ (1983). Capgras' syndrome. *American Journal of Psychiatry, 140,* 969-978.

Bisiach E, Rusconi ML, and Vallar G (1991). Remission of somatoparaphrenic delusion through vestibular stimulation. *Neuropsychologia, 29,* 1029-1031.

Bonhoeffer K (1901). *Die akuten Geisteskrankheiten der Gewohnheitstrinker.* Gustav Fischer, Jena, Germany.

Bonhoeffer K (1904). Der Korsakowsche Symptomenkomplex in seinen Beziehungen zu den verschiedenen Krankheitsformen. *Allgemeine Z Psychiatry, 61,* 744-752.

Brady N, Campbell M, and Flaherty M (2004). My left brain and me: A dissociation in the perception of self and others. *Neuropsychologia, 42,* 1156-1161.

Breen N, Caine D, and Coltheart, M (2001). Mirrored-self misidentification: Two cases of focal onset dementia. *Neurocase, 7,* 239-254.

Brenner C (1974). *An Elementary Textbook of Psychoanalysis.* Anchor Books, Garden City, NY.

Breznitz S (1983), ed. *The Denial of Stress.* International Universities Press, New York.

Brock S, and Merwarth HR(1957). The illusory awareness of body parts in cerebral disease. *AMA Archives of Neurology and Psychiatry, 77,* 366-375.

Buck R (1999). The biological affects: A topology. *Psychological Review, 106,* 301-336.

Buss LW (1987). *The Evolution of Individuality.* Princeton University Press, Princeton, NJ.

Capgras J, and Reboul-Lachaux J (1923). Illusion des sosies dans un délire systématisé chronique. *Bulletin de la Société Clinique de Médicine Mentale, 2,* 6-16.

Cappa S, Sterzi R, Vallar G, and Bisiach E (1987). Remission of hemineglect and anosognosia during vestibular stimulation. *Neuropsychologia, 25,* 775-782.

Cardeña E (1994).The domain of dissociation. In SJ Lynn and JW Rhue, eds., *Dissociation: Clinical and Theoretical Perspectives,* pp. 15-31. Guilford Press, New York.

Chalmers DJ (1995). Facing up to the problem of consciousness. *Journal of Consciousness Studies, 2,* 200-219.

Chalmers D (1996). *The Conscious Mind: In Search of a Fundamental Theory.* Oxford University Press, New York.

Christodoulou GN (1977). The syndrome of Capgras. *British Journal of Psychiatry, 130,* 556-564.

Coltheart M (2002). Cognitive neuropsychology. In H Pashler and J Wixted, eds., *Steven's Handbook of Experimental Psychology,* Vol. 4. *Methodology in Experimental Psychology,* 3rd ed., pp. 139-174. John Wiley, New York.

Cory GA, Gardner R (2002). *The Evolutionary neuroethology of Paul MacLean: Convergences and frontiers.* Praeger, New York.

Conway MA, and Tacchi PC (1996). Motivated confabulation. *Neurocase, 2,* 325-339.

Courage ML, and Howe ML (2002). From infant to child: The dynamics of cognitive change in the second year of life. *Psychological Bulletin, 128,* 250-277.

Courbon P, and Fail G (1927). Syndrome d'illusion de Frégoli et schizophrénie. *Bulletin de la Société Clinique de Médecine Mentale, 15,* 121-124.

Craig AD (2002). How do you feel? Interoception: The sense of the physiological condition of the body. *Nature Review Neuroscience, 3,* 655-666.

Craig AD (2003a). Interoception: The sense of the physiological condition of the body. *Current Opinion in Neurobiology, 13,* 500-505.

Craig AD (2003b). Pain mechanisms: Labeled lines versus convergence in central processing. *Annual Review of Neuroscience, 26,* 1-30.

Craig AD (2003c). A new view of pain as a homeostatic emotion. *Trends in Neurosciences, 26,* 303-307.

Craig AD (in press). Interoception and emotion: A neuroanatomical perspective. In M Lewis, JM Haviland-Jones, and LF Barrett, eds., *Handbook of Emotion,* 3rd Ed., Guilford Press, New York.

Cramer P (1991). *The Development of Defense Mechanisms: Theory, Research, and Assessment.* Springer-Verlag, New York.

Cramer P (2006). *Protecting the Self: Defense Mechanisms in Action.* Guilford Press, New York.

Cramer P, and Briliant (2001). Defense use and defense understanding in children. *Journal of Personality, 69,* 297-322.

Crick FHC (1994). *The Astonishing Hypothesis.* Basic Books, New York.

Crick F, and Koch C (1990). Towards a neurobiological theory of consciousness. *Seminars in Neurosciences, 2,* 263-275.

Critchley M (1953). *The Parietal Lobes.* Hafner Press, New York.

Critchley, M (1955). Personification of paralyzed limbs in hemiplegics. *British Medical Journal, 30,* 284-287.

Critchley, M (1974). Misoplegia or hatred of hemiplegia. *Mount Sinai Journal of Medicine, 41,* 82-87.

Cummings, JL (1985). Organic delusions: Phenomenology, anatomical correlations, and review. *British Journal of Psychiatry,* **146**, 184-197.

Cutting, J (1978). Study of anosognosia. *Journal of Neurology, Neurosurgery, and Psychiatry, 41,* 548-555.

Dally P, and Gomez J (1979) Capgras: Case study and reappraisal. *British Journal of Medical Psychology, 52,* 291-295.

Damasio, AR (1999). *The Feeling of What Happens: Body and Emotion in the Making of Consciousness.* Harcourt Brace, New York.

DeLuca, JA (2000). Cognitive neuroscience perspective on confabulation. *Neuro- Psychoanalysis, 2,* 119-132.

Dennett, D (1991). *Consciousness Explained.* Little, Brown, Boston.

De Veer MW, Gallup GG, Theall LA, van den Bos R, and Povinelli DJ. (2003). An 8-year longitudinal study of mirror self-recognition in chimpanzees (Pan troglodytes). *Neuropsychologia, 41,* 229-234.

Devue et al. (2007) Here I am: The cortical correlates of visual self-recognition. *Brain Research, 1143,* 169-182.

Dorpat, T L (1985). *Denial and Defense in the Therapeutic Situation.* Jason Aronson, New York.

Dostoyevsky, FM (1976). *The Double.* Prideaux Press, Letchworth, UK.

Edelman, GM (1989). *The Remembered Present: A Biological Theory of Consciousness.* Basic Books, New York.

Edelman GM (1992). *Bright Air, Brilliant Fire: On the Matter of the Mind.* Basic Books, New York.

Edelman GM (2004). *Wider than the Sky: The Phenomenal Gift of Consciousness.* Yale University Press, New Haven, CT.

Ellis HD, and Young AW (1990). Accounting for delusional misidentifications. *British Journal of Psychiatry, 157,* 239-248.

Engel AK, Fries P, Krieter P, Konig P, Brecht M, and Singer W (1999). Temporal binding, binocular rivalry, and consciousness. *Consciousness and Cognition, 8,* 128-151.

Engel AK, Fries P, and Singer W (2001). Dynamic predictions: Oscillations and synchrony in top-down processing. *Nature Reviews Neuroscience, 2,* 704-716.

Engel AK, and Singer W (2001). Temporal binding and the neural correlates of sensory awareness. *Trends in Cognitive Sciences, 5,* 16-25.

Federn P (1952). *Ego Psychology and the Psychoses.* Basic Books, New York.

Feinberg TE (1997a). Anosognosia and confabulation. In TE Feinberg and MJ Farah, eds., *Behavioral neurology and neuropsychology,* pp. 369-390. McGraw-Hill, New York.

Feinberg TE (1997b). The irreducible perspectives of consciousness. *Seminars in Neurology, 17,* 85-93.

Feinberg TE (2000). The nested hierarchy of consciousness: A neurobiological solution to the problem of mental unity. *Neurocase, 6,* 75-81.

Feinberg TE (2001a). *Altered Egos: How the Brain Creates the Self.* Oxford University Press, New York.

Feinberg TE (2001b). Why the mind is not a radically emergent feature of the brain. *Journal of Consciousness Studies, 8,* 123-145.

Feinberg TE (2008). The nested hierarchy theory of consciousness (NHTC).*Toward a Science of Consciousness,* April 8-12. Consciousness Research Abstracts, p. 158. Presented at *Toward A Science of Consciousness,* Tucson, Arizona 04/09/08.

Feinberg TE (In press). Confabulation, the self, and ego functions: The "Ego Dysequilibrium Theory." In W Hirstein, ed., *Confabulation: Views from Neuroscience, Psychiatry, Psychology and Philosophy.* Oxford University Press, New York.

Feinberg TE, DeLuca J, Giacino JT, Roane DM, and Solms M. (2005). Right hemisphere pathology and the self: Delusional misidentification and reduplication. In TE Feinberg and JP Keenan, eds., *The Lost Self: Pathologies of the Brain and Identity,* pp. 100-130. Oxford University Press, New York.

Feinberg TE, Eaton LA, Roane DM, Giacino JT (1999). Multiple Fregoli delusions after traumatic brain injury. *Cortex, 35,* 373-387.

Feinberg TE, and Giacino J (2003). Confabulation. In TE Feinberg and M Farah, eds., *Behavioral neurology and neuropsychology,* 2nd Ed., pp. 363-372. McGraw-Hill, New York.

Feinberg TE., Haber LD, and Leeds NE (1990). Verbal asomatognosia. *Neurology, 40,* 1391-1394.

Feinberg TE, and Keenan JP (2005). Where in the brain is the self? *Consciousness and Cognition, 14,* 661-678.

Feinberg TE, and Roane DM (1997). Anosognosia, completion and confabulation: The neutral-personal dichotomy. *Neurocase, 3,* 73-85.

Feinberg TE, and Roane DM (2003). Anosognosia. In: TE Feinberg and MJ Farah, eds., *Behavioral Neurology and Neuropsychology,* 2nd Ed., pp. 345-362. McGraw-Hill, New York.

Feinberg TE, Roane DM, and Ali J (2000). Illusory limb movements in anosognosia for hemiplegia. *Journal of Neurology, Neurosurgery, and Psychiatry, 68,* 511-513.

Feinberg TE, Roane D, Schindler RJ, Kwan PC, and Haber LD (1994). Anosognosia and visuoverbal confabulation. *Archives of Neurology, 5,* 468-473.

Feinberg TE, Schindler RJ, Flanagan NG, and Haber LD (1992). Two alien hand syndromes. *Neurology, 42,* 19-24.

Feinberg TE, and Shapiro RM (1989). Misidentification-reduplication and the right hemisphere. *Neuropsychiatry, Neuropsychology, and Behavioral Neurology, 2,* 39-48.

Fenichel O (1945). *The Psychoanalytic Theory of Neurosis*. W.W. Norton, New York.

Finney J (1955).*The Body Snatchers*. Dell, New York.

Flanagan O (1993). *Consciousness Reconsidered*. MIT Press, Cambridge, MA.

Fotopoulou A, Conway M, Griffiths P, Birchall D, and Tyrer S (2007). Self-enhancing confabulation: Revisiting the motivational hypothesis. *Neurocase, 13,* 6-15.

Fotopoulou A, Conway MA, and Solms M (2007). Confabulation: Motivated Reality Monitoring. *Neuropsychologia, 45,* 2180-2190.

Fotopoulou A, Solms M, and Turnbull O (2004). Wishful reality distortions in confabulation: A case report. *Neuropsychologia, 42,* 727-744.

Fraiberg, S. (1959). *The Magic Years*. New York: Scribners.

Freeman W, and Watts JW (1942). *Psychosurgery*. Charles C Thomas, Springfield , IL.

Freud A (1936). *The Ego and the Mechanisms of Defence*. Hogarth Press and Institute of Psycho-Analysis, London.

Freud S (1891). On Aphasia. A critical study by Dr. Sigmund Freud. In E Stengel, ed. *Sigmund Freud on Aphasia, Authorized Translation by E. Stengel* (1953), International Universities Press, New York.

Freud S (1900). *The Interpretation of Dreams*. Translated by A A Brill (1913). Macmillan, New York.

Freud S (1923). *The ego and the id*. Standard Edition (1961) London: Hogarth Press. 19, pp. 3-66.

Freud S (1937). Analysis terminable and interminable. Standard Edition, *23,* 216-253. London: Hogarth Press, 1961.

Freud S (1923). *The Ego and the Id*. The Standard Edition of the Complete Psychological Works of Sigmund Freud, (1961) Vol. 19 (1923-1925). pp. 3-66.

Freud S (1930). *Civilization and Its Discontents*, p. 66. The Standard Edition of the Complete Psychological Works of Sigmund Freud Vol. 21. Hogarth Press, London. (1930 [1929]), Civilization and Its Discontents. *Standard Edition, 21,* 64-145. London: Hogarth Press, 1961.

Fried I, MacDonald KA, and Wilson CL (1997). Single neuron activity in human hippocampus and amygdala during recognition of faces and objects. *Neuron, 18,* 753-765.

Fries P, Roelfsema PR, Engel AK, König P, and Singer W (1997). Syncronization of oscillatory responses in visual cortex correlates with perception in interocular rivalry. *Proceedings of the National Academy of Science, 94,* 12699-12704.

Frith CD, and Frith U. (1999) Interacting minds—A biological basis. *Science, 286,* 1692-1695.

Frith U, and Frith CD. (2003) Development and neurophysiology of mentalizing. *Philosophical Transactions of the Royal Society of London B, 358,* 459-473.

Fromm E (1951).*The Forgotten Language.* Grove Press, New York.

Fujiwara E, and Markowitsch H (2005). Authobiographical disorders. In TE Feinberg and JP Keenan, eds., *The Lost Self: Pathologies of the Brain and Identity,* pp. 65-80. Oxford University Press, New York.

Fuster JM (2003). *Cortex and Mind: Unifying Cognition.* Oxford University Press, New York.

Gallagher S (2000). Philosophical conceptions of the self: Implications for cognitive science. *Trends in Cognitive Science, 4,* 14-21.

Gallagher S (2003). Self-narrative in schizophrenia. In T Kircher and A David, eds., *The Self in Neuroscience and Psychiatry,* pp. 336-357.Cambridge University Press, New York.

Gallup GG (1970). Chimpanzees: Self recognition. *Science, 167,* 86-87.

Gallup GG (1979). Self-awareness in primates. *American Scientist, 67,* 417-421.

Gazzaniga MS (1985) *The Social Brain.* Basic Books, New York.

Gazzaniga MS (2000). Cerebral specialization and interhemispheric communication: Does the corpus callosum enable the human condition? *Brain, 123,* 1293-1326.

Gazzaniga MS, and LeDoux, JE (1978). *The Integrated Mind.* Plenum, New York.

Gerstmann J (1942). Problem of imperception of disease and of impaired body territories with organic lesions. *Archives of Neurology and Psychiat*ry, *48,* 890-913.

Geschwind N (1965). Disconnexion syndromes in animals and man. *Brain, 88,* 585-644.

Geschwind DH, Iacoboni M, Mega MS, Zaidel DW, Cloughesy T, and Zaidel E (1995). Alien hand syndrome: Interhemispheric motor disconnection due to a lesion in the midbody of the corpus callosum. *Neurology, 45,* 802-808.

Gill MM (1963).*Topography and Systems in Psychoanalytic Theory.* (Psychological Issues, Monograph 10). International Universities Press, New York.

Gleason TR, Sebanc AM, and Hartup WW (2000).Imaginary companions of preschool children. *Developmental Psychology, 36,* 419-428.

Globus GG (1973). Unexpected symmetries in the "World Knot." *Science, 180,* 1129-1136.

Globus GG. (1976). Mind, structure, and contradiction. In GG Globus, G Maxwell, and I Savodnik, eds., *Consciousness and the Brain—A Scientific and Philosophical Inquiry,* pp. 271-293. Plenum Press, New York.

Gluckman LK (1968). A case of Capgras syndrome. *Australian and New Zealand Journal of Psychiatry, 2,* 39-43.

Goldstein K (1939). *The Organism: A Holistic Approach to Biology Derived from Pathological Data in Man.* American Book Company, New York.

Gottfried JA (2006). Smell: Central nervous processing. *Advances in Otorhinolaryngology, 63,* 44-69.

Göncü A, and Gaskins S (2007). *Play and development: Evolutionary, sociocultural, and functional perspectives.* Lawrence Erlbaum, Mahwah, NJ.

Gross CG (2002). Genealogy of the "Grandmother Cell". *The Neuroscientist, 8,* 512-518.

Gross CG (2008). Single neuron studies of inferior temporal cortex. *Neuropsychologia, 46,* 841-852.

Gross CG, Rocha-Miranda CE, and Bender DB (1972). Visual properties of neurons in inferotemporal cortex of the macaque. *Journal of Neurophysiology, 35,* 96-111.

Halligan PW, Marshall JC, and Wade DT (1993). Three arms: A case study of supernumerary phantom limb after right hemisphere stroke. *Journal of Neurology, Neurosurgery, and Psychiatry, 56,* 159-166.

Halligan PW, Marshall JC, and Wade DT (1995). Unilateral somatoparaphrenia after right hemisphere stroke: A case description. *Cortex, 31,* 173-182.

Happé F (2003). Theory of mind and self. *Annals of the New York Academy of Science, 1001,* 134-144.

Harlow JM (1848). Passage of an iron rod through the head. *Boston Medical and Surgical Journal, 39,* 389-393.

Harrington A (1987). *Medicine, Mind, and the Double Brain: A Study in Nineteenth-Century Thought.* Princeton University Press, Princeton, NJ.

Harris PL (2000). *The work of the imagination.* Blackwell, Malden, MA.

Hirstein W (2005). *Brain Fiction: Self-Deception and the Riddle of Confabulation.* MIT Press, Cambridge, MA.

Hirstein W, and Ramachandran VS (1997). Capgras syndrome: A novel probe for understanding the neural representation of the identity and familiarity of persons. *Proceedings of the Royal Society of London, Series B, 264,* 437-444.

Hoff EV (2004-2005). A friend living inside me—The forms and functions of imaginary companions. *Imagination, Cognition, and Personality, 24,* 151-189.

Hogrefe G-J, Wimmer H, and Perner J (1986). Ignorance versus false belief: A developmental lag in attribution of epistemic states. *Child Development, 57,* 567-582.

Howe ML, and Courage ML (1997). The emergence and early development of autobiographical memory. *Psychological Review, 104,* 499-523.

Hubel DH (1988). *Eye, Brain, and Vision.* Scientific American Library, New York.

Hubel, D. H., and Wiesel TN (1977).The Ferrier Lecture: Functional architecture of macaque monkey visual cortex. *Proceedings of the Royal Society of London B., 198,* 1-59.

Hubel D H, and Wiesel TN (1979). Brain mechanisms of vision. *Scientific American, 241,* 150-162.

Hundert EM (1989). *Philosophy, Psychiatry and Neuroscience: Three Approaches to the Mind.* Oxford University Press, New York.

Hwang J-P, Yang C-H, and Tsai S-J (2003). Phantom boarder symptom in dementia. *International Journal of Geriatric Psychiatry, 18,* 417-420.

Jackson JH (1884). Evolution and dissolution of the nervous system. Croonian Lectures delivered at the Royal College of Physicians, March. In J Taylor, ed., *Selected Writings of John Hughlings Jackson,* Vol. 2, pp. 45-75 (1958). Basic Books, New York.

James W (1904) Does 'Consciousness' Exist? *Journal of Philosophy, Psychology, and Scientific Methods, 1,* 477-491.

James W (1983) *The Principles of Psychology.* Harvard University Press, Cambridge, MA.

James W (1892). *Psychology. The Briefer Course.* University of Notre Dame Press, Notre Dame, Indiana.

James W (1890) *The Principles of Psychology.* Henry Holt and Company, New York.

Janet P (1889). *L'automatisme psychologique.* Felix Alcan, Paris.

Janet P (1904). Amnesia and the dissociation of memories by emotion. *Journal de Psychologie, 1,* 417-453.

Janet P (1907). *The Major Symptoms of Hysteria.* Macmillan, New York.

Jenkins MA et al. (1997). Neuropsychiatric factors in the illusion of visitors among geriatric patients: A case series. *Journal of Geriatric Psychiatry and Neurology, 10,* 79-87.

Johnson MK (1991). Reality monitoring: Evidence from confabulation in organic brain disease patients. In GP Prigatano and GL Schacter, eds., *Awareness of Deficit after Brain Injury: Clinical and Theoretical Issues,* pp. 176-197. Oxford University Press, New York.

Johnson MK, Hayes SM, D'Esposito M, and Raye CL (2000). Confabulation. In J Grafman and F Boller eds. *Handbook of Neuropsychology,* 2nd Ed., pp. 383-407. Elsevier Science, Amsterdam, Netherlands.

Johnson S (2001). *Emergence.* Scribner, New York.

Joseph AB (1986). Focal central nervous system abnormalities in patients with misidentification syndromes. In GN Christodoulou, ed., *The Delusional Misidentification Syndromes* (pp. 68-79). Bibliotheca Psychiatrica No 164, Karger, Basel.

Joseph R (1986). Confabulation and delusional denial: Frontal lobe and lateralized influences. *Journal of Clinical Psychology, 42,* 507-518.

Kandel ER, Schwartz JH, and Jessell TM (2000) *Principles of Neural Science,* 4th Ed. McGraw-Hill Medical, New York.

Kaplan-Solms K, and Solms M (2002). *Clinical Studies in Neuro-Psychoanalysis.* Karnac Books, London.

Kant I. (1993). *Critique of Pure Reason.* Everyman, London.

Kasahara H et al. (2005). Perspectives on phantom boarder symptom. *Psychogeriatrics,* **5,** 103-107.

Kass JH (1989). Why does the brain have so many visual areas? *Journal of Cognitive Neuroscience, 1,* 121-135.

Keenan JP, Gallup GG, and Falk D (2003). *The Face in the Mirror: The Search for the Origins of Consciousness.* Harper Collins/Ecco, New York.

Keenan JP, Nelson A, O'Connor M, and Pascual-Leone A (2001). Self-recognition and the right hemisphere. *Nature, 409,* 305.

Keenen JP, Wheeler MA and Ewers M (2003). The neural correlates of self-awareness and self-recognition. In T Kircher and A David, eds., *The Self in Neuroscience and Psychiatry,* pp. 166-179. Cambridge University Press, New York.

Keenan, JP, Wheeler MA, Gallup GG, and Pascual-Leone A. (2000). Self-recognition and the right prefrontal cortex. *Trends in Cognitive Science, 4,* 338-334.

Keenan JP, Wheeler M, Platek SM, Lardi G, and Lassonde M. (2003). Self-face processing in a callosotomy patient. *European Journal of Neuroscience, 18,* 2391-2395.

Kihlstrom JF (1994). One hundred years of hysteria. In SJ Lynn and JW Rhue, eds., *Dissociation: Clinical and Theoretical Perspectives,* pp. 365-394. Guilford Press, New York.

Kim, J (1998). *Mind in a Physical World. An Essay on the Mind-Body Problem and Mental Causation.* MIT Press, Cambridge, MA.

Kim, J (1992). "Downward causation" in emergentism and nonreductive physicalism. In A Beckermann, H Flohr, and J Kim, eds., *Emergence or Reduction? Essays on the Prospects of Nonreductive Physicalism,* pp. 119-138. Walter de Gruyter, New York.

Kim, J (1995). The Non-Reductivist's Troubles with Mental Causation. In J Heil, and A Mele, eds., *Mental Causation,* pp. 189-210. Clarendon Press, Oxford

King S (2001). *Steven King's Danse Macabre*. Berkley Trade, New York.

Kircher TTJ et al. (2001). Recognizing one's own face. *Cognition, 78*, B1-B15.

Kircher T, and David A, eds. (2003). *The Self in Neuroscience and Psychiatry*. Cambridge University Press, New York.

Koch C (2004). *The quest for consciousness*. Roberts, Englewood, CO.

Koestler A (1967). *The Ghost in the Machine*. Hutchinson, Harmondsworth, UK.

Koestler A (1978). *Janus: A Summing Up*. Random House, New York.

Kopelman, MD (1980) Two types of confabulation. *Neurology, Neurosurgery, and Psychiatry, 43*, 461-63

Korsakoff, SS (1889). *Psychic Disorder in Conjunction with Peripheral Neuritis*. Translated and republished by M Victor and PI Yakovlev (1955). *Neurology, 5*, 394-406.

Kraepelin, E. (1904). *Lectures on Clinical Psychiatry*. Translated by T. Johnstone. Bailliere, Tindall, & Cox, London.

Kraepelin, E. (1907). *Clinical Psychiatry: A Textbook for Students and Physicians*. Translated by A. R. Diefendorf. Macmillan, New York.

Kraepelin, E. (1919). *Dementia Praecox and Paraphrenia*. Translated by R. M. Barclay. E. & S. Livingstone, Edinburgh, UK.

Kumral E, and Özturk Ö (2004). Delusional state following acute stroke. *Neurology, 62*, 110-113.

Lakoff G and Johnson M (1980) *Metaphors We Live By*. University of Chicago Press, Chicago.

Leary MR, and Tangney JP (2002).The self as an organizing construct in the behavioral and social sciences. In MR Leary and JP Tangney, eds., *Handbook of Self and Identity*, pp. 3-14.Guilford Press, New York.

Lebrun Y (1987). Anosognosia in aphasics. *Cortex, 23*, 251-263.

Ledoux J (1996). *The Emotional Brain: The Mysterious Underpinnings of Emotional Life*, Simon & Schuster, New York.

LeDoux J. (2002). *Synaptic Self: How Our Brains Become Who We Are*. Viking Press, New York.

Legrand D (2007). Pre-reflective self-as-subject from experiential and empirical perspectives. *Consciousness and cognition, 16*, 583-599.

Leiguarda R, Starkstein S, and Berthier M (1989).Anterior callosal haemorrhage. A partial interhemispheric disconnection syndrome. *Brain, 112*, 1019-1037.

Leslie AM (1987). Pretense and representation: The origins of "theory of mind." *Psychological Review, 94*, 412-426.

Leslie AM, Friedman O, and German TP (2004). Core mechanisms in "theory of mind." *Trends in Cognitive Sciences*, 8, 528-533.

Levine DN, Calvanio R, and Rinn WE (1991) The pathogenesis of anosognosia for hemiplegia.*Neurology*, 41, 1770-1781.

Levine DN, and Grek A (1984). The anatomic basis for delusions after right cerebral infarction. *Neurology*, 34, 577-582.

Lewis L. (1991). Role of psychological factors in disordered awareness. In GP Prigatano and DL Schacter, eds., *Awareness of Deficits after Brain Injury: Clinical and Theoretical Issues*. Oxford University Press, New York.

Lewis M (1992). *Shame, the Exposed Self.* The Free Press, New York.

Lewis M (1995). Aspects of self: From systems to ideas. In P Rochat ed., *The Self in Infancy: Theory and Research*, pp. 95-115. Elsevier, Amsterdam.

Lewis M (1997). The self in self-conscious emotions. *Annals of the New York Academy of Sciences*, 818, 119-142.

Lewis M (2003). The emergence of consciousness and its role in human development. *Annals of the New York Academy of Sciences*, 1001, 104-133.

Lewis M, and Brooks-Gunn J (1979). Toward a theory of social cognition:The development of self. In I Uzgiris ed., *New Directions in Child Development: Social Interaction and Communication During Infancy*, pp 1-20. Jossey-Bass, San Francisco, CA.

Lewis M, and Ramsay D (2004). Development of self-recognition, personal pronoun use, and pretend play during the second year. *Child Development, 75,* 1821-1831.

Lewis M, Sullivan MW, Stanger C, and Weiss M (1989). Self development and self-conscious emotions. *Child Development, 60,* 146-156.

Lindeman E (1945). Symptomatology of acute grief. *The American Journal of Psychiatry, 101,* 141-148.

MacDougall D (1907). Hypothesis concerning soul substance together with experimental evidence of the existence of such substance. *American Medicine, 2,* 240-243.

MacLean, P.D. (1973). A triune concept of the brain and behavior. In: Boag, T. and Campbell, D. (eds). *The Hincks Memorial Lectures.* Toronto: University of Toronto Press, pp. 6-66.

MacLean, P.D. (1990). *The Triune Brain in Evolution: Role in Paleocerebral Functions.* New York: Plenum.

Malloy PF, and Richardson ED (1994). The frontal lobes and content-specific delusions. *The Journal of Neuropsychiatry and Clinical Neurosciences, 6,* 455-466.

Markowitsch HJ. (2003). Autonoetic consciousness. In T Kircher and A David, eds., *The self in neuroscience and psychiatry*, pp. 180-196. Cambridge University Press, New York.

McGlynn SM, and Schacter DL (1989). Unawareness of deficits in neuropsychological syndromes. *Journal of Clinical and Experimental Neuropsychology*, 11, 143-205.

McGeown WJ, Shanks MF, Guerrini C, and Venneri A (2008). Confabulation, Temporal Consciousness and Self reference, presented at the Twenty-sixth European Workshop on Cognitive Neuropsychology. Bressanone. Italy, January.

McKay R, Langdon R, and Coltheart M (2005). "Sleights of mind": Delusions, defences, and self-deception. *Cognitive Neuropsychiatry*, 10, 305-326.

McKay R, Langdon R, and Coltheart M. (2007). Models of misbelief: Integrating motivational and deficit theories of delusions. *Consciousness and Cognition*, 16, 932-941.

Meares, R. (1999). The contribution of Hughlings Jackson to an understanding of dissociation. *American Journal of Psychiatry*, 156, 1850-1855.

Meehl P (1966). The compleat autocerebroscopist: A thought experiment on Professor Feigl's mind/body identity thesis. In PK Feyerabend and G Maxwell, eds., *Mind, Matter and Method*, pp. 103-180. University of Minnesota Press, Minneapolis.

Melloni L, Molina C, Pena M, Torres D, Singer W, and Rodriguez E (2007). Synchronization of Neural Activity across Cortical Areas Correlates with Conscious Perception. *The Journal of Neuroscience*, 27, 2858-2865.

Mendez MF (1992). Delusional misidentification of persons in dementia. *British Journal of Psychiatry*, 160, 414-416.

Merker B (2007). Consciousness without a cerebral cortex: A challenge for neuroscience and medicine. *Behavioral and Brain Sciences*, 30, 63-134.

Mesulam, M-M (2000). *Principles of Behavioral and Cognitive Neurology* 2nd ed. Oxford University Press, New York.

Metzinger T (2003). *Being No One: The Self-Model Theory of Subjectivity*. MIT Press, Cambridge, MA.

Miller BL, Seeley WW, Mychack P, Rosen HJ, Mena I, and Boone K (2001). Neuroanatomy of the self: evidence from patients with frontotemporal dementia. *Neurology*. 57, 817-821.

Molchan SE, Martinez RA, Lawlor BA, Grafman JH, and Sunderland T (1990). Reflections of the self: Atypical misidentification and delusional syndromes in two patients with Alzheimer's disease. *British Journal of Psychiatry*, 157, 605-608.

Morgane PJ, Galler JR, and Mokler DJ (2005).A review of systems and networks of the limbic forebrain/limbic midbrain. *Progress in Neurobiology, 75,* 143-160.

Morgane PJ, and Mokler DJ (2006). The limbic brain: Continuing resolution. *Neuroscience and Biobehavioral Reviews, 30,* 119-125.

Morowitz HJ (2002). *The emergence of everything.* Oxford University Press, New York.

Moscovitch M, and Melo B (1997). Strategic retrieval and the frontal lobes: Evidence from confabulation and amnesia. *Neuropsychologia, 35,* 1017-1034.

Moskowitz JA (1972). Capgras' syndrome in modern dress. *International Journal of Child Psychotherapy, 1,* 45-64.

Movshon, JA, Adelson, EH, Gizzi, MS, and Newsome, WT (1985) The analysis of moving visual pattern. In C Chagas, R Gattass, and V Gross, eds., *Pattern Recognition Mechanisms,* pp. 117-151. Springer, New York.

Nagel T (1986). *The View from Nowhere.* Oxford University Press, New York.

Nagera H (1969). The imaginary companion: Its significance for ego development and conflict solution. *The Psychoanalytic Study of the Child, 24,* 165-196.

Nauta WJH (1958). Hippocampal projections and related neural pathways to the midbrain in the cat. *Brain, 81,* 319-340.

Nauta WJH (1973).Connections of the frontal lobe with the limbic system. In LV Laitinen and KE Livingston, eds., *Surgical Approaches in Psychiatry,* pp. 303-314. Medical and Technical Publishing, Lancaster, PA.

Nauta WJH, and Haymaker W (1969). Hypothalamic nuclei and fiber connections. In W Haymaker, E Anderson, and WJH Nauta, eds., *The Hypothalamus,* pp. 136-209. Charles C. Thomas, Springfield, IL.

Nelson K (1992). Emergence of autobiographical memory at age 4. *Human Development, 35,* 172-177.

Nelson K (1993). The psychological and social origins of autobiographical memory.*Psychological Science, 4,* 1-6.

Nieuwenhuys R (1996). The greater limbic system, the emotional motor system and the brain. *Progress in Brain Research, 107,* 551-580.

Nieuwenhuys R (1998) Overall functinal subdivision of the mammalian brain. 2023-2097. In R Nieuwenhuys, HJ ten Donkelaar, and C Nicholson, eds. *The Central Nervous System of Vertebrates,* Vol. 3, pp. 551-654. Springer-Verlag, Berlin.

Nieuwenhuys R et al. (1988-1989). Core and paracores; Some new chemoarchitectural entities in the mammalian neuraxis. *Acta Morphologica Neerlando-Scandinavica, 26,* 131-163.

Nieuwenhuys R, Voogd J, and van Huijzen C (2007). *The Human Central Nervous System,* 4th ed. Springer, New York.

Nimchinsky EA, Gilissen E, Allman JM, Perl DP, Erwin JM, and Hof PR (1999). A neuronal morphologic type unique to humans and great apes. *Proceedings of the National Academy of Science, 96,* 5268-5273.

Northoff G, and Bermpohl F (2004). Cortical midline structures and the self. *Trends in Cognitive Sciences, 8,* 102-107.

Northoff G, Heinzel A, de Greck M, Bermpohl F, Dobrowolny H, and Panksepp J (2006). Self-referential processing in our brain—A meta-analysis of imaging studies on the self. *Neuroimage, 31,* 440-457.

Northoff G, Schneider F, Rotte M, et al. (2007). Differential parametric modulation of self-relatedness and emotions in different brain regions. *Human Brain Mapping,*

Panksepp J (1998). *Affective Neuroscience: The Foundations of Human and Animal Emotions.* Oxford University Press, New York.

Panksepp J (2007). Emotional feelings originate below the neocortex: Toward a neurobiology of the soul. *Behavioral and Brain Sciences, 30,* 101-103.

Pattee HH (1973). The physical basis and origin of hierarchical control. In HH Pattee ed., *Hierarchy Theory. The Challenge of Complex Systems.* George Braziller, New York.

Perry JC (1990). *Defense mechanism rating scales (DMRS),* 5th ed. Manual published by author, Cambridge, MA.

Perry JC, and Bond M (2005). Defensive functioning. In JM Oldham, AE Skodol, and DS Bender, eds., *The American Psychiatric Publishing Textbook of Personality Disorders,* pp 523-540. American Psychiatric Press, Washington, D.C.

Phan KL, Taylor SF, Welsh RC, Ho SH, Britton JC, and Liberzon I. (2004). Neural correlates of individual ratings of emotional salience: A trial-related fMRI study. *Neuroimage, 21,* 768-780.

Phillips J (2003). Schizophrenia and the narrative self. In T Kircher and A David, eds., *The self in neuroscience and psychiatry,* pp. 319-335. Cambridge University Press, New York.

Phillips ML, Howard R, and David AS (1996). "Mirror, mirror on the wall, who . . . ?": Towards a model of visual self-recognition. *Cognitive Neuropsychiatry, 1,* 153-164.

Piaget J (2002). *Play, Dreams and Imitation in Childhood.* W. W. Norton, New York.

Platek SM, Keenan JP, Gallup GG, Jr, and Mohamed FB (2004). Where am I? The neurological correlates of self and other. *Cognitive Brain Research, 19,* 114-122.

Platek SM et al. (2006) Neural substrates for functionally discriminating self-face from personally familiar faces. *Human Brain Mapping, 27,* 91-98.

Poe EA (1839) William Wilson. *Burton's Gentleman's Magazine.* October, 1939.

Povinelli DJ (1995). The unduplicated self. In P Rochat ed, *The Self in Infancy*, pp. 161-192. North-Holland, Amsterdam.

Povinelli DJ, and Simon BB (1998) Young children's understanding of briefly versus extremely delayed images of self: Emergence of the autobiographical stance. *Developmental Psychology, 34*, 188-194.

Powers RG (1976). Introduction. In Jack Finney, *The Body Snatchers*. Gregg Press, Boston, MA.

Premack D G. and Woodruff G (1978). Does the chimpanzee have a theory of mind? *Behavioral and Brain Sciences, 1,* 515-526.

Prentice NM, Manosevitz M, and Hubbs L (1978). Imaginary figures of early childhood; Santa Claus, Easter Bunny, and the Tooth Fairy. *American Journal of Orthopsychiatry, 48,* 618-628.

Putnam FW (1989). *Diagnosis and Treatment of Multiple Personality Disorder*. Guilford Press, New York.

Putnam FW (1994). Dissociative disorders in children and adolescents. In SJ Lynn and JW Rhue, eds., *Dissociation: Clinical and Theoretical Perspectives,* pp. 175-189. Guilford Press, New York.

Quiroga RQ, Kreiman G, Koch C, and Fried I (2008). Sparse but not "grand-mother-cell" coding in the medial temporal lobe. *Trends in Cognitive Sciences, 12,* 87-91.

Quiroga RQ, Reddy L, Kreiman G, Koch C, and Fried I (2005). Invariant visual representation by single neurons in the human brain. *Nature, 435,* 1102-1107.

Ramachandran VS, and Blakeslee S (1998). *Phantoms in the Brain. Probing the Mysteries of the Mind*. William Morrow, New York.

Ramnani N, and Owen AM (2004). Anterior prefrontal cortex: Insights into function from anatomy and neuroimaging. *Nature Reviews Neuroscience, 5,* 184-194.

Revonsuo A (2006). *Inner Presence*. MIT Press, Cambridge, MA.

Rizzolatti G, and Craighero L (2004). The mirror-neuron system. *Annual Review of Neuroscience, 27,* 169-192.

Rochat P (1995). Early objectification of the self. In P Rochat, ed, *The Self in Infancy: Theory and Research*, pp. 53-71. North-Holland/Elsevier Science, Amsterdam.

Rochat P (2001). *The Infant's World*. Harvard University Press, Cambridge, MA.

Rochat P (2003). Five levels of self-awareness as they unfold early in life. *Conscious and Cognition, 12,* 717-731.

Rowan E (1984). Phantom boarders as a symptom of late paraphrenia. *American Journal of Psychiatry, 141,* 580-581.

Rubin EH, Drevets WC, and Burke WJ (1988). The nature of psychotic symptoms in senile dementia of the Alzheimer type. *Journal of Geriatric Psychiatry and Neurology*, 1, 16-20.

Ryle, G (1949). *The Concept of Mind*. Hutchinson, London.

Salthe SN (1985). *Evolving Hierarchical Systems: Their Structure and Representation*. Columbia University Press, New York.

Sanders B (1992). The imaginary companion experience in multiple personality disorder. *Dissociation*, 5, 159-162.

Sanides F (1970). Functional architecture of motor and sensory cortices in primates in the light of a new concept of neorcortex evolution. In CR Noback and W Montagna eds., *The Primate Brain*, pp. 137-208. Appleton-Century-Crofts, New York.

Schafer R (1968). The mechanisms of defense. *International Journal of Psycho-analysis*, 49, 49-62.

Schilder P (1950). *The Image and Appearance of the Human Body*. International Universities Press, New York.

Schmitz TW, Kawahara-Baccus TN, and Johnson SC (2004). Metacognitive evaluation, self-relevance, and the right prefrontal cortex. *Neuroimage*, 22, 941-947.

Schnider A (2003). Spontaneous confabulation and the adaptation of thought to ongoing reality. *Nature Reviews Neuroscience*, 4, 662-671.

Schnider A, von Daniken C, and Gutbrod K (1996). Disorientation in amnesia. A confusion of memory traces. *Brain*, 119, 1627-1632.

Schnider A, Gutbrod K, Hess CW et al. (1996). Memory without context: Amnesia with confabulations after infarction of the right capsular genu. *Journal of Neurology Neurosurgery, and Psychiary*, 61, 186-193.

Schnider A, and Ptak R. (1999). Spontaneous confabulators fail to suppress currently irrelevant memory traces. *Nature Neuroscience*, 2, 677-681.

Schnider A, Ptak R, and von Daniken C et al. (2000). Recovery from spontaneous confabulations parallels recovery of temporal confusion in memory. *Neurology*, 55, 74-83.

Schore AN (2005). Back to basics: Attachment, affect regulation, and the developing right brain: Linking developmental neuroscience to pediatrics. *Pediatrics in Review*, 26, 204-17.

Schore AN (2000) Attachment and the regulation of the right brain. *Attachment and Human Development*, 2, 23-47.

Schore AN (2003a). *Affect Regulation and the Repair of the Self*. W.W. Norton, New York.

Schore AN (2003b). *Affect Dysregulation and Disorders of the Self*. W.W. Norton, New York.

Searle JR (1984). *Minds, Brains and Science*. Harvard University Press, Cambridge, MA.

Searle JR (1992). *The Rediscovery of the Mind*. MIT Press, Cambridge, MA.

Searle JR (2000). Consciousness. *Annual Review of Neuroscience, 23,* 557-578.

Seeley WW, and Miller BL (2005). Disorders of the self in dementia. In TE Feinberg and JP Keenan, eds., *The Lost Self: Pathologies of the Brain and Identity*, pp. 147-165. Oxford University Press, New York.

Seeley WW et al. (2006) Early frontotemporal dementia targets neurons unique to apes and humans. *Annals of Neurology, 60,* 660-667.

Sellars W (1963). *Science, Perception, and Reality*. Routledge and Kegan Paul, London.

Semrad E (1967). The organization of ego defenses and object loss. In DM Moriarity ed., *The Loss of Loved Ones*, pp. 126-134, Charles C Thomas, Springfield, IL.

Shanks MF, and Venneri A (2002). The emergence of delusional companions in Alzheimer's disease: An unusual misidentification syndrome. *Cognitive Neuropsychiatry, 7,* 317-328.

Shenker JI, Wylie SA, Fuchs K, Manning CA, and Heilman KM (2004).On-line anosognosia: Unawareness for chorea in real time but not on videotape delay. *Neurology, 63,* 159-160.

Sherrington C (1947). *The Integrative Action of the Nervous System*. Yale University Press, New Haven, CT.

Simon HA (1973). The organization of complex systems. In HH Pattee, ed. *Hierarchy Theory. The Challenge of Complex Systems*. George Braziller, New York. pp. 1-27.

Singer DG, and Singer JL (1990). *The House of Make-Believe: Children's Play and the Developing Imagination*. Harvard University Press, Cambridge, MA.

Singer W (1999). Neuronal synchrony: A versatile code for the definition of relations? *Neuron, 24,* 49-65.

Singer W (2001). Consciousness and the binding problem. In PC Marijuán ed., Cajal and Consciousness: Scientific Approaches to Consciousness on the Centennial of Ramón y Cajal's Textura, *Annals of New York Academy of Sciences, 929,* 123-146.

Singer W, Engel AK, Kreiter AK, Munk MHJ, Neuenschwander S, and Roelfsema PR (1997). Neuronal assemblies: Necessity, signature and detectability. *Trends in Cognitive Sciences, 1,* 252-261.

Skouteris H, and Robson N (2006). Young children's understanding of photo self-representations. *Australian Journal of Educational and Developmental Psychology, 6*, 50-59.

Solms M (2000). A psychoanalytic perspective on confabulation. *Neuro-Psychoanalysis, 2*, 133-138.

Spangenberg KB, Wagner MT, and Bachman DL (1998). Neuropsychological analysis of a case of abrupt onset mirror sign following a hypotensive crisis in a patient with vascular dementia. *Neurocase, 4*, 149-154.

Sperry R W (1966). Brain bisection and mechanisms of consciousness. In JC Eccles, ed., *Brain and Conscious Experience*, pp. 298-313. Springer-Verlag, New York.

Sperry RW (1984). Consciousness, personal identity and the divided brain. *Neuropsychologia, 22*, 661-673.

Sperry R W (1990). Forebrain commissurotomy and conscious awareness. In C Trevarthen, ed., *Brain Circuits and Functions of the Mind*, pp. 371-388. Cambridge University Press, New York.

Sperry RW, Zaidel E, and Zaidel D (1979). Self recognition and social awareness in the deconnected minor hemisphere. *Neuropsychologia, 17*, 153-166.

Staton RD, Brumback RA, and Wilson H (1982). Reduplicative paramnesia: A disconnection syndrome of memory. *Cortex, 18*, 23-36.

Stern DN (1985). *The Interpersonal World of the Infant*. Basic Books, New York.

Strawson G (2000). The phenomenology and ontology of the self. In D Zahavi, ed., *Exploring the Self: Philosophical and Psychopathological Perspectives on Self-Experience*, p. 39. John Benjamins, Amsterdam and Philadelphia.

Stuss D, and Benson DF (1985). *The Frontal Lobes*. Raven Press, New York.

Stuss, DT, Alexander MP, Lieberman A., and Levine H (1978). An extraordinary form of confabulation. *Neurology, 28*, 1166-1172.

Stuss DT, Gallup GG, and Alexander MP (2001). The frontal lobes are necessary for "theory of mind." *Brain, 124*, 279-286.

Stuss DT, Picton TW, and Alexander MP (2001). Consciousness, self-awareness, and the frontal lobes.In SP Salloway, PF Malloy, and JD Duffy, eds., *The Frontal Lobes and Neuropsychiatric Illness*, pp. 101-109. American Psychiatric Publishing, Washington, D.C.

Stuss DT, Rosenbaum RS, Malcolm S, Christianna W, and Keenan JP (2005). The frontal lobes and self-awareess. . In TE Feinberg and JP Keenan, eds., *The Lost Self: Pathologies of the Brain and Identity*, pp. 50-64. Oxford University Press, New York.

Sugiura M, Watanabe J, Maeda Y, Matsue Y, Fukuda H, and Kawashima R

(2005). Cortical mechanisms of visual self-recognition. *Neuroimage, 24,* 143-149.

Sugiura M, Sugiura M, Sassa Y, Jeong H, Miura N, Akitsuki Y, Horie K, Sato S, Kawashima R (2006) Multiple brain networks for visual self-recognition with different sensitivity for motion and body part. *Neuroimage, 32,* 1905-1917.

Suwanwela NC, and Leelacheavasit N (2002). Isolated corpus callosal infarction secondary to pericallosal artery disease presenting as alien hand syndrome. *Journal of Neurology, Neurosurgery and Psychiatry, 72,* 533-536.

Svendsen M (1934). Children's imaginary companions. *Archives of Neurology and Psychiatry, 32,* 985-999.

Talland, GA (1961). Confabulation in the Wernicke-Korsakoff syndrome. *Journal of Nervous and Mental Diseases, 132,* 361-381.

Talland, GA (1965). *Deranged Memory.* New York: Academic Press.

Taylor M (1999). *Imaginary Companions and the Children Who Create Them.* Oxford University Press, New York.

Taylor M, and Carlson SM (1997). The relation between individual differences in fantasy and theory of mind. *Child Development, 68,* 436-455.

Taylor M, Carlson SM, Maring BL, Gerow L, and Charley CM (2004). The characteristics and correlates of fantasy in school-age children: Imaginary companions, impersonation, and social understanding. *Developmental Psychology, 40,* 1173-1187.

Taylor M, and Mannering AM (2007). Of Hobbes and Harvey: The imaginary companions created by children and adults. In A Göncü and S Gaskins, eds., *Play and Development: Evolutionary, Sociocultural, and Functional Perspectives,* pp 227-245. Lawrence Erlbaum, Mahwah, NJ.

Teller P (1992). Subjectivity and knowing what it's like. In A Berckermann, H Flohr, and J Kim, eds., *Emergence or Reduction? Essays on the Prospects of Nonreductive Physicalism,* pp. 180-200. Walter de Gruyter, Berlin and New York.

Terr L (1990). *Too Scared to Cry: Psychic Trauma in Childhood.* Basic Books, New York.

Tulving E (1985). Memory and consciousness. *Canadian Psychology, 26,* 1-12.

Tulving E (1987). Multiple memory systems and consciousness. *Human Neurobiology, 6,* 67-80.

Tulving E (2002a). Episodic memory: From mind to brain. *Annual Review of Psychology, 53,* 1-25.

Tulving E (2002b). Chronesthesia: Conscious awareness of subjective time.In DT Stuss and RT Knight, eds., *Principles of Frontal Lobe Function,* pp. 311-325. Oxford University Press, New York.

Turk DJ, Heatherton TF, Kelley WM, Funnell MG, Gazzaniga MS, and Macrae CN (2002). Mike or me? Self recognition in a spilt-brain patient. *Nature Neuroscience, 5*, 841-842.

Turnbull OH, Berry H, and Evans CEY (2004). A positive emotional bias in confabulatory false beliefs about place. *Brain and Cognition, 55*, 490-494.

Tye M (1997). *Ten Problems of Consciousness: A Representational Theory of the Phenomenal Mind*, MIT Press, Cambridge, MA.

Uddin LQ, Iacoboni M, Lange C, and Keenan JP (2007). The self and social cognition: The role of cortical midline structures and mirror neurons. *Trends in Cognitive Sciences, 11*, 153-157.

Uddin LQ, Kaplan JT, Molnar-Szakacs I, Zaidel E, and Iacoboni M (2005) Self-face recognition activates a frontoparietal "mirror" network in the right hemisphere: an event-related fMRI study. *Neuroimage, 25*, 926-935.

Ullman M. Motivational and structural factors in denial of hemiplegia (1960). *Archives of Neurology, 3*, 306-318.

Vaillant GE. (1971). Theoretical hierarchy of adaptive ego mechanisms: A 30-year follow-up of 30 men selected for psychological health. *Archives of General Psychiatry, 24*, 107-118.

Vaillant, GE (1977). *Adaptation to Life*, Little, Brown, Boston, MA; reprinted with a new preface in 1995 by Harvard University Press, Cambridge, MA.

Vaillant, GE (1992). *Ego Mechanisms of Defense: A Guide for Clinicians and Researchers*, American Psychiatric Press, Washington, D.C.

Vaillant, GE (1993).*The Wisdom of the Ego*, Harvard University Press, Cambridge, MA.

Vallar G, and Ronchi R (2009). Somatoparaphrenia: A body delusion. A review of the neuropsychological literature.*Experimental Brain Research, 192*, 533-551.

Van Der Horst L (1932). Uber die Psychologie des Korsakowsyndroms. *Monatschriften Psychiatry and Neurology, 83*, 65-84.

Venneri A, Shanks MF, Staff RT, and Della Sala, S (2000). Nurturing syndrome: A form of pathological bereavement with delusions in Alzheimer's disease. *Neuropsychologia, 38*, 213-224.

Vié, J (1930). Un trouble de l'identification des personnes: L'illusion des sosies. *Annales Médico-Psychologiques (Paris), 88*, 214-237.

von der Malsburg C (1995). Binding in models of perception and brain function. *Current Opinion in Neurobiology, 5*, 520-526.

Wallerstein RS (1985). Defenses, defense mechanisms, and the structure of the mind. In HP Blum, ed., *Defense and Resistance: Historical Perspectives and Current Concepts*, pp. 201-225. International Universities Press, New York.

Watson JD, and Crick FHC (1953). A structure for deoxyribose nucleic acid. *Nature, 171,* 737-738.

Weinstein EA (1991). Anosognosia and denial of illness. In GP Prigatano and DL Schacter, eds., *Awareness of Deficit after Brain Injury: Clinical and Theoretical Issues,* pp. 240-257. Oxford University Press, New York.

Weinstein EA (1996). Symbolic aspects of confabulation following brain injury: Influence of premorbid personality. *Bulletin of the Menninger Clinic, 60,* 331-350.

Weinstein EA, Cole M, Mitchell M, and Lyerly OG (1964). Anosognosia and aphasia. *Archives of Neurology, 10,* 376-386.

Weinstein EA, and Friedland RP (1977). Behavioral disorders associated with hemi-inattention. In EA Weinstein and RP Friedland, eds., *Advances in Neurology.* Vol. 18, pp. 51-62. Raven Press, New York.

Weinstein EA, and Kahn RL (1955). *Denial of Illness.* Charles C. Thomas, Springfield, IL.

Weinstein EA, and Kahn RL (1959). Symbolic reorganization in brain injuries.In S Arieti, ed., *American Handbook of Psychiatry,* Vol. 1, pp. 964-981. Basic Books, New York.

Weinstein EA, Kahn RL, and Malitz S (1956). Confabulation as a social process. *Psychiatry, 19,* 383-396.

Weinstein EA, Kahn RL, and Morris GO (1956). Delusions about children following brain injury. *Journal of the Hillside Hospital, 5,* 290-298.

Weinstein EA, and Lyerly OG (1968). Confabulation following brain injury. *Archives of General Psychiatry, 18,* 348-354.

Welch-Ross MK (1995). An integrative model of the development of autobiographical memory. *Developmental Review, 15,* 338-365.

Wheeler MA, Stuss DT, and Tulving E. (1997). Toward a theory of episodic memory: The frontal lobes and autonoetic consciousness. *Psychological Bulletin, 121,* 331-354.

Whitehead AN (1925). *Science and the Modern World.* Free Press, New York.

Williams HW, and Rupp C. (1938). Observations on confabulation. *American Journal of Psychiatry, 95,* 395-405.

Willick MS (1985). On the concept of primitive defenses. In HP Blum, ed., *Defense and Resistance: Historical Perspectives and Current Concepts,* pp. 175-200. International Universities Press, New York.

Wimmer H, and Perner J (1983). Beliefs about beliefs: Representation and constraining function of wrong beliefs in young children's understanding of deception. *Cognition, 13,* 103-128.

Woolley JD (1997). Thinking about fantasy: Are children fundamentally different thinkers and believers from adults? *Child Development, 68,* 991-1011.

Wolfram S (2002). *A New Kind of Science.* Wolfram Media, Champaign, IL.

Zaidel E, Iacoboni M, Zaidel DW, and Bogen JE (2003).The callosal syndromes. In KM Heilman and E Valenstein, eds. *Clinical Neuropsychology,* 4th ed., pp. 347-403. Oxford University Press, New York.

Zeki S (1993). *A Vision of the Brain.* Blackwell, Oxford.

Zeki S (2008). The disunity of consciousness. *Progress in Brain Research, 168,* 11-18, 267-268.

INDEX

Note: *f* denotes figure and *t* denotes table.

The Norton Series on Interpersonal Neurobiology
Allan N. Schore, PhD, Series Editor
Daniel J. Siegel, MD, Founding Editor

The field of mental health is in a tremendously exciting period of growth and conceptual reorganization. Independent findings from a variety of scientific endeavors are converging in an interdisciplinary view of the mind and mental well-being. An interpersonal neurobiology of human development enables us to understand that the structure and function of the mind and brain are shaped by experiences, especially those involving emotional relationships.

The Norton Series on Interpersonal Neurobiology will provide cutting-edge, multidisciplinary views that further our understanding of the complex neurobiology of the human mind. By drawing on a wide range of traditionally independent fields of research—such as neurobiology, genetics, memory, attachment, complex systems, anthropology, and evolutionary psychology—these texts will offer mental health professionals a review and synthesis of scientific findings often inaccessible to clinicians. These books aim to advance our understanding of human experience by finding the unity of knowledge, or consilience, that emerges with the translation of findings from numerous domains of study into a common language and conceptual framework. The series will integrate the best of modern science with the healing art of psychotherapy.